C. NORTHCOTE
PARKINSON

THE RISE OF BIG BUSINESS

WEIDENFELD
AND NICOLSON

LONDON

First published in Great Britain by
Weidenfeld and Nicolson
11 St John's Hill London SW11

ISBN 0 297 77327 5

Printed and bound in Great Britain by
Morrison & Gibb Ltd, London and Edinburgh

Contents

Preface

Big Business is the modern Leviathan, overshadowing the world in which we live. We hear the words spoken with bated breath and in every language, uttered sometimes with awe, sometimes with hatred, but seldom with precision. Big Business is said to influence governments and politics, peace and war. It supports this, condemns that, expects inflation or prepares for a slump. But few who use the words have the least idea of what they mean. Who are the Big Businessmen and what do they do? Which companies are important and why? Beyond what level can Business be described as Big? Those who admire and those who vituperate are alike at least in their ignorance. The major industrial group is a central feature of our economy and a potent influence on our daily lives but it is almost too big to notice. Few of us could name the first six groups in their order of importance. Few of us could name the key men in the key industries. Few of us know a thing about it.

If we realize our lack of information and go to the library or book-store we shall find there sections devoted to economic history, to commerce, to technology and to business administration. These and adjacent shelves do in fact contain books which shed some light on the subject but mostly, as it were, by accident. The authors are intent on something else and refer only in passing to the organizations which dominate our industrial society. The economic historian begins with chapters on agriculture and Tudor legislation, goes on to talk of coal and textiles and ends with chapters on trade unionism and co-operative societies. Much of our economic history is written from a socialist standpoint, the ill-treatment of labour being its central theme and the Factory Acts representing so many legislative triumphs over the wicked employer. A glance at the index of any history will reveal the fact that no individual enterprise is of much interest in itself except as a target for industrial unrest or government intervention. Somewhere in the same section of the library we come across the histories which are published about individual firms. These are the stuff of history and invaluable for reference but they are at once too local and too dated. They appear to have been printed at the firm's expense in 1926 or 1934, their frontispieces showing the bewhiskered Founder of the Firm, their last illustration a photograph of the new research wing and tennis courts. Much has happened, however, since 1934 and the book about one chemical plant fails, as a rule, to show its relationship to the industry as a whole. How did the modern Leviathan come into existence? We have no idea and this sort of book will often leave us no better informed.

Under 'Commerce' we find manuals of accountancy and book-keeping, with hints on filing, correspondence and audit. There are volumes on commercial law and more books again on the legal complexities which lie between employer and employed. Under 'Technology' there are shelves of information about alloys and fuel, about electronics and dyes. There are excellent books written for the intelligent apprentice or workman, books on how to strip an engine or fit a lock, manuals on lubrication and joinery, manuals on welding and glass. There are even histories of technology, mostly of recent date, with fascinating information about what was invented where and by whom. Glancing through the chapter headings we find ourselves often on the fringe of Big Business but never at the heart. Last of all, perhaps, we find the most recent books of all, the manuals on business administration, on data processing and retrieval, on automation and cybernetics. We are now in the world of the computer and the binary system, lost in a maze of technicalities and jargon. But here again the books are intended for the office worker just as the older manuals were meant for the plumber's mate and the metalworker's apprentice. We are studying the more recent tools (or playthings) of Big Business. We are not studying Big Business itself.

If we turn from the bookshelves to the daily and weekly press we find a wealth of current information but here the whole emphasis is on investment. In the financial columns and financial weeklies we read of conflicts and mergers, of debentures and equities, of prospects and dangers, of profit and loss. Here again we may feel that we are on the fringes of Big Business. The share prices quoted are an indication of what is happening, the expert prognostication seeks to foreshadow what will happen next. If we are investors our money is at stake and the facts given are those we want to know. But this is no guide to the world of Big Business even if it completes the knowledge of those who already understand it. Turn where we will, we find no picture of what has happened and is happening. The book we want is simply not in existence.

If you are a young man or woman and about to go into business your first need is to look at the picture as a whole. Before plunging into the jungle you need a map. What are the most important organizations, how did they begin and where are they going? If you are already in business, you need to know where you stand in relation to your competitors and how your national industry compares with that in other countries. Are you even in the right line of business? Is your industry destined to expand or is it bound to decline? In what direction should you move? To what other organization should you transfer? How should you qualify for some other business career and where would be the strategic centre from which to operate?

Suppose, on the other hand, that you are already a director or senior manager, totally absorbed in the problems of the group to which you belong. You have worries, maybe, about finance, new developments, coming legislation, industrial unrest and public relations. You have enough to do at the office without letting your eyes wander over the whole field of industry. And yet a general background knowledge may be vitally important. You are in competition, you know, with companies which manufacture the same or similar goods. Will the time come when you may have to compete with yet other companies – with organizations of which you have barely heard, using different raw materials to make a different product – one which might supersede the one you have now to sell? Is it not important to see the world as a whole, a single market of the future?

The attempt was made in a previous book, *Big Business* (published in 1974), to satisfy the needs of these different readers, providing a guide to the Big Business of today essential, surely, to all who engage in it but useful even to those on the fringe of it, to those with responsibilities merely as consumers and voters. In compiling that book, something was done towards providing at least an outline knowledge of the subject. If we are to defend Big Business let us know what it is we are to uphold. If we are to criticize, let it be for the right reasons. If we are to plunge into the business jungle let us survey its boundaries and area, let us mark on the map its opportunities and pitfalls, its mountains and volcanoes, its dangers and chances, its lowlands and swamp. If we are already in the jungle, on the other hand, struggling to progress or even seeking merely to survive, our need is to rise on occasion above the treetop level, see the jungle as a whole and recover our sense of direction. These are the needs we sought to fulfil. That book provided a general picture of Big Business in the world of today.

What was Big Business, however, for the purposes of that book? In the historical process commerce comes before industry and it is from the profits of commerce that industry is financed. With commerce comes banking and both were established before industry could become important. In the sense I used the expression, Big Business is based upon industry. My concern was with the large industrial complex or group, the giant overshadowing the modern economic landscape. It might be arguable that agriculture is Big Business when applied, shall we say, to a million acres. It could be thought that banking is Big Business and is a foundation on which industry is based. It would be easy to prove that shipping lines and railways are Big Business and that no major modern industry could have been established without them. In that book, nevertheless, these organizations were discussed only briefly, not because they are unimportant but because each deserves a volume of its own. I similarly ignored industrial concerns which no longer exist. While admitting that, say, pyramid building must have been Big Business in ancient Egypt, I concluded that it is not of interest to the readers for whom that book was planned. For the same reason I excluded the business which is done in fully Socialist countries, as also in industries elsewhere which have been nationalized. I concede that the scale of these operations is large but it is not the sort of business in which my readers would be interested. There is no means, moreover, by which it can be fairly compared with any other form of enterprise. To keep *Big Business* down to a useful size its scope had to be confined within a certain field. It could deal only with organizations of broadly the same type, capitalist and planned to supply a market, not socialist and planned to execute a policy.

That book was designed to meet a need in education and also in the supply of necessary information to an intelligent public. It began, however, in the present and touched only lightly on the process which brought Big Business into existence. In this book the attempt is made to fill in the background. This may seem remote history and therefore irrelevant but a glance at the chapter headings will serve to show that their content is still very much to the point. The process by which the established industries came into being is not very different, we may suppose, from the way in which new industries will be founded. The way in which millions have been made in the past is the pattern, most likely, for the success stories of the future. Apart from that, however, our knowledge of the business jungle must be incomplete if we have no knowledge of how its main features came into existence. In this book I have tried to provide that background knowledge, in so far as any one book can cover the whole story. What I could not do was bring the story down to the present day. The period studied ends virtually in 1971. Much has happened since then, but one has to call a halt somewhere. It has altogether been an interesting, if daunting, task and the reader is asked to remember that it is necessarily selective, the topics chosen following a logical or chronological sequence but no pretence being made of telling the whole story. Much is included but as much again left out, not as trivial but merely from lack of space.

C. NORTHCOTE PARKINSON

Part I   THE BACKGROUND

1 Agriculture and Commerce

Business is usually defined as the pursuit of an occupation or trade; more narrowly, the purchase and sale of goods with the object of making a profit. It becomes recognizable at the point where financial motives emerge, disentangled from military, political and social considerations. It becomes Big Business when pursued on the grand scale, reaching a point when the business concerned becomes a power in the land, perhaps even rivalling the government in wealth and influence. The isolation of the business motive is a distinctive feature of the modern as opposed to the medieval world. Medieval institutions which still exist, the Papacy being perhaps the biggest of them, have all the functions of Big Business but with other functions interwoven and often predominant. It is these other functions, religious, social, charitable and diplomatic, which prevent us from readily identifying the nature of the business as opposed to the other activities which are being pursued. The older monastic orders and the older universities are similarly in business but again with a variety of other objects in view and with as many changes in emphasis over the centuries. City guilds and livery companies date in the same way from a period when institutions were less specialized. What distinguishes the Big Business of today is not so much its scale as its sharp dissociation from other aspects of life. Its functions in our day have been almost purely economic. In this respect changes might seem to be inevitable but it is fair to add that they have hardly yet begun.

The early chapters of this book are, of necessity, historical and the

3

author is faced, therefore, with the historian's chief difficulty. This centres upon his foreknowledge of how the story is to end. Whether he recognizes the fact or not, the historian's narrative, for all but the most recent period of history, is apt to be coloured by his awareness of the events which are to follow. Writing of the old regime in France, he is too often at pains to identify the causes of a revolution which will later overwhelm the society he seeks to describe. But Louis xv and his ministers could not foresee the revolution and were not interested, therefore, in its causes. Their concern was with other and more urgent problems and a historian who fails to explain these, being aware all the time of the revolution they should have been seeking to prevent, is in danger of writing nonsense. The same peril confronts the economic historian who knows that nineteenth-century Britain is to be the scene of an industrial revolution. Interpreting earlier centuries in the light of that foreknowledge, he gives vast space to the most trivial of inventions and dwells at length on every nascent industry. These were the beginnings of industrial Britain and all credit is due to the ingenuity, persistence and enterprise which would make the coming changes possible. Where we go wrong is in making it seem that these precursors were as important in their own day as they may seem to be in retrospect. For all these early industrialists were overshadowed by other contemporary business men, by the folk who really mattered at the time. And while some of these, as we know, were merchants, the greater number of them and certainly the biggest of them, were landowners. Knowing that the Corn Laws would be repealed, knowing that the landowners could be penalized and eventually ruined by their political opponents, historians have tended to underestimate their importance during the period when their position seemed unassailable. Big Business of the seventeenth and eighteenth centuries was the business of landownership. Here again it may be objected that the economic aspects of agriculture were often confused by other considerations, political, sporting and social, and so indeed they were. The fact remains, however, that the British landscape was dominated by men of vast influence and wealth. It was these, not the industrialists, who were the Big Businessmen of the day.

Our failure to understand the business of landownership is due in part to the Edwardians. The country-house life of recollection and hearsay is the life lived by people who might live in the country but whose income was derived from the cities. These elegantly idle people, perhaps cultured, perhaps bored, were rootless *rentiers*, often spending more on their estates than the land was worth. Our ideas are further coloured by the visits we have paid to historic and stately homes, our impressions formed by architecture and art and by the beautifully furnished rooms in which titled folk used so beautifully to live. The country mansion may be a museum now but it was never a museum before, nor even a home in the more intimate sense, not at least until its effective life was ending. It was rather a centre from which a vital business was organized, a lively and bustling head office with executives and accountants, copying clerks and a transport pool. The economic purpose was central to an organization which admittedly played a part also in politics, religion, justice and war. There was a revenue to be collected and spent, trees to be planted and land to be drained, leases to sign and game to preserve. Directorships in an estate were hereditary, to be sure, but how could they be otherwise? No one can plant oak trees except for his grandchildren. Here was a whole way of life and business and the landowners were the men (and women) to whom the business belonged.

When we study landownership as the earliest form of Big Business we do well to look, first of all, to Britain. There were bigger land-owners elsewhere, as for example in Russia, but Britain, unlike most other countries, underwent successive and large-scale changes of land-ownership. The result was gradually to replace medieval robber barons by businessmen whose political and legal activities rested upon a solid basis of management, production and marketing. The larger castles, each built as the headquarters of what we should now call an armoured brigade, turned into centres of agricultural and commercial activity. The process began with the Wars of the Roses (1455–85), in the course of which some noble families were killed off. It continued with the dissolution of the monasteries in the reign of Henry VIII, which created a new class of landowners endowed with more wealth than ancestry. It was completed during the Civil Wars of the seventeenth century when property changed hands again, leaving the astute as successors to the loyal and the brave. The effect was to establish an aristocracy that was peculiar to Britain, a class of landowners who were seldom 'noble' in

the European sense, whose younger brothers were often lawyers or clergy, whose own outlook was more managerial than military. The peculiar strength of eighteenth-century Britain lay in the close alliance of the peerage with the gentry, with the professions and the City. Social exclusiveness there may have been but it seldom stood in the way of policy or finance. Men who mattered usually (not always) agreed with each other in the main purposes of trade and war.

Big Business in eighteenth-century Britain was represented, in the first place, by families whose wealth gave them power and whose power served to enhance their wealth. There were other families of comparable or even greater fortune who lacked political ambition and these might be thought to form a separate group. To take the politically prominent families first, these are dealt with at length in a book published in 1865,[1] from which the following extract is highly significant:

... So powerful has been the action of these circumstances, so engrained is in England the preference for these houses, that the thirty-one families whose histories we have related supply at this moment one clear fourth of the English House of Commons ... A careful analysis shows that the thirty-one families at this moment supply one hundred and ten members ... (and) ... have, in fact, as great a direct power as the whole kingdom of Ireland, double that of Scotland, five times that of London, as much as that of London and the forty next greatest cities. I believe it to be beyond all shadow of doubt that when we have added the great Irish and the great Scotch proprietors, it will be found that sixty families supply, and for generations have supplied, one-third of the House of Commons, one-third of the ultimate governing power for an Empire which includes a fourth of the human race.

Of the families listed eleven had been fairly important in the Middle Ages. These were the Percys, Greys, Stanleys, Clintons, Talbots, Manners, Grenvilles, Herberts, Somersets, Berkeleys and Howards. Eight families rose to prominence under Henry VIII. These were the Vanes (or Fanes), Cavendishes, Stanhopes, Pagets, Montagus, Russells, Cecils and Seymours. Six families gained power during the seventeenth century. These were the Lowthers, Fitzwilliams, Osbornes, Spencers, Villiers and Petty-Fitzmorurices; to which group may be added the two ducal families deriving illegitimately from Charles II, the Fitzroys

and Lennoxes, and the Bentincks who came to England with William
III. There followed, in the eighteenth and nineteenth centuries, the
Leveson-Gowers, the Barings and the Grosvenors, closing this particular
list to all eternity. It should not be taken too seriously and it could well
be that some families have been wrongly omitted, but the general
picture is accurate and the weight of aristocratic influence is if anything
under-estimated by the exclusion of cousins, sons-in-law and depen-
dents. The aristocracy that had established itself by 1688 was very much
the same in 1865 with but three families added. While an analysis of
these families' representation in Parliament may be impressive, a list of
their ministerial posts would be more impressive still. These were
families whose position rested upon a very solid wealth derived from
landownership.

There were other families, however, whose wealth was not matched
by their political aspirations. When the 'New Doomsday Survey' of
1873 was compiled the fact emerged that four-fifths of the kingdom
belonged to seven thousand people. It also appeared that sixteen people
in England and Scotland had rentals of over £100,000 a year.[2] Listed
alphabetically, they were the following:

	Acres	£s rental
Marquis of Anglesey	25,505	107,361
Duke of Bedford	87,507	141,577
Duke of Buccleuch	458,739	216,026
Marquis of Bute	116,668	231,421
Lord Calthorpe	6,470	122,628
Earl of Derby	56,598	150,326
Duke of Devonshire	198,665	180,990
Earl of Dudley	25,554	123,176
Earl Fitzwilliam	115,743	138,801
Marquis of Londonderry	50,323	100,118
Duke of Norfolk	44,638	269,698
Duke of Northumberland	186,297	176,048
Sir Lawrence Palk, Bt	10,109	190,275
Duke of Portland	162,235	124,925
Sir John Ramsden, Bt	72,448	175,631
Duke of Sutherland	1,358,546	141,679

There are several defects in this list, one being the exclusion of Ireland, another being the fact that some returns include, while others omit, rentals from town property. Nor must we forget that most of these magnates had other sources of income. With these limitations noted, however, we may find the list of interest. It illustrates the fact that the ownership of Scottish mountains might be financially irrelevant. The vast areas thus owned by the Earl of Breadalbane, Sir James Matheson, the Earl of Seafield and the Earl of Fife did not qualify them for inclusion in the list. Had a return been made of Irish lands some more families would have been listed, especially perhaps the Earls of Portland, Athlone, Galway and Albermarle, descendants of William III's immediate followers.

If the landed estate was the symbol of established wealth, the town house in London was the symbol of that wealth deployed for a political purpose. The family which kept out of sight (ambition curbed, perhaps, by the execution of an ancestor) would never have more than a local importance. To play for safety would thus mean a town house in York or Exeter, Dublin or Bath. London was the scene preferred, inevitably, by those who played for high stakes and their town properties lay originally in the City itself. Fear of the plague hastened their withdrawal from there, the more important folk moving to what is still called the Strand, the river shore between London and Westminster. Taken in sequence, moving upstream, these houses in 1600 were Essex or Leicester House, Arundel House, Somerset House, the Savoy, Russell House, Durham House, Norwich House, York House and Northumberland House, with Whitehall beyond Scotland Yard and Lambeth House beyond that again. These and other great houses were primarily to be reached by river, their owners going to court for favours, to the City for money and sometimes to the Tower for treason. The Strand lost some of its appeal with the Fire of London (1666) and more again from the development of the coach and the paved highway. When Samuel Pepys bought his first coach (second-hand) in 1668 he was taking a modest part in the movement which was to create the West End. It was the horsed carriage which led the aristocracy away from the river and into the area which centres upon St James's Palace. Their leader in the movement was the Earl of Clarendon, whose house in Piccadilly passed to the Duke of Albermarle.

His early imitators and neighbours included the Earl of Burlington, Lord Berkeley and Sir Thomas Bond, all of whose names are imprinted on the streets. The development of Mayfair proper began in 1662 when the St James's Street area was granted on lease to Henry Jermyn, Earl of St Albans. It was he who planned St James's Square with King Street, York Street, Charles Street and Jermyn Street among the thoroughfares adjacent. The Soho area was granted to the Duke of Monmouth in 1677 but passed in 1700 to William Bentinck, Earl of Portland, the friend and adviser to William III, and this is the origin of the BBC's address in Portland Place.

Bloomsbury owes its plan and street names to the Russell family.[3] Their story begins with James Russell, first Earl of Bedford (1486–1555), whose services to Henry VIII were rewarded by grants of monastic land in Devon, Bedfordshire and London. With the draining of the fens the Thorney estate eclipsed the Tavistock estate but both were eclipsed in turn by the value of the Long Acre and Convent (or Covent) Garden properties which had belonged to the Abbey of Westminster. Like other great families they had their town house but they realized, from an early date, that their London property was essentially an investment. They began to develop it in 1630, building the Piazza at Covent Garden, with St Paul's church overlooking what would eventually become the fruit and vegetable market. Meanwhile Thomas Wrothesley, the first Earl of Southampton, had also been rewarded for his services to Henry VIII. He thus acquired the Manor of Bloomsbury, another area of monastic property extending as far as Tottenham Court Lane. Following the Russell example the fourth Earl of Southampton (1607–67) built a piazza which is now Bloomsbury Square. He had no son, however, and his second daughter married the second son of the fifth Earl of Bedford, bringing with her as dowry the manors of Bloomsbury and St Giles. Another fortunate marriage brought the ownership of the Rotherhithe Docks and the Wells' Brothers shipbuilding yard. As for Bloomsbury, the Russells began to build Bedford Square in 1774. Russell Square followed in 1805–14 and then Tavistock Square, built by Thomas Cubitt in 1822. Cubitt went on to build Gordon Square, Woburn Square and all the adjacent streets, consolidating what had become an enormously valuable estate of 119 acres in the heart of London. Similar if smaller investments were made, mostly after 1763, by the Cavendishes, Harleys and Portmans.

The Grosvenor's rise to eminence began with Sir Thomas Grosvenor (1656–1700), third baronet of Cheshire, who married Mary Davies, daughter and heiress to a London scrivener. Her dowry included the manor of Ebury and some fields adjoining Park Lane. These potentially urban properties developed slowly, being worth over £2,000 a year in 1722, nearly £7,000 in 1779 and £12,000 in 1802. It was later still, in 1826, that the second Earl Grosvenor, first Marquis of Westminster, planned what has since been called Belgravia. To him and to his descendants, Dukes of Westminster, we owe the Grosvenor Hotel, Grosvenor House, Grosvenor Gardens, Belgrave Road and St George's Road, with the squares called respectively Eaton, Chester, Eccleston, Warwick and St George's. It was this London property which made the first Duke at one time the richest man in England. His chief adviser in developing the Westminster estate was George Trollope, the estate agent and founder of the firm which still exists and which is also one parent of the contracting firm of Trollope & Colls. Victorian Big Business owed much to men like George Trollope, who founded his agency in 1778. (Colls & Sons, the contractors, established their business in 1840 and then joined with George Trollope & Sons to form Trollope & Colls Ltd.) It was said of Trollope that he rarely visited Grosvenor House and that the Duke never visited his office. It was the agent's business to know where the Duke would be at any given time; whether at Tattersalls, at Ascot or in the precincts of the House of Lords. It was in such surroundings that business used to be done. Not the least of an agent's business was the maintenance of the town house itself, its coach-house and stables. These great town houses played a central part in the London Season until the years which followed World War I. Then they began to disappear, the town houses of the Grosvenors, Lansdownes and Devonshires being demolished to make room for hotels and offices. By 1930 only four of the great houses remained – Apsley, Bridgewater, Londonderry and Holland. Now there is only the one, Apsley House, and that is a museum except for the flat on the top floor which is still occupied by the Duke of Wellington.

These London mansions had been the symbols of political power but many of the landed families had a still greater influence elsewhere.

London's West End they had to share but the provincial city nearest their principal seat was often a place they could partly own and entirely dominate. Manchester grew thus under the protection of the canal-building Duke of Bridgewater. Liverpool was similarly over-shadowed by the Earls of Derby and Sefton, Derby and Eastbourne by the Dukes of Devonshire, Sheffield by the Dukes of Norfolk and Cardiff by the Marquises of Anglesey. Lord Calthorpe owned the greater part of Edgbaston, Birmingham's fashionable suburb, Sir Laurence Palk owned most of Torquay and the Clintons most of Blackpool. In the sunset period of British landownership the great incomes came not from agricultural but from urban land development. As from about 1860 the industrialists were becoming important, with fortunes and peerages derived from engineering, textiles and beer, but they had to share some of their wealth with the landowners. Of the provincial towns it appeared that sixty-nine largely belonged to the old nobility and thirty-four to untitled gentry whose wealth was almost comparable. It has been very justly observed[4] that 'only those land-owners who had an industrial source of income remained impregnably wealthy'. One might add that these, a fortunate few, were probably more wealthy than any of the great families had ever been before. A Duke of Westminster of about 1890 might be less powerful than his ancestors had been but his three hundred servants at his principal – but not his only – residence represented a peak of luxury which no one else has enjoyed before or since (see the diagram on page 12).

As Big Business was at first based upon landownership, it is relevant to ask how the great estates used to be run. There was no uniformity about this but the Bedford estates were administered on a system which may have been fairly typical[5] and which can be represented dia-gramatically.

The Earl's revenue came to the Receiver-General from his Stewards and Agents, who had it from Bailiffs who had collected it from tenants. The Receiver-General supplied money as required to the Earl and his personal staff through the Gentleman of the Privy Purse. He also supplied money to the Steward of the household, who in turn supplied the other officers through whom the servants were paid and the whole house provisioned. The actual hierarchy was certainly more complex and variable than the diagram. One basic fact, however, is

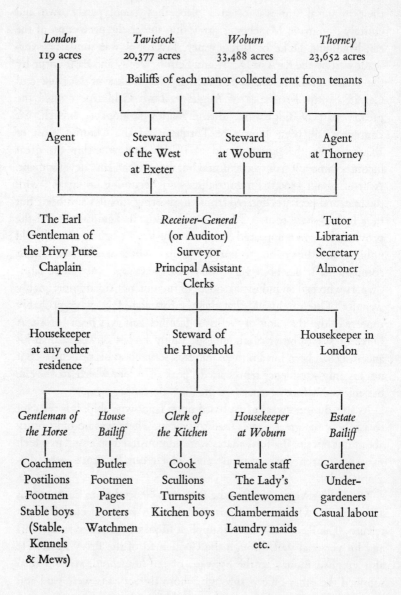

London	Tavistock	Woburn	Thorney
119 acres	20,377 acres	33,488 acres	23,652 acres

Bailiffs of each manor collected rent from tenants

Agent	Steward of the West at Exeter	Steward at Woburn	Agent at Thorney

The Earl Gentleman of the Privy Purse Chaplain	Receiver-General (or Auditor) Surveyor Principal Assistant Clerks	Tutor Librarian Secretary Almoner

Housekeeper at any other residence	Steward of the Household	Housekeeper in London

Gentleman of the Horse	House Bailiff	Clerk of the Kitchen	Housekeeper at Woburn	Estate Bailiff
Coachmen Postilions Footmen Stable boys (Stable, Kennels & Mews)	Butler Footmen Pages Porters Watchmen	Cook Scullions Turnspits Kitchen boys	Female staff The Lady's Gentlewomen Chambermaids Laundry maids etc.	Gardener Under-gardeners Casual labour

that most of the household moved with the Earl between Woburn and London so that the steward of the household was responsible for both residences, at least when the earl was there. In this particular household the chaplain was also tutor, librarian, secretary and almoner, but this need not have been so. The office of gentleman of the horse was usually filled by a young man of good family, who went on to become agent, perhaps, on one of the estates. The footmen belonged to him when attending the earl's carriage but to the house bailiff when indoors, a plentiful source of friction. The gardener became more independent in course of time and was eventually paid more than the steward of the household. The Earl of Bedford did not become a duke until 1694, from which time his entourage may well have increased. Other dukes certainly had more servants and we read that the Duke of Chandos had four tables at Cannons; the Duke's, the chaplain's, the household officers' and that of the gentleman of the horse.[6] The same nobleman retained Pepusch as his 'Master of the Music' with Handel as organist (1718–20) for his private chapel.

From what we learn of the eighteenth-century household at the ducal level we soon come to realize that the country house was the head office of a complex organization. It was also the focal point of a whole countryside:

Winter or summer, the country houses of the aristocracy were the centres of local social life whenever the family were in residence. A constant stream of visitors rode up the drive to pay their respects, discuss business or politics, or to present requests and complaints. The consumption of food and wine and the employment of servants were necessarily on a massive scale ... When the second Duke of Kingston was at Thoresby for twelve weeks in 1736 the household expenses came to £1,477 of which £307 was spent on meat, and the first Duke of Dorset reckoned up his expenses at more than £257 when visited briefly at Knole by the future George II, then Prince of Wales ... At Audley End the bill for wages of indoor staff was over £500 in 1773, and in 1759 the Marquis of Rockingham spent £2,050 on housekeeping and £2,536 on his stables and kennels.[7]

Central to estate administration was the office of receiver-general, commissioner or auditor. Its importance varied with the ability of the occupant and the habits of his noble master. Some landowners entrusted their business to a London banker like Richard Hoare, at the sign of the golden bottle in Fleet Street, leaving their auditors to do little more than check the accounts. Others had a barrister or solicitor as chief agent and left all business to him. Others, more active, did their own business and trusted nobody. It was for the nobleman to decide whether he would be managing director or chairman of the board but there was, in any case, a mass of work to be done by somebody. Big Business began in the office of the man who did it and his legacy to the later industrialist was his system of accountancy.

On visiting Belvoir the Duke (of Bedford) was much impressed by his fellow nobleman's system of household statistics. The Duke of Rutland's agent had quickly produced a return on the number of persons (including servants) who had dined at Belvoir in the past year. The number was 18,000. He had also been able to calculate such matters as the average cost of feeding and lodging Belvoir's establishment and the average consumption of bread.[8]

Here were the beginnings of statistical method and the final result was the emergence of the land agent as a professional man in his own right; not a solicitor with experience of estate management but a man especially qualified in that particular business. The process began with the foundation of the Institution of Surveyors in 1868. It became the Royal Institution when chartered in 1881, by which date the membership numbered five hundred. As from about 1870 many surveyors became land agents (the standard book on the subject[9] appeared in 1898), but the land agents had no society of their own until 1902. The active founders were Colonel Halifax Wyatt, agent for the Earl of Sefton, and Mr E. G. Wheler, commissioner for the Duke of Northumberland. Membership rose to nearly nine hundred in four years and a qualifying examination was introduced in 1921.[10] Organizations are apt to take formal shape when their actual importance is dwindling.

A landed aristocracy was not peculiar to Britain but it was the British landowners who most nearly foreshadowed the Big Business of the future. There were nobles elsewhere in Europe whose family pride prevented them knowing too much about trade or commerce. They might know the land over which they hunted and they might admit to an interest in horses and game but they were apt to leave the sordid details to their underlings. English owners of Irish land were sometimes as remote from economic reality, intent only on their military and political aspirations. There were English landowners, for that matter, who would tolerate the bad farming and habitual arrears of a tenant who was politically loyal, while others would make farming give way to sport. More aristocrats, however, had an eye to finance and knew no substitute for money. Where profit was concerned they seldom let pride of ancestry stand in their way. Nor was there ever in Britain a rigid distinction of rank which divided the nobility from the gentry or the gentry from the middle class. The merchant became a landowner and the landowner's younger brother might go to sea. When class distinctions began to harden, as they did in the later nineteenth century, it was because the landowners were beginning to lose their grip.

Landownership could be Big Business then, especially when some of the land was urban. To what extent could the same be said of commerce? The bigger profits came from trade with America and the West and East Indies, the expansion in business beginning with the reign of Charles II. Virginia and Maryland, which had exported 20,000 lbs of tobacco in 1619, had increased this to nine million lbs in the 1660s and to thirteen million by 1700, two-thirds of which was re-exported. Sugar imports into London, which had been negligible before the Civil Wars, rose to 148,000 cwt in 1663–9 and 371,000 cwt in 1699–1701, a third of it being re-exported.[11] In spite of setbacks in time of war, the business continued to grow and some considerable fortunes were made out of it. The sugar magnates included the Longs of Jamaica, Richard Pennant, who became Lord Penrhyn, and the Lascelles, who were to be the forbears of the Earls of Harewood. Still more important politically was the Gladstone family of Liverpool which used its West Indian fortune to gain a baronetcy in 1846 and provided Britain with one of its most famous prime ministers. Few merchants, however, had this sort of success and not one of them founded a family of the first rank. By 1761 there were between fifty and sixty merchants in the House of Commons, the number rising slowly towards the end of the century. 'The domination of land was almost unimpaired, nevertheless, and even in 1832 about three-quarters of the Members could be said to be concerned entirely or mainly with land.[12]

The East India trade, nationalized from the outset, provided only a few individual fortunes of any consequence. Sir Josiah Child (1630–99) was a notable chairman of the East India Company and wealthy enough to acquire Wanstead Abbey in 1673 and marry his elder daughter to the Marquis of Worcester. It was his grand-daughter, Elizabeth Howland, who married Wriothesley Russell in 1695, adding the Child and Howland fortunes to the already enormous property of the Dukes of Bedford. The most successful East India family was un-questionably that of Pitt. Founder of the Pitt fortunes was Thomas (1653–1726) who began his career as an interloper in the East Indies trade but ended as governor of Madras. His fortune sufficed to make his son Earl of Londonderry and his grandson became prime minister and Earl of Chatham. The second Earl of Chatham also had an im-portant career but was less distinguished than his younger brother, who became prime minister at the age of twenty-four but died unmarried in 1806, the family then disappearing from both the peerage and the political scene. Later representatives of the East India Company in-cluded Sir Charles Grant whose son of the same name became Lord Glenelg. These and other directors of the company were often eclipsed in fortune, however, by generals and still more so by admirals. Fortunes were made from prize-money by seamen like Edward Boscawen, Peter Rainier, George Elphinstone (ancestor to the Marquis of Lansdowne) and Edward Pellew. But the county families founded by these heroes were never in the millionaire class.

Fortunes of this sort could be made in several ways but there was only one way in which the money could be invested. Whatever his profession or trade had been, the man of wealth had to end as a landowner. Only then could he be accepted as one whose wealth was secure, whose status was unquestioned, whose future was assured. Landownership set the seal on any solid success. Only with the acquisition of an estate could it be said of a man that he had finally, and unquestionably, arrived.

The solid ramparts of Big Business in its landowning form were first breached not by the merchants but by the bankers. There was enough middle-class pressure to bring about the repeal of the Corn Laws in 1846. This was a blow to agriculture but there was a comparable shock in 1847 when one of the ducal houses suddenly collapsed. Richard Plantagenet Temple Nugent Brydges Chandos Grenville, second Duke of Buckingham and Chandos, the owner of well over 50,000 acres, an exponent of scientific cultivation and a landlord known as the 'Farmers' Friend', was compelled to sell most of his property. It did not mean the end of the family. It did not even prevent the third Duke from becoming Secretary of State for the Colonies (1867-8). The effect, however, was to shake the whole fabric of landowning society. That the land of an agricultural theorist should come on the market might surprise nobody, but ducal estates seldom changed hands except by inheritance.

Whatever the cause, the sale of such large acreages of land was almost unprecedented, and it offered an opportunity for rich men without estates to acquire them and join the envied ranks of the landowners. The most ready buyers were the bankers. Thus we find that the Duke's Aston Clinton estate at Tring was bought by Sir Anthony de Rothschild, and the neighbouring estate of Aston Abbots was acquired by Samuel James Lloyd of the Manchester banking firm of William, Jones, Lloyd and Co., later better known as the Westminster Bank. Samuel Lloyd was later created Lord Overstone. In Hampshire another banker, Alexander Baring, was busy carving out an estate. Earlier he had paid the heirs of the last Duke of Bolton £64,200 for the Itchener Stoke estate. Now he added to it the Duke of Buckingham's lands at Itchen Abbas ...
Another noted banker who was an enthusiastic purchaser of land was Henry Drummond of the Charing Cross Bank ... he finished up with the Albury estate in Surrey. He had no male heir and the estates subsequently passed into the hands of the dukes of Northumberland when Drummond's daughter married Algernon George Percy, who was to become the sixth Duke ...[13]

From being Big Business in itself the agricultural estate was becoming a status symbol, a decorative amenity for somebody whose income was derived from another source. The result was that estates in the 1860s were often sold at forty or even sixty-five years' purchase, being no longer regarded as an investment at all. The great days of landownership were over. By 1865 Lord Overstone (1796-1883), with a fortune of five million, was supposed to be one of the wealthiest men in the world, his position as a landowner merely incidental to his position as a financier.
Most significant of the banking families were the Barings and that for three reasons. In the first place their rise to eminence began at an early period when the task was more difficult. In the second place they actually established themselves as members of the governing group,

the only new family to do so after 1688. In the third place their family link with the United States foreshadowed much that would happen in the twentieth century. Dutch in origin, the seventeenth-century Barings are first heard of at Gröningen, Overyssel, where Pastor Francis Baring was born. He eventually settled in England and his son John set up a cloth-making business in Devonshire. John's third son, Francis (1740–1810), established a merchant house in London which became Baring Brothers & Co. A member of Parliament, a director and later chairman of the East India Company, a close friend of Lord Shelburne, Francis was made a baronet in 1793. His second son, Alexander (born in 1774), went to the USA where he purchased extensive lands in Pennsylvania and Maine and married the eldest daughter of Senator William Bingham of Philadelphia, then considered to be the richest man in the USA. From Bingham this daughter, the future Lady Ashburton, inherited 900,000 dollars. Alexander was given a peerage in 1835, by which date his second son, Francis, had married the daughter of the Duke of Bassano, Napoleon's Secretary of State. The second Baron Ashburton (1799–1864) married a daughter of the sixth Earl of Sandwich, another grandson of Sir Francis became Chancellor of the Exchequer and Baron Northbrook, while a third became Bishop of Durham. When we discover that Baring is still the family name of Baron Ashburton, the Earl of Cromer, Baron Howick of Glendale, Baron Northbrook and Baron Revelstoke, we realize that the Barings' achievement has been unique.

The bankers were the first to break into the closed circle of land-ownership. They were followed by the industrialists. Some 246 new peerages were created between 1886 and 1914, three-quarters of them going to leaders of industry and five of them to brewers. Mr W. H. Smith became Lord Hambledon, Mr Cunliffe-Lister became Lord Masham, Mr William Armstrong (the armament king) became Lord Armstrong of Cragside and the owner of 16,000 acres in Northumberland. When we learn, finally, that Sir Edward Guinness (Lord Iveagh from 1891) the Irish brewer, bought 17,000 acres in Suffolk from His Highness the Maharajah Duleep-Singh, we can fairly conclude that the old order had collapsed. The change was accurately reflected in the membership of the House of Commons where landowners were replaced by company directors. With Estate Duty (or Death Duty, as it was called) introduced in 1894, increased in 1907 and raised to twenty-five per cent in 1909, the pressure on the owners of property began. It was applied more heavily amidst the casualties of World War I and it was estimated in 1921 that a quarter of England must have changed hands,[14] the vendors including the Dukes of Rutland, Beaufort, Northumberland and Westminster and the Marquises of Northampton and Bath. To illustrate the process of spoliation one might instance the eleventh Duke of Bedford, forced to sell Thorney and Covent Garden, whose death in 1940 led nevertheless to a demand for £3,000,000 in death duties. The twelfth Duke died in 1953 and the demand this time was for £4,000,000. The thirteenth (and present) Duke then sold most of Bloomsbury to pay for the restoration of Woburn, which was thrown open to the public and made to pay for itself with the help of three million visitors over the first eleven years.

If there was a moment in history when the reign of the great landowners came to an end it was perhaps the year 1881 when the Derby was won by an American horse, Iroquois, owned by a Mr Lorillard. Until then the ownership of racehorses had been more or less confined to the aristocracy. The Ascot meeting, dating from the reign of Queen Anne, had been revived and made fashionable by the Duke of Cumberland. During a typical day's racing at Newmarket in the late eighteenth century nearly every horse would have a titled owner. Ducal owners remained important throughout the nineteenth century, the Duke of Westminster being especially prominent as the century approached its end. But the success of Iroquois was no isolated and accidental event. Jack Hammond's horse, St Gatieu, was the winner in 1884 and worse was to follow with Orby's win in 1907, for that horse's owner, Mr Richard Croker, was an Irish-American, a New York politician, rugged, opinionated and ruthless. Lemberg, by contrast, the winner in 1910, was owned by an Australian whose fortune derived from the Broken Hill Silver Mines. With racing results such as these the last citadel of aristocracy might be thought to have fallen. It is a question, however, whether such a conclusion might be justified. The pillars of the turf when the twentieth century began were clearly the Prince of Wales, the Duke of Westminster, the Duke of Portland and the Earl of Rosebery. When Lord Derby's Sansovino won the Derby in 1924, moreover, he was repeating the success of his ancestor (the

founder of the race) whose horse won it in 1787. We should also remember that the list of the world's wealthiest men, as published by the American newspapers in 1923, was headed by Henry Ford and John D. Rockefeller but the Duke of Westminster was in third place. He was ahead, and had always been ahead, of the Vanderbilts, a fact made apparent at Epsom and Ascot. If it was true that the millionaires had forced their way in, it was far from obvious that the aristocrats had been wholly excluded. They fought for survival and some of them are fighting still.

2 Transport

As agriculture comes before commerce, so commerce comes before industry. But commerce depends in turn upon a means of transport. The merchant must load his goods on a camel or horse, in a waggon or a ship. In the countries where Big Business originated, the early emphasis was always on water transport, to which the road system was ancillary. A ship or rivercraft has always offered the cheapest means of carrying the heavy load and it is cheaper still when aided by the current, tide or wind. It soon became obvious that the horse which tows a laden canal boat is propelling more than the cartload it can move when on the road. So the history of transport is largely, though not entirely, the story of ships and harbours, docks and charts. This is an aspect of economic history which scholars have mostly agreed to ignore, leaving us with a vast gap in our historical knowledge. We know enough, however, to dismiss at the outset some legends which are commonly believed. One of these concerns the existence of seafaring peoples, of folk with an inborn gift for navigation, of men with the sea in their blood. In so far as these hereditary aptitudes exist they are confined to the seaports. The maritime historian has thus to deal with the specialized communities which have grown up near the quayside. Historically these groups have been committed to an age-long conflict with the sea itself, a conflict in which ships and men innumerable have been lost. In a trade so hazardous and picturesque there has been little scope until recently for Big Business. Shipowners and seafaring men have been concerned with the romance of travel, with the beauty of the ships and the perils of the storm. While fortunes have undoubtedly been made by shipowners and even occasionally by master mariners, their motives have seldom been purely economic. Where danger is imminent wealth matters less than life. Partly for this and partly for other reasons there has been from the earliest times a sharp distinction between the shipowner and the merchant, between the owners and the crew.

The legal relationships of those who traded overseas were first defined comprehensively in the Laws of Oleron which may or may not have been drawn up by King Richard 1 in about 1194. Whatever the exact truth about their origin, they do seem to date from that period and they do distinguish clearly between the several parties concerned in a ship. In earlier law it had been assumed that a ship's master should be at least a part owner of the vessel. As from the date of this Code there was no such assumption and the several articles define his duty towards both his owners and those who had freighted the ship. There was a further inference that the owners would be plural. Because of the risks involved the investor evidently preferred to distribute his interest between several ships, being unable or at least unwilling to bear the consequences of any one being a total loss. Fragmentation of the risks meant fragmentation of the profits and while fortunes were made from overseas trade the shipowners were never involved in the Big Business of any century except, possibly, the nineteenth. For nearly the whole of the sailing-ship era the vessels were relatively small and each one divided by law into sixty-four parts. Big profits, when made, were associated with big risks and high insurance rates. Some British ship-owners ended, nevertheless, as country gentlemen with estates near London, Bristol or Liverpool. The biggest ships, from about 1600 to 1813, were in the service of the East India Company which also chose to hire rather than own its tonnage; and while the company itself was in Big Business its affairs had been nationalized from the outset. Members of the company's 'Shipping Interest', as distinct from the company itself, were men of substance in London but not of the millionaire class, nor were they given scope for any daring speculation. The stability of their business owed much to the development of marine insurance during the eighteenth century. Lloyd's Coffee House was moved to the Royal Exchange in 1774 and the forms of marine insurance policy were standardized in 1779. The great man among the underwriters of that period was John Julius Angerstein (1735-1823), Pitt's friend and financial adviser, whose collection of pictures forms the nucleus of the collection in the National Gallery. In so far as anyone made an enormous fortune out of shipping in the age of sail, it was the great underwriters, Angerstein, 'Dicky' Thornton and Sir Francis Baring. It must be remembered, however, that these were financiers whose interests were by no means confined to shipping.

Without being more than moderately successful in their own interests, the British shipowners did build up the structure of trade which made the industrial revolution possible. By the eve of the French Wars, in 1792, there were over 16,000 vessels on the British Register. Of these a large number were small craft employed in the coastal trade or in the trade with Ireland. Among the coasters, however, were the colliers which plied between Newcastle and London, vessels of some size and of great importance. From the same ports and from Hull were maintained the associated trades with the Netherlands and the Baltic. Ships of smaller tonnage traded with France and the Mediterranean, some reaching the ports of the Levant. Ships from the West Country, from Poole, Dartmouth and Teignmouth, were prominent in the Newfoundland fisheries. The slave trade to Africa, America and the West Indies was based upon Bristol, London and Liverpool, the lion's share going increasingly to Liverpool. Ships for the West Indies sailed mostly from London, especially after the West India Docks were opened in 1801, but some also sailed from Bristol, Liverpool, Glasgow and Belfast. Liverpool was the leading port in the trade with Boston, New York and Philadelphia, improving its position as the demand rose for raw cotton in Lancashire. London came second, but fewer ships sailed from Bristol than from Ireland. One other port which deserves mention is Falmouth, not for its trade but for its role as the base for the Post Office packets which crossed the Atlantic. Other packets sailed from Harwich, London, Holyhead and Milford, maintaining a regular and frequent service to Ireland, to European ports, to Gibraltar and Malta. In the development of trade the overseas mail service played an important part and it was well established when British industries were still in their infancy.

While trade expanded, however, and while port facilities improved, the sailing ship changed very little between 1600 and 1800. Significant progress in design began first in the USA where fast sailing vessels were built around Boston and on the Lower Merrimac from about 1793. Construction reached a peak of activity in 1810. 'It took rum to build ships in those days; a quart to a ton by rough allowance; and more to launch her properly.' These were good sailing vessels but they were bettered for speed by the privateer schooners and brigs which took part in the war of 1812. When the war ended these turned into the Baltimore clippers of the Smyrna trade; vessels which brought grapes and oranges to the USA in time for Christmas. From these developed the fast sailing ships of 1840 and a growing demand for speed. In 1841 John Griffith of New York lectured on ship design and produced a model in which certain radical changes were proposed. The result was that Howland and Aspinwall ordered the *Rainbow*, first of the true Yankee clippers. She had concave water lines at the bow, a fine stern and a greater length (in proportion to her breadth) than many designers thought safe. At sea from 1845, she did not founder, in fact, until 1848 and other ships had been launched meanwhile with similar characteristics. First of these was *Sea Witch* (1845) of 907 tons register, with low freeboard, raking masts and considerable sheer. Others followed, like *Samuel Russell*, *Architect* and *Memnon* and all were designed for the China tea trade, a business in which speed was a great advantage. The whole situation was changed, however, with the discovery (1848) of gold in California. With the gold rush of 1849 every ship available sailed for the voyage round the Horn. The veterans among them ended derelict at San Francisco, their crews having gone to the gold-fields. With frantic haste other ships were built at New York and Boston. This is the moment in history when we first hear of the shipbuilding firm of Roosevelt & Joyce.

The gold rush soon ended but its effect had been to bring American clippers into the Pacific. From San Francisco they headed for China, entering the tea trade but now from the opposite direction. Ships were then designed for that trade with emphasis not only on speed but also on strength. Built of soft wood at a low cost, they were distinguished by their good lines and sail design, their deck winches and patent sheaves and their light manilla (not hemp) running gear. With small and miscellaneous crews of 'Dagoes, Dutchmen, Scouwegians and niggers', driven by bully captains and bucko mates, these white-decked and shining clippers broke one record after another. By dint of blasphemy, belaying pins, marlinspikes and revolvers these ships thrashed round the Horn and then careered back on the homeward run. With the repeal of the British Navigation Act in 1849 the American clipper *Oriental* entered the British tea trade, reaching the London docks in ninety-seven days from Hong Kong. This started the British builders on the quest for speed and they responded by launching composite-built ships with wood planking on an iron frame. The Americans were defeated in 1856 and their last entry, *Sea Serpent*, was beaten by both *Ellen Rodger* and *Fiery Cross* in 1859. From 1860 began the classic age of British tea clippers, many of them built on the Clyde, others at Blackwall, Liverpool, Glasgow and Dumbarton. The most exciting finish was in 1866 with five clippers docking almost together after a ninety-nine day passage. *Ariel* made the record outward passage in 1866–7, eighty-three days from Gravesend to Hong Kong. There were twenty-seven ships racing in 1870, a record number, and *Cutty Sark* among them, but that was the year in which the first steamships appeared. Numbers dwindled after that, the last voyage under sail taking place in 1881. For speed and beauty the final prize might have to be divided between *Hallowe'en*, *Thermopylae* and *Cutty Sark*, the first for the best passage of all time (89 days), the second for winning on four occasions and the last-named for logging a twenty-four-hour run of 363 nautical miles with a maximum speed of $17\frac{1}{2}$ knots. Of all these magnificent ships *Cutty Sark* is the last survivor, permanently docked at Greenwich.

It would be easy to dismiss this classic period of sail as a picturesque anachronism. The tea races took place, after all, when steamships had already come to predominate on other routes. These semi-sporting events might seem irrelevant, therefore, to the growth of modern industry and alien to all caculations of profit and loss. Such a conclusion would, however, be wrong for three reasons. First and foremost the early steamship was a sailing ship with the addition of an auxiliary engine. Even in 1875 the White Star Line's *Britannia* and *Germanic* were fully rigged, and years would pass before sails were finally discarded. Apart from that we have to realize that, far from being wasted, the work done on the design of the clipper hull was a preparation for the ships of the future and for ships, indeed, which are still being built. More than that, the later composite or iron sailing ships marked the transition from timber to steel construction although some of the clipper features were retained. In the second place, the sailing ship did not disappear overnight but remained in use until the end of the nineteenth century. The period 1880–1900 thus saw the development of the big four-masted barque, usually built for the Australian wool trade. There were some famous ships during this last phase, such as the *Torrens* in which Joseph Conrad sailed as mate and, in 1893, the *Dalgonar*, which was saved from destruction by fire in 1896. One of the last of these vessels crossed the battlefield during the action near the Falkland Islands in 1914. In the third place, several of the great shipping lines were founded in the days of sail and are still very much in business. Perhaps the most important of these is the firm of Wilcox & Anderson, founded in 1815 and renamed the Peninsular Company in 1837. It became the Peninsular and Oriental Steam Navigation Company after its merger in 1840 with the Trans-Atlantic Steamship Company and under this name it has traded ever since, dominating the routes to India and the Far East and, latterly, to Australia. Although it was the steamship which made Big Business possible at sea, it was the sailing ship which prepared the way and (incidentally) supplied the steamship with its coal on the long-distance trade routes where there was no coal to be had at the other end.

The sailing clipper and the steamship developed side by side on different routes and for different purposes. It is a question, incidentally, whether the clipper ship would even have been possible without the steam tug. Earlier ship designs had been a compromise between what was needed on the high seas and what was needed in an estuary or harbour mouth. As soon as tugs became generally available (from about 1850) the design could become more specialized on the assumption that ships in confined waters would never be under sail. It was the tug which first appealed to the British Admiralty and it was the tug which first gained the approval of the British shipowners. For the steamship in its early form there was otherwise less support in Britain than in the USA. The development of British canals and roads had lessened the importance of river travel for passengers. As for goods, the early steamships were all but useless, their cargo space being mostly filled with machinery and coal. The United States, by contrast, had unlimited uses for the steamship, having no roads or canals and a tremendous system of navigable lakes and rivers flanked by forests full of timber fuel. Great scope existed for passenger services on the Hudson, Delaware and Potomac, but even greater scope on the Mississippi and its tributaries which offered 44,000 miles of waterway much of it, without steamships, being hardly navigable at all. If the first successful steamboat was the *Charlotte Dundas*, placed on the Forth and Clyde Canal in 1802, it was Fulton's *Clermont* (of 1807) which established the first regular passenger service, that between Albany and New York. It was mainly in the USA, therefore, that the river steamship developed.

The first steamship appeared on the Mississippi in 1814 and many others followed, mostly built at Pittsburgh or Cincinnati. There were more than two hundred of them by 1834, fast and lightly built vessels of shallow draught, powerfully engined and at work in a highly competitive trade. Between 1816 and 1848 some 233 paddle-wheel steamboats blew up in American waters, sometimes as many as a dozen a year, with casualties running to thousands. Speeds were worked up to 25 knots and the question was soon being asked whether steamships could not be used at sea. The first steamship to attempt the Atlantic crossing was the 350-ton *Savannah* of New Jersey, sailing in May 1819. This experiment was a failure, her passage being no better than average and her engines running for only eighty hours out of twenty-nine and a half days. The truth was that success with the early steamship demanded a short passage with sheltered waters and plenty of points at which to refuel. Such conditions existed on the Clyde, where British marine engineering had its birthplace, but the river had to be artificially deepened before its potentialities could be realized. First of the Clyde steamboats was the *Comet* of 1811, and ten in all had been built by 1815. These were all quite small, the first regular sea-going steam vessel being the 90-ton *Rob Roy* of 1818, built by William Denny of Dumbarton, with engines by David Napier of Glasgow. She operated for the next two years between Greenock and Belfast. Still more successful was the *Aetna* ferry boat which ran for fifteen years (from 1817) between Liverpool and Tranmere. Encouraged by the results obtained on the Clyde and the Mersey, Messrs J. & C. Wood built the *James Watt* of 420 tons for the London and Leith Line (1821) and next year saw the beginning of Mr Napier's regular steamship service between Liverpool, Greenock and Glasgow. In these relatively sheltered waters the ships were developed which would later attempt the Atlantic.

If there was to be an ocean-going steamship the Atlantic was the only possible ocean in which to experiment. The passage was relatively short – three to five weeks under sail – and there was coal available at either end together with marine engineers capable of doing repairs. After some unsuccessful attempts the Atlantic was finally conquered in 1838. In that year the *Sirius*, of 700 tons with 320 hp engines built by Thomas Wingate of Glasgow, and chartered by the British and American Steam Navigation Company, sailed for New York on 4 April. Three days later the *Great Western* of 1,340 tons, designed and built by Mr Patterson of Bristol, with 440 hp engines built by Maudslay, Sons & Field of London, sailed for the same destination. Amid mounting excitement both reached New York on 23 April. Using 655 tons of coal, the *Great Western* had achieved a sixteen-day passage, reaching a maximum speed of 8.2 knots. She bettered her record on the homeward voyage, taking only fourteen days to make the crossing and logging a maximum speed of 9 knots. On her second voyage she did better still, taking fourteen days, sixteen hours on the outward, and twelve days, fourteen hours on the homeward passage. The case for the ocean-going steamship had been proved. A ship like the *Great Western* could offer a faster passage than any sailing ship. What was more to the point, she could do it with regularity, advertising beforehand the day of arrival. She had, of course, no space for cargo but she was ideally suited for passengers and mail. The directors of the Great Western Company were discreetly jubilant and when the Admiralty advertised in October 1838, inviting tenders for the North American mails, they confidently put in their bid. They failed, however, to secure the contract. It was given, instead, to Mr Samuel Cunard, a native of Halifax, Nova Scotia.

Coming to Britain in 1830, Cunard had met Mr Robert Napier of Glasgow, through whom he was introduced to Mr George Burns of Glasgow and Mr David MacIver of Liverpool. These men formed the syndicate which underbid the Great Western Company, offering to undertake two voyages a month between Liverpool and the United States, carrying the mails in return for a subsidy of £55,000 a year.

Later, the number of ships was raised to four and the subsidy to £81,000. The first four ships, all built of wood on the Clyde and all engined by Robert Napier, were *Britannia*, *Acadia*, *Caledonia* and *Columbia*. These went into service on 4 July 1840 and were soon followed by the *America*, *Niagara* and other ships, all of 1,820 tons and 680 hp, logging an average speed of $10\frac{1}{4}$ knots. Further development beyond this point depended upon greater size and improved means of propulsion. It was realized that a larger ship would save, proportionately, on engine and fuel space, but no larger ship could be built of timber. Could a ship be built of iron? River vessels and canal boats had already been built of iron and yards for building in this material had already been established by Fawcett & Preston at Liverpool and by William Laird & Sons at Birkenhead. But doubts were expressed about iron-built ships at sea. What would happen about compass deviation? And what about barnacles and seaweed? As for improved means of propulsion, the limitations of the paddle-wheel were obvious, especially when the ship rolled, burying the one wheel and jerking the other into the air. Could a screw propeller be used instead? Successful experiments and trials from 1836 led to the launching of the *Archimedes* in 1839 and the Admiralty's construction of the *Rattler*. For all practical purposes that problem had been solved and the other objections to the iron ship were soon shown to be unfounded.

The success of the Cunard Line, combined with the progress made in iron construction and screw propulsion, encouraged the Great Western Steamship Company to build a notable successor to the *Great Western*. This was the *Great Britain* of 2,984 tons and 1,000 hp built again to the design of Mr Patterson. With a length of 322 feet over all and 51 feet extreme breadth, she was far larger – and especially far longer – than any ship previously built. Screw-propelled and built of iron throughout, she had six masts, only one of them square-rigged, and her emergence from dock (not without difficulty) was the sensation of the year 1843.

So great, indeed, was the interest felt in this vessel that, on her arrival in the Thames, Her Majesty and Prince Albert with great numbers of the nobility, and thousands of other persons, paid her a visit. Nor was her fame confined to England, forming as she did the subject of discussion among the learned and scientific societies of Europe, which was taken up with unusual fervour in the United States of America when it became known that she was to be employed as one of the Transatlantic steamers destined to eclipse the still celebrated American sailing clippers.[1]

She had, in fact, a remarkable career and one not entirely ended. Thirty years after completion she was still in service but in the Australian trade. When judged to be worn out she was left as a hulk in the Falkland Islands. Forgotten for a lifetime, she was then rediscovered, and funds were raised to tow her back to her home port of Bristol. She survived that last voyage and ended (1970) in the dock from which she had been brought forth and which her hull exactly fits. To overcome one of the objections to an iron ship she had originally been sheathed in oak and coppered, the wood serving to separate the copper and iron. What is extraordinary is that the oak has survived to this day without the copper. She will remain now as a monument to the enterprise of her original owners.

Other and bigger ships entered the Atlantic passenger service but there is no need, for the present purpose, to follow these later developments. As from 1843 the problem of the transatlantic passage had been solved. In a highly competitive business the speed of the crossing was bound to improve. This process has continued and is continuing in terms of air travel, but no subsequent improvement has been as important as the first discovery that a big screw-driven iron ship can cross the Atlantic with the regularity of a ferry boat. From about 1843 it was possible for business men to travel rapidly between London and New York. The mails had become dependable and fast, not throughout the world but on this particular route. It was now seen to be inevitable, however, that the steamship should conquer the other oceans in turn. The process was actually a slow one, but from 1870, when the Suez Canal came into use, it became possible to organize business on a world basis with regular contact between head office and branches. Between civilized countries travel was ceasing to be an adventure and was becoming a routine. The Cunard and White Star lines were to flourish in rivalry for years to come, with the competition to face of other shipping lines based on the United States, the Netherlands and France. From the point of view of business there had come into existence a certain community of the countries facing on the Atlantic, a community emphasized among those to which the English language was common. For all practical purposes the Atlantic had ceased to be a barrier.

Britain of the industrial revolution depended largely on its coastal shipping for internal transport and this service extended, of course, to the navigable rivers. The most important of these were and are the Thames, the Severn, the Trent and the Mersey. When industries grew up in the Midlands, sited in relation to coal and iron supplies, there was scope for canal builders. The first demand was to connect the industrial region with the nearest river system; the second to connect the four river systems with each other. The British canal builders could look to many precedents in antiquity but the most impressive example before them was that of the Languedoc canal built in the reign of Louis XIV and opened in 1681; an astonishing achievement with 119 locks spread over 144 miles. Still in use, it connects the Garonne with the Mediterranean via Toulouse, rising at one point to 620 feet above sea level. If we exclude the Exeter and Topsham canal, built in Tudor times, the Canal Age in Britain begins more modestly with James Brindley's canal between Worsley and Manchester built for the Duke of Bridgewater in 1759–60. Its success led to the subsequent construction of the Bridgewater Canal (1762–72) connecting Manchester with Liverpool, and finally to the completion by 1777 of the Grand Trunk Canal between the Trent and the Mersey. This was connected with the Severn by the Staffordshire and Worcester Canal and the Severn with the Thames by another canal in 1782. These successive developments joined together the main river systems but the Thames could only be reached from the north by a circuitous route. This defect was made good by the construction of the Grand Junction Canal connecting the Thames more directly with the Birmingham area and the Trent. These developments were paralleled in Scotland by the construction of the Forth and Clyde Canal in 1790.

Up to this point each canal fulfilled an obvious need, attracted a volume of traffic and brought dividends to the shareholders. Once the engineering work had been done, largely by Irish labour, a canal needed only a small and inexpensive staff of lock keepers, toll collectors and maintenance men. The older and more profitable canals thus paid dividends of up to 75 or even 100 per cent with an average, perhaps, of 48 per cent. Support for them had come originally from the industrialists to whom the canals would be useful. Conspicuous among these were Josiah Wedgwood of Burslem, Thomas Bentley of Liverpool, Matthew Boulton of Birmingham and Richard Arkwright of Cromford but other interested tradesmen were, many of them, in a smaller way of business. Almost as active from the beginning were the great landlords, the Duke of Bridgewater's example being followed by Lord Middleton, the Earl of Moira, the Earl of Dudley, Earl Gower, the Marquis of Buckingham, the Duke of Grafton and many others. The dividends announced and the powerful directors named were enough to encourage the smaller investors among whom the purchase of canal shares became, in about 1790, a sort of mania. By the nature of things, however, the obviously profitable canals were those first undertaken, each subsequent venture being a shade less promising than its predecessor. If the older canals like the Ewewash paid 48 per cent on average, the dividends from canals completed between 1790 and 1800 averaged 13 per cent or less. That was also the Grand Junction dividend but other later canals, unfinished in 1800, mostly paid only 3 or 4 per cent, while some begun after 1800 paid little or nothing.[2] The last canals, completing the system, were opened between 1830 and 1840 but with hopeless prospects from the start. For a brief period, from about 1770 to 1830, the canals played an important part in the industrial revolution. They carried the bulk commodities: timber, bricks, slate, cotton, iron ore and corn. Above all they carried the coal from the pit to the town, providing fuel for the steam engines and raw material for the gasworks.

Much money was made and lost in canal shares but no one concerned can be said to have engaged in Big Business. The first big canal company, the Trent and Mersey, raised a capital of £130,000, the supporters each subscribing £2,000 or less, and this was the pattern very generally followed. The real profit went to the manufacturers and landowners, to the users rather than to the owners of the system. The indirect benefits were immense and widespread, involving to begin with, a great reduction in the price of coal. Among the most profitable canals was the Bridgewater, Brindley's masterpiece, which still flourished after many others had failed. Its owner, the Earl of Ellesmere, complained in 1845 'that I own the last canal or nearly which can be said to exist in England, and I do not suppose anybody in Manchester would give me three years purchase for the article.'[3] The Earl's pessimism was groundless and that canal was earning him £40,000 clear in 1857, the year of his death. This most unusual success, at that period, depended upon a heavy local traffic making use of a short canal. At least one canal, the Glamorganshire (from Merthyr Tydfil to Cardiff) was frankly planned for the users' benefit, the dividend being limited to 8 per cent and all further profit going to reduce the tolls. As for the carriers, the owners of the canal boats and horses, they seem to have earned no more than a decent living. The only carrying firm to have survived is that of Pickfords who had begun with waggons but took to the waterways in about 1790, specializing in the traffic between London and Manchester, with sidelines to Bristol and Leicester. It might seem, at first sight, that canal carriage was a business to which steam power might have been applied. The difficulty was, however, that any foaming bow-wave would have destroyed the canal banks which were lined merely with puddled clay.

Little use was made of the canals for passenger traffic although passenger boats were not unknown and must have offered an ideally smooth ride. It is a question, however, whether canals took the shortest route or went where most people would want to go. Quite apart from that, the development of the canal system was paralleled by the development of the mail coach which would travel twice as fast to cities which no canal would ever serve. The story of the highways is of great significance but it is highly complex, demanding of the historian an expert knowledge of Roman history, civil engineering, coach design, horse-breeding, harness manufacture and postal systems. There were practically no wheeled vehicles in Britain between the withdrawal of the Roman legions and the reign of Elizabeth I and there was little occasion, therefore, for maintaining the roads. For people who rode or walked there was need only for bridges and alehouses and these were provided with loving care and ingenuity. When carts and coaches appeared again the art of roadmaking had been forgotten and years were to pass before the problem was solved. The highway existed as a right of way and there were penalties for encroachment but horses go well on bare earth and do little damage to the surface. When waggons multiplied, however, there was a demand for a better sort of road, partly at least because the waggons had rutted and ruined what surface there was. Parishes were made responsible for the roads which passed through them and were told to see that they were fit for use.

What nobody knew was what, exactly, the parishioners were supposed to do about it.

The ancient main roads of England are five in number and all radiate from London. The longest is the Great North Road which runs via Stamford, Newark, Doncaster and Durham to Berwick and so to Edinburgh. Shortest is the road via Canterbury to Dover and so to France. There are then the two roads which lead to Ireland, the one via Bath and Bristol, the other by Coventry, Lichfield, Chester and Holyhead. There is, finally, the road via Salisbury to Plymouth. These were the post roads from the reign of Henry VIII, whose master of the posts was Brian Tuke. Along them the mails were taken by postboys, mounted and armed, whose distinctive badge of office was the horn they carried, the sound of which gave warning of their approach. Along these same roads passed waggons carrying goods or passengers, and noblemen, well attended, on their way to court. Very occasionally there were troops to be seen on the move, with waggons again for their baggage and (a new problem) their train of artillery. Civil engineering was imported from Holland during the Civil Wars, but the roads were still imperfect when the General Post Office was re-established in 1660 with Henry Bishop – who introduced the postmark – as postmaster-general. The postal service was a royal monopoly and a rival 'penny post' set up in the London of 1680, for local use only, was sternly suppressed as contrary to the law.

The speeding up of communications after 1660 was largely due to the development of cavalry during the Civil Wars. As late even as the sixteenth century the armoured knight fought singly, mounted on an immensely strong and expensive horse, trained for battle by the techniques still practised at the Spanish School in Vienna. With the invention of the musket the horseman lost much of his importance and social status, becoming for a time little more than a mounted infantry-man, mobile on the march but no longer dominant on the battlefield. The knight became an officer and his horse was presently harnessed to the plough, supplanting oxen in an agricultural revolution to which historians have paid surprisingly little attention. The more expensive horses were now bred for the racecourse and the hunting field, the Arab strain producing speed instead of armour-carrying strength, so when cavalry tactics were revived by Prince Rupert his men were mounted on horses which reflected Charles I's interest in flat-racing at Newmarket. Their opponents were as well mounted and it was Oliver Cromwell who finally produced the finest cavalry in Europe, once more the decisive arm in battle. In this their greatest achievement, Cromwell and his imitators (like Marlborough) owed much to Rupert and as much again to Britain's first great author on horse breeding and training, William Cavendish, Duke of Newcastle (1592–1676), whose famous textbook was published at Antwerp in 1657 and the English edition ten years later. The end of the Civil Wars and the restoration of Charles II brought many of these hunters on to the market for the Lifeguards and Horseguards could not use them all. The revival of trade also created a demand for a better postal service and for better means of travel by road. It is said to have been Sir Kenelm Digby (1603–65) who saw what was needed and built four of the great London coaching inns, the Black Swan in Holborn, the Bell, the Black Bull and the George and Blue Boar.[4] As from this time stage coaches began to provide a more or less regular means of transport on the main roads and between the principal cities. They were drawn by horses which could gallop, given a road on which speed was possible without danger to the coach, and given a coach which would travel fast without danger to the passengers.

For the first quarter of the eighteenth century coaches were indifferently designed and had to grind their way over the bad roads for which the parishes were responsible. The system was unworkable because the country folk were being asked to give their time and money to maintain communications in which they had no interest. It was nothing to them that other folk wanted to reach London from Oxford. All they wanted themselves was a track along which to drive their pigs to market. Let those who wanted a good road find a way to maintain it! The answer was to set up toll-gates and make the passing coaches pay for the roadmaking.

Turnpike companies were granted Parliamentary powers to erect gates and toll bars, and to mulct the actual users of the roads in return for remaking and maintaining some particular stretch of highway. Between 1700 and 1750 as many as four hundred Road Acts were passed; between 1751 and 1790 sixteen hundred! This was the principal machinery by which land communications were steadily improved throughout the Hanoverian epoch ... By 1750 the stagecoach, drawn by two or four horses, was lighter and more rapid; but it still had no springs ... Stoppages and overturns were frequent ... in 1775 the Norwich Coach was waylaid in Epping Forest by seven highwaymen, of whom the guard shot three dead before he himself was killed at his post ...[5]

Highwaymen found their place in literature with Gay's *Beggar's Opera* of 1728. Dick Turpin was hanged at York in 1739 but robberies became less frequent during the later years of the century. This improvement in safety was due in part to the activity of Henry Fielding, magistrate for Westminster from 1748, his work being continued thereafter by his half-brother, Sir John Fielding, who died in 1780. Among the highwaymen executed during this period, one Isaac Dorking read *The Beggar's Opera* while in the condemned cell. In 1773 Sir John asked Garrick to cease presenting the play, no doubt because of its bad influence. Whether robbed or not, however, the coaches gradually improved in both speed and safety. By 1741 there was a 'flying coach' between Birmingham and London; by 1751 an 'expedition coach' between London and Norwich and, soon afterwards, a coach from Liverpool which could cover the 206 miles to London in a mere three days. In the story of eighteenth-century road travel the crucial date, however, is 1784 and the central figure is John Palmer of Bristol. His first success was in obtaining a royal licence for the two Bristol theatres which his father owned and which he himself managed.

... This at once raised them to the status of Covent Garden, Drury Lane and the King's Theatre in the Haymarket, not only in the eyes of the *beau monde* visiting the fashionable city of Bath, but for members of the theatrical profession, seeking engagements outside London. The Orchard Street Theatre took the proud title of Theatre Royal and became the scene of Sarah Siddon's first triumph in tragedy and of innumerable plays performed by Garrick's great rival, Henderson, who acted there and in Bristol for several seasons.

To operate both theatres successfully with one company of actors meant a great deal of travelling about between Bath and Bristol. Mrs Siddons often complained of being exhausted when obliged to rehearse in Bath on a Monday before going on to act in Bristol on the same day, and then having to return to Bath after a drive of twelve miles, 'to represent some fatiguing part there' on the Tuesday evening. Palmer arranged for her to travel by post-chaise from one theatre to the other in the shortest possible time and with the least amount of strain on her nerves; but this was expensive, and it was even more expensive and difficult to bring actors down from London, to get a prompt reply to any letters, contracts or other kind of mail sent by post from the West of England to the capital.[6]

It is interesting that the first effective demand for a passenger transport system should have come from an impresario. He was fortunate, however, to gain the ear of William Pitt, the young prime minister, who agreed to his proposal that the mails should in future go by passenger coach. The postboy, riding a horse or driving a mail cart, was replaced by the guard on the rear seat of the mail coach. And just as the postboy paid no road toll, neither – on Palmer's insistence – did the mail coach; and the object of the horn (now to be three feet long) was to ensure that the toll-gate should open before the coach arrived. Palmer presented his scheme in 1782 and the first experimental mail coach left Bristol for London in August 1784. The coach's success was immediate and services were quickly established to Liverpool, Manchester, Leeds, Swansea, Dover, Oxford, Chester and Carlisle. There were two hundred mail coaches on the road by 1812. The practice had been for the mail to leave London at midnight but Palmer, who in 1786 was given direction of the whole service, changed the hour of departure to 8pm. The coaches, built for speed, were all made by Mr Vidler in Millbank. To his works they returned in the morning after delivering the mails to the London Post Office, and they were cleaned, greased and overhauled before going back into service – replaced by a spare coach, indeed, if in need of repair. The coaches did not belong to the Post Office but to contractors who supplied the horses also, four to a coach, and the coachmen. The red-uniformed guard, on the other hand, was employed and armed by the Post Office and travelled with his feet on the locked mail box to which he had no key. In contrast with the other vehicles on the road the mail coaches were all uniformly painted in maroon and black with scarlet wheels and the royal arms on the door panels. They represented the Royal Mail and the horn – a badge of office – is still painted on aircraft to which the mail is entrusted. A possibly unexpected result of Palmer's work was the disappearance of the highwayman. There seems to have been scarcely an instance of a mail coach being waylaid – although the increase in traffic may have been as important a safeguard in itself.

The use of horses evolved and coaches developed but the turnpikes did not improve to the same extent. This was not so much from lack of care as from lack of knowledge. Scientific road making begins in Britain with Thomas Telford (1757–1834), engineer of the Ellesmere and Caledonian Canals and builder of Scottish roads, who was appointed Surveyor of the London-Holyhead road in 1815. Telford believed in constructing a solid 'pavement' of large stones as foundation for the road metal, the result being that his highway cost £1,000 a mile and was not finished until 1829. His work was much admired and he went on to make other main roads on the same expensive principles, as also the Menai Bridge (opened in 1826) which shortened the journey to Holyhead. Contemporary with him was John Loudon McAdam (1756–1836), Surveyor of the Bristol roads from 1815 and author of the road making textbook. Caring less about the solid foundation, McAdam concentrated on the texture of the surface. He pointed out that the coach wheel actually rests, at any given time, on one inch of its iron tyre. Any stone, therefore, of more than one inch in diameter will be displaced rather than rolled in by the wheel's passing. Stone must therefore be broken down to that size to form the road's surface, which could then be laid even on soft ground. 'I never use large stones on the bottom of a road,' he explained, 'I would not put a large stone in any part of it.' Telford's roads, which have lasted very well, were better than the traffic would justify, and it was McAdam's methods which prevailed. He became Surveyor-General in 1827 and there was a tremendous system of turnpike roads by the time of his death; 22,000 miles by 1840.

With highways at last really suited to fast horses and light vehicles we find the Brighton–London road in 1819 claiming some 70 stage coaches a day . . . and its fifty odd miles covered with post-chaises and private carriages of all kinds. By 1835 – the year before McAdam died – coaching had reached its zenith with some 700 Royal Mail coaches and 3,300 stage coaches running regularly all over Britain, the best of them travelling at ten miles – sometimes more – an hour with records of timekeeping and punctuality that no form of mechanical travel has exceeded, or even equalled. William Chaplin, most important of the coach proprietors (who became Member of Parliament for Salisbury) had 1,300 horses at work; Edward Sherman, of the 'Bull and Mouth' Inn, St Martin's-le-Grand, had about 700; in all some 150,000 horses were working British coaches, giving employment to 30,000 men as coachmen, guards, horse-keepers and yard-hands.[7]

The great days of the stage and mail coaches were all too brief. Perfection was the prelude to collapse. In 1835 a peak of achievement was reached in coach design, harness, punctuality and speed. The assembly of the mail coaches as they set off from the London Post Office was one of the sights of London. Their annual parade on the king's birthday was one of the events of the year. The king's highway had become a source of national pride.

... The coach time-tables give the most reliable evidence as to the condition of the roads. The fast mail coach from London to Holyhead ran from 1785 to 1808 and made the journey of 278 miles 7 furlongs in 38 hours. After the opening of the Menai Bridge in 1826 the time was reduced at first to $32\frac{3}{4}$ hours, and in 1830 to 29 hours 17 min., the length then being $260\frac{1}{2}$ miles. In its last two years, 1836 and 1837, the time was 26 hours 55 min. The coach left London at 8 p.m.: it rested at Birmingham for breakfast from 7.8 to 7.43 a.m.; it was at Shrewsbury at noon; at Bangor from 8.20 to 8.25 p.m.; it arrived at Holyhead at 10.55 p.m. The average speed, including stoppages, was 9.68 miles per hour.

The highest coach speeds were attained on shorter routes in more level country, where the competition between rival companies was keener. Thus the Independent Tally-Ho in 1830, on the run from London to Birmingham, had a minimum speed of 12 miles an hour and did one stage at the rate of $18\frac{3}{4}$ miles an hour; its average rate for the 109 miles was $14\frac{1}{4}$ miles per hour.[8]

The year 1830, however, which saw these astonishing performances on the road was also the year in which the mails on the Manchester to Liverpool route were transferred to the railway. As from then the railway system developed quickly, train fares being lower than coach fares by 1837. The horses used on the Exeter, Southampton and Gosport routes were offered for sale at Bagshot in 1838. The London to Birmingham line was opened in that year and the coach ceased to run in 1839. The last daily run of the London coach to Norwich and Newmarket took place in 1846 and the last mail coach left Manchester in 1858. The great days of the highway were over and the main roads by 1880 were overgrown in places and virtually out of use. Coaches survived for a time in remote parts of the country, ancillary to the rail system. Horsed vehicles were essential, moreover, to reach the railway station, as many still living can remember. Apart from that the carriage remained the status symbol of wealth and tremendous attention was paid to the gleam of the paintwork, the smartness of the livery, the polish of the leather, and the costliness of the horses.

Of whatever size, they must have quality, action, proud carriage, irreproach-able heads, necks and tails; in a word the symmetry of the ideal Arab, with the true action that 'steps and goes'. They must be a perfect match in colour, height and action; admirably broken yet full of courage. In a word, they must have the appearance of fiery dragons, with the docility of trained chargers . . .[9]

In those last years the horsed vehicle was ceasing to be a means of transport and was in process of becoming a toy.

The coach had made Big Business technically possible and was essential even to those who were planning the railway lines. But was this form of transportation a big business in itself? The answer must be that it was not. Coaches were mostly owned by small proprietors and companies, each based upon a coaching inn with stabling for perhaps a hundred horses. There were two big contractors, however, William Chaplin and Eward Sherman. The London Bull and Mouth was Sherman's base of operations, his most famous coach the Shrewsbury 'Wonder' which did the journey by day in fifteen hours.

A stud of one hundred and fifty horses was kept exclusively for the use of this famous coach and people who travelled by it never forgot the excitement it caused, boasting of the journey for the rest of their lives. Sam Hayward, its celebrated coachman on the run from Birmingham to Shrewsbury, used to bring the coach up the steep hill of Wyle Cop at a gallop, turn the horses in their own length and drive them through the archway into the yard of the Lion at a smart trot, with only an inch to spare on either side of the vehicle and all the outside passengers ducking their heads for fear of being scalped. 'I think I'll get off,' one nervous outsider was said to have murmured, only to be told, 'You be damned!' as Hayward performed this astonishing feat with absolute precision and great pride in his own skill . . .

Sherman's tough and tight-fisted methods of running his business brought him great prosperity. He rebuilt the Bull and Mouth in 1830, greatly extending the accommodation for the huge number of travellers coming in and going out every day, and he also built underground stables beneath the yard, big enough to hold seven hundred horses. In this he was imitating William Chaplin, whose business was even more extensive and whose knowledge of horses and every-thing to do with coaching far exceeded that of anyone else in the field.[10]

Chaplin's empire centred upon the Swan with Two Necks in Lad Lane off Gresham Street but he owned three other inns and extensive stabling at Hounslow, Purley and Whetstone. He was said to own eighteen hundred horses and employ two thousand men. He horsed fourteen of the twenty-seven mail coaches which left London each night – that is, on the first stage in and out of the capital. But he also owned his own line of coaches, painted in red and black, which served on a number of routes from Birmingham to Dover. Unlike other proprietors, Sherman included, Chaplin quickly realized what railway competition was going to mean. He sold out his interests and invested his fortune in the railway line from London to Southhampton. He was to be a director of that company for the next twenty years.

Chaplin came nearer to Big Business than did anyone else in the coaching world but his career illustrates the limitations (as well as the finish) of that form of enterprise. A business which depends on horses must require the daily attention of the proprietor himself, a man, in Chaplin's case, who had begun in his father's stables on the Dover Road. He was concerned with the coaches on sixty-eight different routes but only over the first (or sometimes the second) stage on each of them. All the horses were thus under his eye from day to day. London was the only point at which so many routes converged and the business there was mostly shared between two coach proprietors. Beyond one or at most two stages out of London each proprietor was concerned with but a single route and in only two stages of it, one in either direction. They could be prosperous but they could not make a fortune, nor could they diversify into other fields of enterprise, for a coaching inn and its stables needed personal supervision for anything up to twenty-four hours in the day. There was a further limitation on their financial success, for this particular form of enterprise was complicated by non-economic motives. When a rival proprietor placed the 'Nimrod' coach on the Shrewsbury route with orders to run the 'Wonder' off the road, there was profit at stake but as much in bets as in fares. The sporting element crept in as a purely aesthetic delight in the perfection of turnout. Horse events can never be a mere matter of economics – and the same is true of sailing ships. Big Business begins after horses and sails have been left behind.

3   Finance, Banking and Insurance

Probably the oldest organization in Big Business is, as we have seen, the papacy. It derived much of its power from the threat of Islam, the pope being a chief symbol of European unity in the face of an external threat. It worked through a network of provincial, diocesan and monastic institutions. It gained in efficiency from the use of Latin as the tongue common to educated men throughout Christendom. It was hampered, however, by its own doctrine of usury, the rule under canon law that the exaction of interest on a loan is sinful. Medieval moneylending was thus officially confined to the Jews, to folk among whom usury had always been lawful. More fortunate than the needier monarchs, the popes had an assured revenue, not only from papal territories but from loyal churchmen everywhere, much of their income coming from the Holy Roman Empire which lay to the north of the Alpine passes. The northward lines of communication were vital, therefore, to both diplomacy and trade. Central to the road system was the province, once the kingdom, of Lombardy, shared between the rival families of Visconti and Gonzaga. The capital of Lombardy was Milan and papal affairs in Germany came inevitably to be handled by the merchant houses of that city. If the payment of papal dues had ever involved the passage of specie-laden packhorses through the Simplon or Brenner Passes, that phase must have been shortlived. It was soon found safer to transact business with a bill of exchange. So Lombard merchants became expert in these paper transactions, their agents going further afield as their business increased, some of them as far as Bruges and London.

Where they settled they tended to trade under the sign of the three golden balls, the Lombard coat of arms. On certain conditions they would sometimes advance the sums with which papal dues might be paid, finding means to profit somehow from transactions in which the charging of interest was illegal and therefore (naturally) unknown. The Lombards came to England in the reign of Henry III (1216–72) and took over the sort of business which had formerly been left to the Jews. The more prosperous of them settled around what is still called Lombard Street, the smaller fry in scattered premises over which the three balls are still to be seen. In Holland a state-owened pawnbroking establishment was called the Lombard and private 'lombards' were declared illegal from 1614.

By the later Middle Ages, from about 1300, the church played a less prominent part in the world of commerce and finance. Trade with the Orient had been re-established, much to the profit of merchants throughout Europe, and the cities began to have a new importance, especially those on the main trade routes to the East: Venice, Genoa, Augsburg, Bruges, London and Bristol. There were merchants in business whose financial position put them almost on a level with royalty. Among the earliest of these was William de la Pole, who in 1332 became the first mayor of Kingston-upon-Hull. It must seem a strange place of origin for a man of such consequence, for Hull had been founded by King Edward I as recently as 1298. William ended, nevertheless, as Knight Banneret and Chief Baron of the Exchequer. His son, Michael, served the Black Prince and John of Gaunt, became baron in 1366 and then Earl of Suffolk. The third Earl was killed at Agincourt, the fourth, who commanded in France against Joan of Arc, became Lord Chancellor and Duke of Suffolk in 1448. John de la Pole, the second Duke, married the sister of Edward IV and made his son heir-presumptive to the throne. Richard de la Pole, afterwards killed at the Battle of Pavia in 1525, was actually recognized as king of England by Louis XII. The family was latterly unfortunate, becoming extinct in Henry VIII's reign, but the startling fact remains that a merchant's descendants could rise as high as they did. Contemporary with William de la Pole was Thomas Blanket of Bristol, a cloth manu-facturer who acquired great wealth and gave his name to an essential item of bedding. He was surpassed in wealth (if not in immortality), however, by William Canyng, also of Bristol, who owned ten ships at one time and employed eight hundred mariners. He was Mayor of Bristol in 1456 and specialized in trade with the German and Baltic ports. The Levant trade he seems to have left to Robert Sturmey, another Bristol merchant and a man of comparable wealth. The Canyngs did not end as members of the nobility but other families were in that respect more fortunate, especially those which had provided a lord mayor of London. Among merchant families later distinguished were those of Holles, Pulteney, Osborne, Greville, Legge, Coventry, Rich, Fitzwilliam, Verney, Gascoyne, Capell, Craven and Gore. As for the Bullens or Boleyns of London, Sir Thomas (1477–1539) became Earl of Wiltshire and his daughter was mother to Queen Elizabeth 1. More than most other countries England offered high rank to families of commercial talent.

The same could not, perhaps, be said of medieval Germany but to this rule there were at least two remarkable exceptions. When Hans Fugger came to Augsburg in 1367 he was no more than a fustian weaver. Such, however, was his success that he married the burgomaster's daughter and, dying in 1409, left a fortune to his sons Andrew and Jacob. They were ennobled in 1452 and it was Ulrich and George, the sons of Jacob, who set up the Golden Counting-House as head office of what was to become a mammoth organization. The growth of the business from 1473 was largely due to the efforts of Ulrich's younger brother, Jacob, whose early training had been in Venice. It was he who developed the spice trade via Portugal and the Fugger mining ventures in Tyrol, Carinthia and Hungary. Despite their interests in silver and copper, the later members of the family were essentially bankers. Branches of the firm were established in cities as far apart as Madrid and Antwerp, Danzig and London. They lent money to the Archduke Sigismund, to Emperor Maximilian 1 and to several of the popes. It was they, finally, who financed the election of Charles v to the imperial throne in 1519, and two of the Fugger partners were subsequently raised to the rank of count. By 1546 the total of the Fugger capital was estimated at sixty-three million florins, a colossal sum by any standard. It was essentially they who financed the Counter-Reformation. From the death of Charles v the Fugger fortunes declined, the more quickly after they had advanced large sums to Philip ii, who became bankrupt in 1557. In one respect they were eclipsed by the rival banking family of Welser, also of Augsburg, for one of the Welser daughters actually married an archduke, affording final proof of how important a banking firm can be.

If not as wealthy as the Fuggers, the Florentine Medici were a great deal more fortunate. They are first heard of in about 1370 but the banking house was not fully established until after 1400. Giovanni dei Medici, founder of the business, died in 1429, leaving to his eldest son Cosimo a finance house with branches as distant as Constantinople and London. He became the virtual ruler of republican Florence, and left the business to his son Piero, whose death in 1469 cleared the path for his younger brother Lorenzo 'the Magnificent'. Lorenzo's efforts brought the Medici to the summit of their political and artistic achievements. By the time of his early death in 1492 he had become Duke of Urbino. As from that period the Medici were central to the complex politics of renascent Italy. Suffice to say that Lorenzo's second son, Giovanni, became pope as Leo XI; another son became Duke of Nemours and his daughter Catherine, queen of France. Alessandro Medici became hereditary Duke of Florence in 1532 and married the daughter of the Emperor Charles V. Lorenzo's cousin Giulio became pope as Clement VII, and Medici of the younger branch became grand dukes of Tuscany in 1569. One of these, Francesco (1541–87), had a daughter, Marie, who also became queen of France and the line became extinct in 1737. The story is a remarkable one from any point of view and it illustrates the way in which Big Business is readily transformed into political power. In the Middle Ages and the renascence the commercially successful family did not remain in business for long. Like the de la Poles, the Fuggers and the Welsers, the Medici family was soon noble and even royal. What they could not have done was to stay out of politics, for the man of wealth who did that was too vulnerable. Beyond a certain point of financial success they had to assume power or face destruction. What remains astonishing is the vigour with which their ambitions were pursued, not without rivalry among themselves. For a banking family to include, at different times, two popes and two queens, not to mention grand dukes, is, and is likely to remain, a record.

Medieval bankers could achieve a princely status but the banks which still exist date, at earliest, from the seventeenth century. The wars of religion left Protestantism finally established and with it the tentative conclusion that usury might be lawful after all and that financial success is a sure indication of divine approval. Doctrines such as these lent added respectability to the Bank of Amsterdam, founded in 1609, and the Bank of Hamburg, founded ten years later. These, like the Bank of Genoa, were municipal, not national banks, as the following description makes clear:

As to the government of the bank (of Amsterdam) it is very solemn and regular. The whole city is bound to make good the money there deposited, and the treasure is secured under four different locks, the keys of which are kept by four of the principal magistrates, one of whom is always the president burgomaster for the time being.[1]

These banks were essentially places of safe custody, their place in London being taken by the Royal Mint, then in the Tower of London, and by the leading goldsmiths, whose vaults were necessarily locked and guarded and who could find space in them for private deposits. Unlike the public custodians of money, who charged for their services, the goldsmiths, who were also moneylenders, offered their depositors a rate of interest. A leader among these in Charles II's time was Alderman Backwell, at the sign of the unicorn in Lombard Street, who offered $3\frac{1}{2}$ or 4 per cent on money at call, 5 per cent on money at fourteen days' notice and 6 per cent on sums at twenty days' notice. He had some distinguished clients, one being the East India Company and another Samuel Pepys, who describes the panic which followed the Dutch attack on the Medway in 1667:

. . . W. Hewer hath been at the banker's and hath got £500 out of Backewell's hands of his own money; but they are so called upon that they will be all broke, hundreds coming to them for money: and they answer him 'It is payable at twenty days – when the days are out, we will pay you'; and those that are not so, they make tell over their money, and make their bags false, on purpose to give cause to retell it, and so spend time. I cannot have my 200 pieces of gold again for silver, all being brought up last night that were to be had, and sold for 24 and 25s a-piece. So I must keep the silver by me . . .[2]

Backwell survived this moment of panic, which ended when the Dutch withdrew. He was less fortunate in consenting to act as financial intermediary, after 1670, between Charles II and Louis XIV. By 1672 there was nearly a million pounds owing to the goldsmiths, at which point the Exchequer, which was empty, ceased payment of interest. Backwell, with whom many of the other goldsmiths banked, was the immediate victim. He went bankrupt and had to flee the country for a time. On his return he wisely secured election to Parliament, which would prevent him being arrested for debt.

One significant fact which Pepys's diary serves to illustrate is that England was then using a bimetallic currency. Its standard coinage had been silver, the original 'pound' being that amount of (troy weight) metal. At the time of the Reformation there were some wild fluctuations in value caused, first of all, by the partial collapse of the papal credit system and, second, by the influx of silver from Spanish America. It was the more difficult for the bankers in that their profession was but recently established and the principles of their art were still in process of discovery. Gold was the better basis for a currency, being virtually indestructible, but gold (as Pepys found for himself) was in short supply. For the time being there were both gold and silver coins in circulation but their relative value varied. The goldsmith bankers who tried to cope with the resulting problems were still to be found in Lombard Street where Martins Bank (now Barclays) at No. 68 still displays the sign of the grasshopper, Sir Thomas Gresham's crest. Wheeler, another Elizabethan goldsmith, had a daughter and sole heiress married to Francis Child (1642–1713), who set up in business at the sign of the marygold in 1681. Alderman Child was the first goldsmith to confine himself to banking, which he did in 1690, following his knighthood in 1689 but before his term of office as lord mayor in 1698–9. He was succeeded by his son, another Sir Francis (?1684–1740) and another lord mayor, who from 1721 headed the firm of Francis Child & Co., which was still prospering in the time of Charles Dickens. Contemporary with the elder Sir Francis was Sir Richard Hoare (1648–1718) who founded Hoare's Bank and became Master of the Goldsmiths' Company as well as lord mayor in 1712, his grandson being another Sir Richard and lord mayor in his turn. Other merchant bankers set up in business during the eighteenth century, notably Thomas Coutts (1735–1822), son of John Coutts, an Edinburgh banker and lord provost in 1742–4, who was founder and sole partner of Coutts & Co., founded in 1778 and flourishing today. As many more of the old houses were doomed to extinction, though, however important they had been in their day. There were bankers enough in the London of Charles II and James II. What was lacking was any central institutions, as in Amsterdam, to give stability to the City as a whole.

The Revolution of 1688 brought a Dutchman to the throne of England, a known Protestant and a sworn foe of Louis XIV. The king's need was for funds with which to wage war against France and various proposals were made for setting up a national bank upon which the government could draw. Charles Montagu, a Lord of the Treasury, accepted the scheme put forward by William Paterson and backed by a body of leading merchants. This plan was not for a City of London bank but for a new bank to be called the Bank of England, the name chosen being a stroke of genius as it claimed from the start a national rather than a local importance. This was not an entirely new idea, however, because the Sveriges Riksbank, the national bank of Sweden, had been founded at Stockholm in 1668. The Act for establishing this new institution was passed in 1694 and empowered the bank to raise £1,500,000 to be lent in the form of banknotes to the Crown at an agreed and guaranteed rate of interest – the beginning, in fact, of the National Debt. The principal subscribers then elected a governor, deputy governor, and twenty-four directors to constitute the court.

At any earlier period than the later years of the seventeenth century the foundation of the bank, upon the lines on which it was established, would have been impossible. After a century-long struggle the Protestant way of regarding Man and his duty to God and his neighbour, had at last prevailed in England, and while it would be preposterous to call the Bank a religious institution, its establishment was nevertheless largely a direct consequence of this radical change in religious outlook. The Church no longer kept the conscience of both rulers and ruled. As for the rulers, anything which was expedient for the survival and growth of the State was right; as for the ruled, each man, with his private conscience for guide, worked out his own salvation within the laws laid down by the State.[3]

Symbol of the bank was Britannia who first appeared as a barbarian maiden on coins of the Emperors Hadrian and Antoninus Pius. She was not seen again until some medallions were struck in 1667 to commemorate the signing of the Treaty of Breda. In that context she figured as a goddess, her face that of Frances Stewart, Charles II's mistress who was afterwards Duchess of Richmond. The Royal Mint used the same effigy for its copper coinage of 1671 and Britannia has ruled the waves ever since. The Bank of Scotland, which struggled for existence from 1695, had a rival in the Royal Bank of Scotland of 1727 and later in the British Linen Company's Bank. These and the banks in Ireland were never of comparable importance. The bank might be that of England but its influence was to cover Britain as a whole.

The Bank of England had at first a monopoly for the issue of bank-notes in England (not Scotland) and, from 1708, no other joint-stock bank might do business in London. Its foundation was followed in 1696–9 by a recoinage of the silver currency which would circulate alongside the banknotes. Gold coins were also in use, the pound piece of 1663 being the supposed equivalent of 20s in silver, but the relative values were unstable and the 'guinea' (struck from gold imported by the African Company) rose to a value of 22s or even, during one crisis, to 28s. The Master of the Mint in 1699–1727 was Sir Isaac Newton and his final effort in 1717 produced a guinea with the stabilized value of 21s, which remained current for the next century. Britain adopted the Gold Standard in 1816, a measure long advocated by the first Earl of Liverpool (1727–1808). A great recoinage followed, leading to the issue of the new gold sovereign and half-sovereign in 1817. From this time the silver coins had only a token value as related to the pound. The currency then remained admirably stable throughout the Victorian era, the only innovation being the appearance of the gothic florin in 1848, a first move towards decimalization. There was an attempt to follow this up with a decimal penny in 1857 but the inconvenience was as obvious then as it is today and the unpopular project was very properly abandoned. The guinea remained only as a theoretical coin in which payment could properly be made to medical men, portrait painters and tailors. Sums paid for racehorses and newspaper articles have always been expressed in the same gentlemanly terms, which have the ad-vantage of confusing foreign visitors. If there is to be a decimalized guinea it is a thing of the future.

Until 1826 the only banks in England other than the Bank of England itself were private firms and partnerships, some in London and some in the provinces. In that year an Act was passed which legalized joint-stock banking outside a radius of sixty-five miles from London. The first banks of this type were founded in Lancaster, Huddersfield, Norwich and Whitehaven.[4] And when the Bank of England's charter came up for renewal in 1833, its monopoly was restricted to note issue, and joint-stock banking was thus legalized even in London. First joint-stock bank to open in London was the National Bank (1833) with a head office in St Helen's Place, Bishopsgate, and a first provincial office at Gloucester. Its original country was in the west of England and south Wales but it soon opened branches in Barnstaple, Devonport and Exeter. It became the National Provincial Bank, absorbing the Union of London and Smith's Bank in 1917. The Westminster Bank comes second historically, having opened in 1834 at 38 Throgmorton Street, with a branch at Waterloo Place – hence its original name of the London and Westminster. It joined with the London & County Banking Co. in 1909, with Parr's Bank in 1918 and with Beckett's (Yorkshire) Bank in 1920. The Midland Bank has its origins in Birmingham. It was founded in 1836, established itself in Warwickshire and Lancashire, added major branches in Derby and Leeds and joined with the Central Bank of London in 1891. Like the Midland, Lloyd's Bank started in Birmingham, based upon the Quaker 'Old Bank' of Lloyd's & Co. and originally did business around Stafford, Rugby, Wolverhampton, Coventry and Shrewsbury. Lloyd's moved to London in 1884, absorbing Bennett, Hoare & Co. (of the black horse sign, already well established in 1677) and also Bosanquet, Salt & Co. Barclays Bank also had Quaker origins but started trading in East Anglia. It began with the amalgamation in 1896 of Barclay, Bevan, Tritton, Ransom, Bouverie & Co., of London and Brighton, with Jonathan Backhouse of Darlington, and Gurney, Birkbeck, Barclay & Buxton of Norwich. The Gurney country covered King's Lynn, Yarmouth, Ipswich and Colchester. Barclays amalgamated with the London Provincial and South Western Bank in 1918. Judged by the total of deposits and the number of branches in 1933, the Midland was then the biggest, with Barclays second and Lloyds third. The National Provincial came fourth on the number of its offices, the Westminster on the size of its deposits. By 1964 Barclays was the biggest, with the Midland second. Through a recent merger (1970) the Westminster and the National Provincial have come together, while Barclays have taken over Martin's, forming what is probably the final pattern. Since 1970 the Big Five have become, in effect, the Big Four. Alongside them and part of the same system were such institutions as the Royal Bank of Australia and the Bank of British North America, the Chartered Bank of India (founded 1853) and the Hong Kong and Shanghai Bank (of 1864). By the mid-nineteenth century London had become the financial centre of the British Isles, of the British Empire, and, for some purposes, of the civilized world.

Of British bankers the most remarkable, from one point of view, was Thomas Coutts, to whom reference has already been made (see page 47) and who had the reputation of being, at one time 'the richest man in England'. Believed at first to be a confirmed bachelor, he married Susan Starkie in 1763. She had been a maidservant in his brother's household, came of farming stock and was scarcely literate. Her three daughters came to be known as 'the three Graces'. The first, Susan, married the Earl of Guildford; the second, Frances, the Marquis of Bute; and the youngest, Sophie, Sir Francis Burdett. Thomas Coutts seems to have fallen in love with Harriot Mellon, the actress, in about 1805. He was then aged seventy, she twenty-eight. Her first stage appearance had been in *The Spoiled Child* played at Ulverstone in 1787, and this title was prophetic at least to the extent that her personal fortune, due to his generosity, amounted eventually to £200,000. When Mrs Coutts died in 1814, Thomas married Miss Mellon within a matter of days and lived with her until his death at the age of eight-six. When she remarried in 1827 her second husband was the Duke of St Albans, descendent of Charles II and Nell Gwynne. On her death in 1837 the Coutts fortune went to Angela Burdett, daughter of Sir Francis, who became, in her own right, Baroness Burdett-Coutts.[5] It was she, reckoned at one time the richest heiress in Britain, who proved a benefactor to a vast number of charities, being among the founders of the National Society for the Prevention of Cruelty to Children and the Royal Society for the Prevention of Cruelty to Animals. She endowed bishoprics in Cape Town, Adelaide and British Columbia, befriended the explorer, H. M. Stanley, and was among the last to entertain General Gordon before he went to the Sudan. Born in 1814, she played an active role in banking as well as in social work, died in 1906 and was buried in Westminster Abbey.

Our present concern is with the financial structure which would make Big Business possible, but some international finance was Big Business in itself. There was more of this in the Middle Ages, more even in the sixteenth century, than there had ever been since. Business (like religion and war) had been nationalized and little remained of European unity whether in finance or anything else. Some rulers were more than national, however; the Hanoverian kings of England retained, for example, their interest in Hanover. Just south of Hanover, ruled by its landgrave (a Hanoverian relative), was the state of Hesse-Cassel, adjacent to which was the small territory of Hanau, near Frankfurt, governed by the Hesse-Cassel heir apparent. The basic industry of Hesse-Cassel lay in the breeding and training of infantry which could be hired out profitably to kings, like those of England, who might be short of troops. As the landgrave had to be compensated (naturally) for each man killed, the Hessians represented a good income for their ruler whose shrewd investments made him one of the richest monarchs of the day. Landgrave Frederick was not more prosperous, however, than his son, Prince William of Hanau, who was financially well advised by Carl Büderus, the official who invented the salt tax. Büderus in turn had dealings on occasion with Mayer Rothschild, a dealer whose place of business was in the Frankfurt ghetto. Mayer had served his apprenticeship with the Oppenheimer Bank in Hanover but afterwards returned to the Judengasse in Frankfurt where he dealt in pawnbroking and second-hand goods, in cottons, in wine and tobacco. He had, in addition, a special interest in old and rare coins, of which Prince William had a collection. When the Landgrave Frederick died in 1785, Prince William, his successor, moved his court from Hanau to Wilhelmshöhe at Cassel. He took with him the beginnings of a financial link with Mayer Rothschild, who eventually became the new landgrave's official agent. He thus became a merchant banker, pawnbroking a thing of the past, and his discounting of drafts on London (the equivalent of cashing cheques) was now on a considerable scale. His growing and diversified business was increasingly handled by his sons as they came of age. There were five of them, each with initiative, energy and a complete concentration on the one thing that mattered to them: money.

As from 1789 the French Revolution posed a threat to the rest of

Europe and more immediately to the small German states which bordered on the Rhineland. Hesse was finally conquered by Napoleon in 1806 and its ruler fled to Schleswig, taking with him all the treasure he could rescue, much else being invested in countries which had themselves been occupied. Mayer assisted the landgrave in saving all that could be saved and then urged him to invest largely in consols. Mayer's son, Nathan, was already in London and admirably placed to transact the business. No other place seemed as safe as London and the landgrave agreed to invest the equivalent of £550,000.

... the agreement with William called for a purchase of consols at an average price of 72. Nathan did not buy at 72. He invested the money for his own account, took a rapid profit and then took a second profit when he bought the prince's consols. These had meanwhile dropped to 62 just as he had foreseen. The saving in price, of course, went into his own pocket.[6]

The money reached Nathan between February 1809 and December 1810. The first consol certificates, to the value of £189,500, reached the landgrave in 1811. Nathan had the use of that sum until then, the use of the remainder until some later date. With these sums he speculated in gold bullion, of which he sold £800,000's worth to the British Government in 1810. The Government's problem was to finance Wellington's army in Spain, and this Nathan now agreed to undertake. For reasons no longer obvious it was decided (so the story goes) to send the gold overland rather than by sea and Nathan is said to have sent it secretly through enemy territory. Whether he did so or not a special 'military guinea' was coined for this purpose in 1813:

This was an exceptional coin – to supply Wellington's victorious army on the Pyrenées a desperate effort was made to secure gold, and from mohurs and pagodas brought from distant India some 80,000 guineas were coined and sent to the front. The people of invaded France had refused Spanish dollars or English paper, and would only take gold – which was therefore provided on a small scale. This coinage was politically profitable, but economically ruinous, for a gold guinea was at this time worth 27s in Bank of England notes at home. This was the very last guinea to be coined.[7]

Whatever profit the Rothschilds made as paymasters of Wellington's army was as nothing, however, compared with their gains in 1815. They had built up a system of couriers which far outdistanced any other method of communication. Nathan, it is said, thus had the news of the Battle of Waterloo some hours before Wellington's despatch arrived. Consols had fallen in price with the news of the action at Quatre Bras. When Nathan sold, as he promptly did, consols fell more steeply, the brokers assuming that he had received early news of a British defeat. When they were at rock bottom Nathan bought through his agents all and more than he had sold, and did so just before the official news sent the price up again. In point of fact the price of consols moved only sluggishly between 69$\frac{1}{16}$ and 71$\frac{1}{2}$ – enough, however, to make a useful profit.

Old Mayer Rothschild had died in 1812, leaving his sons tactically deployed across Europe. Nathan was established in London, his office in St Swithin's Lane, his mansion in Piccadilly. James Rothschild had settled in Paris, acquiring as residence the Palais Fouché in the rue Laffitte which had been the town house of Napoleon's chief of police. His wealth was estimated at six hundred million francs. He became Baron Rothschild, the owner (incidentally) of the Laffitte vineyards. Salomon Rothschild came to Vienna in 1819 and became indispensable to Metternich, acquiring vast estates and a title of nobility. Carl Rothschild became the leading banker of Italy, financier to the king of Naples, to the rulers of Tuscany and Sardinia and even to the pope himself. As for Amschel, the eldest of the five, he inherited the family bank in Frankfurt and became a baron in his turn and a friend of Bismarck. What is most significant about the Rothschilds is not the success of each branch of the family, but the fact that they became a European institution, useful to their several countries but still allied with each other. They remain important to this day but their later history is not to the present purpose. What their example proves is that it was possible, from 1815, to engage in Big Business. Theirs was not, however, the sort of business with which we are concerned. From 1810 at latest the Rothschilds were solely interested in finance, their estates being incidental to their main obsession. They were heirs, in effect, to the Medici or the Fuggers but cannot be ranked among the captains of industry. Their means of communication sufficed for purposes of international banking but theirs was not yet a world of large-scale production. What they did provide was the financial basis upon which later industries would be founded.

All but two of the Rothschild banks have disappeared: Naples in 1861, Frankfurt in 1901 and Vienna (the Creditanstalt) in 1938. As against that, N. M. Rothschild & Sons are still to be found in St Swithin's Lane between Lombard Street and Cannon Street Station. They are still a partnership, not a company, and still central to the world of finance. They do not, however, stand alone and some mention must be made of their rivals. Baring Brothers, already mentioned on pages 17-18, are the oldest of the merchant bankers, having begun business in 1763, and they remain a leading 'American house' as contrasted with the Rothschilds whose interests are in Europe. The firm of J. C. Hambro of 41 Bishopsgate was founded in 1838 by Joachim Hambro of Copenhagen and retains a traditional connection with Scandinavia, although interested in Europe generally and in some parts (but not all parts) of South America. Hambros financed the foundation of the kingdom of Italy, as also the establishment of the present dynasty of Greece. Of the same age as Hambros is Morgan Grenfell, founded in London by George Peabody, an American, and now parent to the whole Morgan Group. Not all the merchant banks are historic, however, and one, S. G. Warburg & Co. of 30 Gresham Street, was founded as recently as 1946. The original partners came, however, from Hamburg, where they had been in business since 1798. Other famous houses are Antony Gibbs & Sons, Goschens & Cunliffe, Layard Brothers & Co. and J. Henry Schroder & Co. There are some sixteen merchant banking firms in London and all have played a significant part in the growth of Big Business. There are similar houses elsewhere in Europe, the Banca Commerciale Italiana of Milan, founded in 1894, being one of them, the Deutsche Bank of Frankfurt another. There are merchant banks of great importance in the Netherlands and others still more influential in Switzerland, but many of these banks represent more the results than the causes of industrial development and it must be agreed that merchant banks are almost peculiar to London.

The merchant bankers and their merchant banks are uniquely British. 'Nowhere in the world is there anything like the London merchant bank,' said the late J. H. Hambro, who called the City 'one hell of a financial mechanism'. The French *banque d'affaire*, the German Handelsbank, the American investment bank prior to the New Deal, had some, but not all, of the features of the classic British merchant bank. Closest to it are Japan's big trading companies, which is no accident: both England and Japan are islands and depend on trade for survival.[8]

When comparing the financial institutions of Britain and the USA we come across two fundamental differences at the outset. To begin with, the American states form a federation but retain, each of them, a measure of independence. The formation of a nationwide banking system is hampered by state laws which prevent a given bank from operating in more than the one state, sometimes in more than the one city. In the second place, the financial and political capitals are not only distinct (like London and Westminster) but are over two hundred miles apart (like London and Manchester). Such a mileage has nowadays dwindled in significance but the historical process has set up a distance, which remains, between Wall Street and Washington. There is lacking the cosy relationship which has traditionally existed between the Treasury, the Bank of England, the banks and the Stock Exchange. When Baring Brothers nearly failed in 1890 the rescue operation was directed by the Chancellor of the Exchequer, the Governor of the Bank of England, Sir Everard Hambro and Lord Rothschild. The crucial meeting lasted forty minutes and, granted that the Prime Minister was sympathetic, the whole affair was closed by an acid comment from Queen Victoria. While Lord Revelstoke, the head of Barings, was more or less killed by this crisis, the scandal was kept within a fairly tight circle of people who knew what they were doing. There was none of the panic, therefore, which resulted from the failure of Overend, Gurney & Co. in 1866. It would be fair to say that the centres of power in the USA of that period were very much further apart.

The scope of this chapter does not allow of a detailed treatment of other countries but banking systems throughout Europe were not, and are not, very different from that of Britain. Most countries have a central bank to which the commercial and private banks look at least for guidance and that central bank has normally the privilege and monopoly of note issue. The Bank of Sweden (1668) seems to be among the oldest and may have been the model for the Bank of England (1694). It was made responsible from the outset to the Rikstag or Parliament, not to the crown or the government of the day. The Banque de France was founded in Paris in 1800 but given its official charter in 1803. It had many provincial sub-offices but had no monopoly of note issue until 1936. Although the Bank of Amsterdam is older than the Nederlandsche Bank, the latter dates from 1814 and is thus older than the Belgian Banque Nationale of 1850 with its main offices at Brussels, Antwerp, Liège and (since 1921) Luxembourg. Italy had its Banca Nazionale nel Regio d'Italia in 1849 but this was superseded by the present Banca d'Italia in 1893. In Switzerland the several cantons issued their own banknotes until 1891 and there were thirty-six banks of issue until 1907. Meanwhile, however, the Schweizerische Nationalbank had been founded in 1905 and was soon afterwards given the note-issuing monopoly. It divides its activities between Berne and Zurich but has a branch in eight other regional centres. West Germany also has a federal structure so that each of its states or *Länder* has a Länderzentralbank. The Deutsche Bundesbank was founded, however, in 1957 and has the exclusive right of note issue. It is also responsible for banking policy throughout the Federal Republic. Its head office is not at the 'provisional' capital of Bonn but at the commercially more important city of Frankfurt-am-Main. It is the successor, of course, to the Reichsbank of Berlin and can regard its present location as a sort of exile.[9]

It is possible to write a history of Big Business with only a passing mention of, say, the Banca d'Italia. It is impossible to avoid a more detailed account of Wall Street, the very centre from which Big Business, in its modern form, derives. The American financial centre is in lower Manhattan:

... The Street itself is seven blocks long, less than half a mile, and the area that contains the greatest of all financial markets is no more than half a mile square. To the north it is guarded by the enormous stone palazzo of the Federal Reserve Bank of New York ... The Street itself begins at Broadway, at the central spine of lower Manhattan, and runs east, gently downhill to the East River. West of Broadway is Trinity Church, Episcopalian, with a tower twenty stories high but so graceful that it seems smaller, so encircled by office buildings that it seems smaller still. West of the Graveyard about and behind Trinity Church is a brick wall dropping down, down some twenty feet to a lower level of the island and Trinity Place, which is home to a stock exchange, a very few financial houses, and the New York University Business School. West of Trinity Place are printing and shipping, loft buildings and the Hudson River.

This is old New York, a disorganized maze of streets with the names common to all the American Colonies: Pine, Cedar, Oak and Stone; Broad Street and Broadway; Liberty Street, New Street, William Street, Maiden Lane, Old Slip, Front Street, South Street. According to legend, there was a real wall here once, where Wall Street runs, guarding the Dutch from the Indians and the Indians from the Dutch.[10]

The wall was apparently built by Peter Stuyvesant in 1653 and marked the boundary of the original settlement, a small town huddled round the southern tip of Manhattan Island. As compared with the other cities of the world, and as contrasted with most of them, New York could expand in only one direction. It was therefore the ideal place for speculation in real estate, a business to which John Jacob Astor, the fur trader, was committed from about 1806. Mr James Roosevelt followed his good example. New York was then a trading and shipping centre, its growing prosperity represented by the Bank of New York (1799), the Manhattan Company, the Mercantile Bank and (in 1811) the Mechanics' Bank. The city's future was secured, however, by the completion of the Erie Canal in 1825, built and owned by New York State, and the Merchants' Exchange was built two years later. It is important to remember, however, that London was still the world's financial centre and one to which the Americans themselves were attracted. George Peabody moved from the USA to London in 1827 and Junius Morgan did the same in 1854. In 1835 Wall Street was mostly destroyed by fire, the Exchequer included, and this was the moment when the Aetna Insurance Company of Hartford, Connecticut, came to the fore. Other companies could not, or did not, meet their liabilities but the Aetna paid up promptly and in full. The director who insisted upon satisfying the policy holders was Mr Joseph Morgan of Hartford and he was soon able to show that this was the very way to attract future business. It was only one aspect of his interest, however, for he was also a director of the Farmers' and Mechanics' Bank which he had helped to found in 1833, stockholder of the Connecticut Steamboat Company and the owner of real estate in Hartford. As a banker, Morgan had to face the crisis of 1837 which followed the abolition of the second Bank of the United States. It had received its charter in 1816 for a twenty-year period and was being successfully managed by Nicholas Biddle of Pennsylvania. President Jackson was unfriendly towards it, however, which led the bank's supporters to apply for a new charter in

1832. The bill passed both houses of Congress but was vetoed by the President. The bank's days were now numbered and the President began to transfer federal deposits to the state banks. The second Bank of the United States closed in 1836 and the 'wildcat' state banks, greatly encouraged, increased their note circulation and lent money on easy terms. When Jackson tried to check this reckless policy, he helped to bring about a sudden panic in 1837. More than six hundred banks failed and with them all the numberless enterprises which had relied on their support. Wall Street of today dates from the aftermath of the fire of 1835 and the panic of 1837. Since that period it has grown with the prosperity of New York itself.

The growth of New York City redoubled after 1840. There were 60,000 immigrants in 1843, 120,000 in 1847 and the population numbered nearly 500,000 by 1850. The rapid expansion of the city brought wealth to the landowners and especially to John Jacob Astor, founder and owner of the American Fur Company. His principle, like that of the Grosvenors in London, was to sell leases but never the free-hold. This policy had made him, by 1847, the richest man in the United States with an estimated fortune of $20,000,000.

His fortune was the colossus of the times; an object of awe to all wealth-strivers. Necessary as manufacturers were in the social and industrial system, they, as yet, occupied a strikingly subordinate and inferior position as an agency in accumulating great fortunes. Statistics issued in 1844 of manufacture in the United States showed a total gross amount of $307,196,844 invested. Astor's wealth, then, was one-fifteenth of the whole amount invested throughout the territory of the United States . . . in every kind of goods which the demands of civilization made indispensable.[11]

In point of fact this $20,000,000 left by John Jacob when he died in 1848 was only the beginning. The fortune left by John Jacob Astor II in 1890 amounted to $150,000,000 and the several branches of the family, later prominent in New York society, have flourished since. Not only in the United States, however, for William Waldorf Astor migrated to England in 1899, acquired the Cliveden estate in Buckinghamshire and was raised to the peerage as Viscount Astor in 1917. He died at Hever Castle in 1919 and the estate and title passed to his elder son, from whom the present Astors are descended.

When Junius Morgan, the son of Joseph, moved to England in 1854, he joined the merchant house of George Peabody & Company, which, with the help of the Bank of England, survived the crisis of 1857 and then prospered during the American Civil War, as did all the firms which had backed the Union. Peabody retired in 1862 and his firm then became J. S. Morgan & Company, the foremost American banking firm in Europe, the firm that was to back Cecil Rhodes against Barney Barnato. This firm was more important than its American counterpart until about 1905 but, Junius having died in 1890, the emphasis of the business gradually shifted towards Wall Street. In 1910 the London firm admitted an English partner and became Morgan, Grenfell and Company. Meanwhile, Junius's son, Pierpont Morgan, who had spent some part of his youth in Europe, came back to the USA in 1856, and set up in business as J. Pierpont Morgan and Company. A subsidiary, Dalney, Morgan and Company, represented J. S. Morgan & Company in the USA. In 1871 Pierpont agreed to go into partnership with Anthony J. Drexel, heir to the Joseph Drexel's important banking house in Philadelphia, which had a branch in Paris but not in London. The result was the establishment of Drexel, Morgan and Company in New York, closely associated with J. S. Morgan of London, Drexel and Company of Philadelphia and Drexel, Hayes and Company in Europe. The New York office of six stories, fronted with white marble was built on the corner of Broad and Wall Streets, central to the financial district. It opened for business during the boom which had followed the American Civil War. The boom period ended with the panic of 1873, a panic so serious that the New York Stock Exchange closed for the first time in its history. The First National Bank of Washington failed and over five thousand business firms collapsed, with a total of over $200,000,000. The failure ushered in a five-year period of depression. The firm least affected was Drexel, Morgan & Company, partly because its policy had been conservative, but mainly because its position was now international. Two subsequent events gave Pierpont Morgan his pre-eminence among financiers. The first was the Treasury's refunding of Civil War bonds in 1871. Half of the total to be refunded ($200,000,000) was handled by Morgan's syndicate, backed in London by Baring Brothers and J. S. Morgan. The second was the Federal bond issue of 1877, $235,000,000 marketed by

Belmont, Rothschilds, Seligman, and Drexel, Morgan & Company, also acting for J. S. Morgan & Company of London. When Drexel, Morgan took over the financing of the New York Central Railroad (1879) and the Northern Pacific (1880) their wealth and power became a legend.[12] By 1933 Morgan partners held 167 directorships in eighty-nine corporations, with total assets of about twenty billion dollars. Among the eighty-nine were fifteen banks and trust companies, seven miscellaneous holding companies, ten railroads, five public utility holding corporations, thirty-eight industrial companies and six insurance companies. Wealth can be assessed but influence on this scale is something which defies measurement.

Since about 1840 Wall Street has represented the power of finance. There are, and have long been, the head offices of the Chase Manhattan Bank, the Manufacturers' Trust, the Guaranty Trust (amalgamated with J. P. Morgan in 1934) and the Bankers' Trust. There is the New York Stock Exchange and close to it the offices of the underwriters or insurance bankers; Morgan, Stanley, Lehman Brothers, Goldman Sachs & Co., Kahn, Loeb & Co. and all the rest, not forgetting Merrill Lynch, Pierce, Fenner & Smith. Wall Street is also the home of the Dow Jones Index and the *Wall Street Journal*. It offers a good living to a number of distinguished lawyers and a hectic career for a lot of news-hungry reporters.

In the vivid, fragrant days before 1929 Wall Street was, though disliked and distrusted by many people, an object of profound veneration to the business world. To become a Morgan partner, or even a Kahn Loeb partner, was for most rising young men of the East practically like becoming a cardinal, only more so. The path was well beaten for any really bright and ambitious youngster and it was often a golden path – St Paul's or Laurenceville, Yale or Princeton, and then the Street. Bankers were really looked up to in those days. Now of course they have to spend most of their time explaining themselves . . .[13]

If the great days ended in 1929, when stocks valued at $89 billion began their fall in value to $17 billion in January 1932, we do well to remember what Wall Street had been before that time of disaster. The development of Big Business in industry had been made possible by the previous development of Big Business in finance.

Closely akin to banking, and as important to industry, is the business of insurance. As applied to ships and cargoes insurance is of medieval origin. The business records of Francesco di Marco, born near Florence in about 1335, have all been preserved and are found to include four hundred insurance policies. The practice of marine insurance spread from Italy to the Netherlands and from there to London. Soon after the Royal Exchange was opened (1570), a Chamber of Assurance was established in which all insurance policies were to be registered, those not so recorded being null and void. Commissioners appointed by the Court of Aldermen were to arbitrate so as 'to end all controversies, doubts and questions concerning assurances'. This procedure was followed from 1575 to 1601, in which year there was an Act of Parliament 'touching Policies of Assurances used among Merchants'. The object of insurance was thus legally defined for the first time, the policy being drawn up on occasions of great adventure to remote parts:

... by means of which policies of assurance it cometh to pass, on loss or perishing of any ship, there followeth not the undoing of any man, but the loss lighteth rather easily upon many than heavily upon few, and rather upon those that adventure not than those that do adventure, whereby all merchants, especially the younger sort, are allured to adventure more willingly and more freely.[14]

The effect of the Act was to set up a Court to deal with insurance cases, the members to include a Judge of Admiralty and the Recorder of London.

Legalities apart, the object in marine insurance was and is to spread the risk as widely as possible. As ships became larger, moreover, the ownership as well as the insurance came to be divided and subdivided. (A knowledge of this practice on Shakespeare's part would have spoilt the plot of The Merchant of Venice.) 'Underwriters' are those whose signatures are added to a policy, taking a proportion of the risk. At some period in the late seventeenth century the underwriters began to frequent the coffee house kept by Edward Lloyd between 1688 and 1726. He moved his establishment to Lombard Street in 1691 and even published 'Lloyd's News', the predecessor of Lloyd's List as it is known today, for the convenience of his customers. The underwriters were still unorganized at that period but there may have been some sort of association by 1760. As an institution Lloyd's took final shape when the subscribers moved their meeting place to the Royal Exchange in 1774. As from then there was a Committee, a standard form of insurance and some qualifications required of new subscribers. Whereas there had been failures in the eighteenth century, some even in 1780, the system was fairly solidly based by about 1810. With the predominance of British shipping under Victoria there was a similar predominance of London marine insurance. Much of the world's shipping was and is covered by policies taken out at Lloyd's – not by that institution as such, but by a large number of underwriters who have accepted the risk between them, abiding by known rules and upholding a professional standard of integrity. The expression 'A1 at Lloyds' is one with world-wide currency.

Fire insurance virtually began with the Fire of London in 1666, a disaster in which 13,000 houses were destroyed. From 1680 a variety of insurance schemes were put forward, the earliest being the Fire Office founded by Nicholas Barbon and afterwards called the Phoenix. The Friendly Society of 1684 was second and a third was the Hand-in-Hand of 1696, which survived until 1905, when it was absorbed by the Commercial Union Insurance Company. The Sun Fire Office opened in 1710 and many others followed, some in London and some in Scotland and the provinces. It was the growth of fire insurance that led to the formation of the earliest fire brigades, established by the insuring companies to extinguish fires in the buildings they had insured. Although less important than marine insurance, the practice of insurance against accident and fire has been a factor in the growth of industry. It has also been one aspect of Big Business, to which life insurance has been more important still. It was calculated in 1945 that a list of corporations in the United States, based on size in terms of assets, would be headed by the Metropolitan Life Insurance Company, The Prudential Insurance Company would come third. Banks and other insurance companies are high in the list and General Motors is only thirteenth, with U.S. Steel next and Ford as low as forty-first. Assets are not necessarily the best measure of importance but facts such as these may serve to remind us that historically finance comes before industry and that even the full development of industry may still leave finance (at least financially) in the lead.

4 Railways and Postal Services in Britain, Europe and Asia

In studying the history of invention one becomes aware of progress on two levels. There are major discoveries made by men of imagination, of vision even, and it is these that attract the notice of historians. There are also innumerable improvements in technique for which no particular craftsman gains the credit, but without which the major discoveries would be – at least temporarily – pointless. John Dee (1527–1608) is said to have discovered electricity but at that time no one was capable of making for him the sort of equipment which an electrician needs. An early design for a submarine dates from the reign of Charles II but who then could have made any such craft with the necessary precision? The problem of ascertaining longitude at sea was solved (in theory) by Sir Isaac Newton but no contemporary of his could make the sort of clock which would be needed. The usual tendency is for technology to lag behind invention, the theory being often easier than the practice.

The two ideas which underlie the railway locomotive are of ancient date but for long inapplicable to any machine which would combine both. The first idea, to place a vehicle on wooden rails, was a commonplace of mining technique from the sixteenth century and quite possibly from the twelfth. The latent energy in steam was observed by Archimedes and again by Leonardo da Vinci but centuries were to pass before the railway age could begin. In the meanwhile rails were laid between hill-sited pitheads and riverside wharves. Laden truckloads of coal would descend suitable inclines by gravity, and were pulled up again, when empty, by the horse who liked the ride down in the dandy-cart but whose stable was at the top. Railways of this sort were to be seen at Newcastle-on-Tyne in 1676, differing little from those seen a hundred years earlier in the Harz mountains or Tyrol.

The first steam engines were also used in mining but solely for the purpose of pumping out the water. As the more accessible strata were exhausted the miners had to go deeper and the problem of drainage became more formidable, first in Germany and later in England. The first steam pump was invented by Thomas Savery (?1650–1715) in 1698 and applied to a Cornish tin mine in 1702. Savery's invention was almost immediately improved by his partner Thomas Newcomen (1663–1729), a Dartmouth ironmonger or blacksmith, whose 'Atmospheric Engine' became generally accepted. One of the successful engines he installed was at Pool Mine in Cornwall, a mile from Dolcoath Mine which was managed in about 1765 by the elder Richard Trevithick, noted engineer and friend and disciple of John Wesley. Trevithick's son, of the same name, born in 1771, was to be still more distinguished. He became engineer of the Ding Dong Mine near Penzance and so improved the steam engine that he was able to construct a steam carriage at Redruth in 1801. 'The engine was called Captain Dick's puffer, from the steam and smoke puffing out of the chimney at each stroke . . .'[1] As in so many instances the design of the machine was ingenious. What was lacking was the machinery for making the working parts. All Trevithick had was a chuck-lathe, hand-lathes and a few drilling machines. The result was that his engine, while quite workable, broke down after a single trial. He then proceeded to build a tramway locomotive at the Penydarran Ironworks near Merthyr Tydfil in South Wales. This engine of 1803–4 was a success and Trevithick was thus the inventor of the locomotive, proving 'the sufficiency of the adhesion of the wheels to the rails for all purposes of traction on lines of ordinary gradient'. Trevithick went on to experiment with a first steam vessel in 1805 and an iron steamboat in 1808. He urged the use of the screw-propeller in 1812 and had ideas as advanced about agricultural machinery. Unfortunately for his place in history he was persuaded to go out to Peru in 1816, his task being to install engines which would pump out the flooded and now useless gold and silver mines both there and in Mexico. Some surprising adventures followed but the war of independence broke out and the Peruvian patriots destroyed the machinery that he had brought from England. He then invented a diving bell with which he salvaged the contents of a frigate which had sunk near Callao. Conscripted into Bolivar's army, he invented a brass cavalry carbine which fired what has since been called a dum-dum bullet. He then went on to Costa Rica, finally returning to England in 1827, where he died penniless in 1833. During his absence from the country James Watt had been accepted as the inventor of the steam engine and George Stephenson as the inventor and founder of the railway. Perhaps a more remarkable man than either of them, Richard Trevithick is all but forgotten.

George Stephenson (1781–1848) was a self-taught mechanic who worked in the Newcastle area and became engineer to the Killingworth Colliery in 1812. Mr Blackett of Wylam Colliery acquired one of Trevithick's locomotives in 1811 – or else one made locally from Trevithick's design. George Stephenson studied this locomotive and produced an improved version of it in 1814. The engine was a success and he was given the task of providing a railroad for Helton Colliery. That also succeeded and he was appointed engineer to the proposed Stockton and Darlington Railway, which opened its service over twelve miles – for passengers as well as goods – in 1825. Such was the success of this experiment with locomotives and rails that a company was formed for building a railway between Manchester and Liverpool. The necessary Bill was presented to Parliament, debated and finally passed. Stephenson was to plan the railroad but the choice of locomotive was to be determined by an open trial between those available. The contest took place in October 1829 and the winner was Stephenson's *Rocket*:

> The genius of the man from Newcastle lay in his ability to co-ordinate the work of others as well as his own ... He was a great engineer, a splendid organizer and a shrewd and determined campaigner, the man of the hour, achieving what no one had done before. This assures his fame for ever, for railways were England's gift to the world and it is beyond all possible doubt that it is to George Stephenson that our thanks are due.[2]

If we accepted the theory that the demand creates the supply we should be mystified over the whole story of how railways developed in England. For in no country was there less obvious need for them. The problem of transporting heavy goods had been triumphantly solved, all the major industrial centres and seaports being linked by canal. The problem of conveying passengers had been solved even more recently. No other country in the world had such splendid coaches travelling with such unexampled speed over such magnificent roads. And if there was any one route singled out for early and costly improvement it had been that between Manchester and Liverpool, the site of one of the earliest canals, to which a well frequented turnpike ran almost parallel. In 1830, nevertheless, the railway opened and was immediately profitable, more, even, from passenger traffic than from goods. As from that date the great railway boom began. Early efforts had been tentative, like the ten-mile line from Monkhead to Kirkintilloch which was finished in 1826, or the Ballochney Railway opened in 1828. From 1832, however, began the effort to connect London with Birmingham, the route which became the London and North-Western Railway of 1846. This was probably Robert Stephenson's masterpiece: 112 miles long, with scarcely a gradient of more than 1/300 and only three curves which impose a speed restriction. Rival to the North-Western, and battling for some of the same territory, was the Great Western, built by Brunel with a wider distance between the rails. The London and South-Western opened in 1840 and so did the first stage of the Eastern Counties. The South-Eastern followed and the Great Northern of 1850. Twelve hundred companies had been formed by 1845; there were 600 railway Bills before Parliament in 1846 and 6,621 miles of railway by 1850, the year in which the Menai Bridge was finished. There were over eighty railway Acts each year (on average) between 1850 and 1860, and 916 Acts during the next five years, bringing the total distance of track to 10,433 miles and the number of locomotives to 5,801. In all essentials the British railway system was finished by about 1870.

The heroes of this tremendous effort are the great engineers, George Stephenson, Isambard Kingdom Brunel and George Rennie. The monuments are the great railway viaducts, tunnels and terminal stations. We hear little, by comparison, of the financiers who raised the capital. It is clear, moreover, that the early companies were formed to build from ten to thirty miles of track only, the patchwork result being joined together as a result of later negotiations. The immediate and certain profit went to the lawyers and surveyors:

If we take together the legal, engineering and parliamentary expenses, for services which are all irrespective of the money paid for land or works, we come to astounding totals. In 1855 it was ascertained that 160 companies had spent in this way a sum of money which, averaged equally among them, would amount to £88,000 each.[3]

Merely to present an unopposed Bill might cost as little as £32,000 but few Bills had as easy a passage. The opposition of landowners was common enough but usually shortlived. As J. B. Snell points out, many of them would oppose a railway bill

... in the confident, happy and well justified expectation that they would be richly bribed to desist. In later years many landowners mastered the technique to a nicety; their opposition was fierce enough to ensure a generous settlement, but not usually so fierce as to risk any actual deviation of the line ... The opposition was never fiercer than on the Liverpool and Manchester, where Stephenson's surveyors were set upon by hired gangs of toughs, hunted by gamekeepers and so chivvied that they often had to work at night, while eagle-eyed lawyers in Parliament scrutinized their plans for any resulting inaccuracies.[4]

On the Liverpool and Manchester line the chief opposition was likely to be offered by the canal proprietors but the opposition of another railway company was at once more probable and more serious, involving legal expenses of up to £200,000. From 1840 the railways came under the general supervision of the Board of Trade, the offices of which were in Parliament Street. Perhaps partly for this reason most civil engineers set up their offices in the same vicinity (where many of them remain), strategically placed between Victoria Station and the Houses of Parliament. That members of the legislature could be bribed is likely enough but the political influence of railway companies was usually more subtle than that, as when important people were offered shares on favourable terms. Shares themselves were speculative and land values were affected by the proximity of lines and stations. It must be remembered, however, that British railway lines were mostly planned to connect towns which already existed, they and the intervening countryside being influenced by noble families and civic authorities that were already there. They were seldom creating land values where there had previously been nothing but desert. This was the limiting factor throughout the British railway boom. Money was made and lost by those who had it to invest but we can point to few fortunes made out of the promotion of railway shares. The word 'millionaire' was first used, italicized, in the American press of about 1843 and referred, of course, to those who had made a fortune in dollars. It could hardly be used in connection with the British railways, so widely were the gains distributed. To that rule there is, however, an exception to be made in the case of George Hudson, the Railway King. It was he who nearly brought Big Business to Britain and there is much to learn from his example of what could and could not be done under Queen Victoria's rule.

George Hudson, born in 1800, had a successful drapery business in York where he founded the York Union Banking Company in 1833, before going on to become lord mayor of that city in 1837. He then became manager of the York and North Midland Railway Company which formed in 1836 and opened a service (from 1839) between York and Normanton. There, from 1841, it connected with the Manchester and Leeds Railway and so, eventually, with Crewe, Birmingham and London. After this modest opening move, Hudson took over the management of the Newcastle and Darlington Line (1842), founded the Midland Railway from Derby to Bristol and London in 1843 and persuaded Parliament in that year to sanction the amalgamation of the York and Newcastle with the Newcastle and Berwick lines. When Hudson had become chairman of the Eastern Counties Railway he controlled an empire which extended, perhaps a little uncertainly, from London to Berwick. His aim was to create the east coast route to Scotland and he was well on the way to doing so. Chosen as MP for Sunderland in 1845 and lord mayor of York again in 1846, he was a man of wealth and influence. His opponents complained that the York city council was a subsidiary of the York and North Midland, its members including the chairman and vice-chairman, together with the company's solicitors, bankers, engineers and chief shareholders. In the House of Commons the 'railway MPs' were said to number 102, Hudson being one of the most influential. But for two obstacles he might have been the first industrial dynast of Britain, the founder of an ennobled family based on railway shares.

Of the two obstacles the first was the very nature of the railway mania. Britain had about two thousand miles of railroad by the end of 1843 and some of the companies were paying a high dividend. There was a rush to register new companies, the new capital authorized rising from £20,000,000 in 1844 to £132,000,000 in 1846 – sums greater than the whole revenue. Six hundred railway Bills were passed in 1846 alone. New ventures were advertised and over-subscribed daily, amid tremendous gambling in the shares and tremendous publicity in the press:

The year 1845 wore on and the mania grew more and more pronounced as the number of new railway companies registered increased week by week. All the leading engineers such as Brunel, Locke, Rennie and Vignolles, found themselves in urgent demand; only 'Old George' Stephenson, in his retirement at Tapton House, kept aloof, but his son Robert made good the deficiency by being connected with thirty-four separate lines! The burly figure of Hudson, surrounded by an admiring group of followers, was often to be seen in Stephenson's offices at 24 Great George Street, Westminster, which were so crowded with persons seeking interview that they presented the appearance of the levée of a minister of State. . . .

Those who could not gain a job from railways contented themselves with speculating in shares. Every class of the community was drawn into the net. A return called for by Parliament, to show the number of persons who had subscribed more than £2000 in railway undertaking included the names of 900 lawyers, 364 bankers, 257 clergymen and 157 Members of Parliament, besides large numbers of noblemen, merchants and manufacturers . . .

The railway prospectuses poured forth from Moorgate Street and Gresham Street: the railway speculators swarmed about Change Alley and Chapel Court. At the Royal Exchange every morning the omnibuses and coaches discharged a flock of stockjobbers from the suburbs. In the provinces similar scenes were enacted. At Leeds four share markets were opened and even York had its own stock exchange.[5]

The mischief was not that the enterprises were unsound but that the current excitement was creating an overvaluation of the shares. Fortunes could be made by the promoters and Hudson himself was in a position to inflate the value of any stock merely by expressing his interest in it. At the peak of his prosperity he held railway shares to the value of about £320,000. As his other property, shares and real estate, came to well over £700,000, he was well in the millionaire class and probably richer than anyone in New York other than John Jacob Astor himself. The whole position was precarious, however, as was obvious to some commentators even at the time.

The second obstacle was more technical than financial. Hudson's aim was to create and control the east coast route to Scotland and he had done so, more or less, by 1844. North of York his position was reasonably secure but his route southward to London was circuitous and vulnerable. In 1846 a group of his rivals, perceiving this, brought forward a Bill, which was passed, for providing a more direct line from London to York. This was to be the Great Northern Railway, a big undertaking which would take some years to complete. Even while Hudson's position seemed secure this rival line was advancing north to Grantham and from there, in 1850, to Shaftholme Junction just north of Doncaster. The line was open to traffic in 1852 and the whole enterprise was crowned by the completion of King's Cross Station in 1853. This might have been enough in itself to destroy Hudson's kingdom but that collapsed for other reasons before the threat of the Great Northern had fully developed. By this time England's main line system was more or less complete and it remained to bring about the amalgamation which would create the North-Eastern Railway in 1854. The main result of Hudson's effort was to make York (his home town) the administrative centre for the east coast route. But for him the railway, like the Great North Road, would have passed through Wetherby and not through York at all. Apart from that he left behind him a legend of success and failure. Many praised him at first far beyond his merits. More finally abused him in terms which he did not deserve. It remains only to describe the extent of his rise and fall.

Hudson had three sons and his plan was to establish them all as country gentlemen. In 1844 he acquired the Octon Estate near Bridlington and another tract of land near Ripon. In 1845 he bought Newby Park from Earl de Grey and Londesborough Park (of about 12,000 acres) from the Duke of Devonshire, together with an adjacent tract of country north of Market Weighton – the area through which any railway line from York to Hull would have to pass.

... When the branch line to Market Weighton was built Hudson erected a private railway station of his own at a point where the tip of the great park reached down to touch the line. Thence he made a carriage track straight as a die for two miles or so across the meadows and up the rising ground between avenue of magnificent trees, to the very doors of Londesborough. There, had time spared him, he planned to build himself a family seat. . . .[6]

For Londesborough he is believed to have paid £500,000, but that was not all. After his election to Parliament he also acquired, in January 1846, a town residence, Albert House, one of two mansions built as a speculation by Sir William Cubitt. It stands on the north side of Knightsbridge and cost £15,000 to buy and another £14,000 to decorate and furnish. It is now the French embassy, less remarkable for its beauty than its size. These various properties were the symbol of Hudson's success, which was further confirmed by some kind words from the Queen herself; words which were no doubt significant. But there is also significance in the fact that no other honour was forthcoming. It is true that the Tory Party, to which he belonged, was out of office from 1846 but there may have been an unspoken objection to him even among the Tories. It would never have done to confer a knighthood on someone who might be suddenly impoverished, or even imprisoned. He received no recognition, anyway, and subsequent events were to justify that apparent neglect.

The boom in British railway shares could not, in the nature of things, have been prolonged indefinitely. Beyond a certain point the capital did not exist and, apart from that, there were other forms of investment available – including railways overseas. The market slackened in 1847 but Hudson and his friends assumed that it would recover the following year. That, however, was the year of revolution and riot, disorders beginning in France and spreading to Germany, Austria, Italy and Poland, with simultaneous unrest in Ireland and even in Britain itself. The result of the depression was not merely a marking down of railway shares but an actual decline in railway traffic. Hudson's business methods had never been especially orthodox and his tendency had been to use newly subscribed capital to pay the dividend on earlier investments. This system broke down when the earnings diminished and it took all the force of Hudson's personality to stay in business for another year. Then his pack of cards collapsed and he was forced to resign his directorships under pressure from the enraged shareholders. There were no criminal or even civil proceedings, his worst ordeal being to explain himself before a coldly silent House of Commons. But what could he say? What excuse could be made for him was made in *The Times*, a newspaper which had never been friendly towards him:

... Mr Hudson's position was not only new to himself, but absolutely a new thing in the world altogether ... Hudson was the William the Conqueror of Railways, and his system of government and equity was rather intuitive than legal. His colleagues knew this. The shareholders knew it. They would have tolerated it to this day without the smallest objection, but for the unlucky circumstance that Hudson has outlived their success. Their shares have sunk to their previous value and many are ruined in consequence; so they now begin to discover that things were not quite as they should have been. We think the King and his subjects are much of a piece. If they deserve indulgence for their losses, he also may be excused for his difficulties. Mr Hudson found himself everything at once – a large shareholder, a trustee for shareholders, an agent for particular transactions, a broker, a contractor, a banker, a confidential friend of landowners, and a good deal more besides. Had he discharged all these functions with perfect fairness, he would have been a little less than an angel, and that he certainly was not.[7]

The end of the story is soon told. Hudson left the country, penniless, in 1854 but was able to return four years later on the strength of an annuity bought for him by his friends. He died, however, in 1871 and there is no monument to his memory.

The author of *The Times*'s editorial ended with a sentence of masterly restraint but he also drew attention, and very rightly, to the central fact that Hudson's position had been at once new and unique. He was the the first British exponent of Big Business. His failure, as contrasted (say) with the success of Cornelius Vanderbilt, was due to the fact that Britain still had an aristocratic form of government and an aristocracy still firmly in the saddle. Hudson's campaign had to be fought across territory on which other forces were well established. His chess-board was already provided with a queen and bishops, castles and knights. He could not create for himself a new millionaire society as at Newport, Rhode Island. He had to make a place for himself in a society which existed and where he himself was very much on approval. There was no real opposition to railways or even to millionaires, but the new-comer had to watch his step. There was no mercy for the breaker of unwritten rules. Nor could the legislature be bought, for its member-ship comprised men far wealthier than Hudson could ever have been. There was corruption enough, heaven knows, but there were limits to it. The verdict on Hudson, pronounced only in the court of opinion, was final and there could be no appeal.

The British railway system existed at least in outline by about 1860. Many refinements were to follow and many additional branch lines. There were sleeping-cars on the east coast Scots express from 1873. Pullman cars were first seen on the Midland route the following year. The first dining-car appeared in 1879 on the GNR service between London and Leeds. The Severn Tunnel was opened in 1886 and corridor trains were introduced by the Great Western in 1892. There was a last golden age of British railways, lasting from then until 1914, since when interest has shifted away from them.

It remains to note how railways came to Europe, Asia and Africa. If one ignores the early experiments it is clear that the development of European railways began in about 1835 and that the most rapid progress was in Germany, which soon had one of the finest systems in the world. The first line was from Nuremburg to Fürth, the next from Dresden to Leipzig (1837) and from Potsdam to Berlin. There were 1,900 miles of track by 1845, 3,777 by 1850. British railways had been planned to meet the needs of existing industry and commerce. German railways, which helped to shape German industry, were influenced from the outset by Bismarck and the High Command. They were strategic, as soon became apparent in time of war. From 1879 they began to pass into state owner-ship and were mostly under Prussian control by 1909. The French railways tended to radiate from Paris in what would soon become a nationalized system, seven companies being amalgamated in 1850 and others after the Franco–Prussian War. Development in Spain was rather belated, and hardly begun in Italy before that country was unified in 1860. Perhaps the greatest feats of engineering were per-formed in Switzerland with the construction of the St Gotthard and Simplon Railways. Most other efforts were dwarfed in scale, however, by the construction of the Trans-Siberian Railway which the Russians began in 1891 and completed in 1915, although it was rivalled by the

Orient Express which offered, from 1883, a way of reaching Constantinople from Paris.

In Asia a beginning was made by Lord Dalhousie, Governor-General from 1847 to 1856, who planned the Indian railway system as a means of unifying the whole sub-continent. While the routes were laid down by his government, and largely followed the roads, the work of construction and administration was left to private enterprise. The first line to be completed ran from Bombay to Thana, as first stage of the route from Bombay to Madras.[8] There followed lines from Calcutta to Lahore, from Karachi to northern India and so to the completion of the network as planned. As Lower Burma was annexed by Dalhousie himself and as British influence soon extended to Malaya and (for railway purposes) to Siam, the question was soon raised as to whether there might not be a connected service between Paris and Bangkok or even between London and Singapore. The last-named project depended upon the scheme for the Channel Tunnel, much discussed during the reign of Napoleon III and then abandoned as a result of his fall. Revived afterwards and agreed in principle, the work was acually begun in 1882. By 1885 there was a mile of tunnel in existence on either side but, relations between the two countries having deteriorated, the work was then abandoned. Whether or not this tunnel should ever come to be made, the more grandiose railway schemes have now been rather overtaken by events. What the possibilities of railway travel were once thought to be can be gathered from *Around the World in Eighty Days*, published by Jules Verne in 1873. The hero of that book, Phileas Fogg, planned to go by rail from Calais to Brindisi via the Mont Cenis route, from Brindisi to Bombay in a P & O steamship, from Bombay to Calcutta by rail, by sea from there to Yokohama and San Francisco, from there by rail to New York and so by sea to London. His bet was that it could be done in eighty days but the original calculation had depended upon the completion of the Great Indian Peninsular Railway between Rothal and Allahabad. In point of fact the completed line fell short of Allahabad by fifty miles and Mr Fogg could get no further without buying an elephant. The first railroad across the United States, however, was already finished (in 1869) and the journey from Oakland to Ogden, from Ogden to Omaha provided no more serious obstacle than a collapsing bridge and a tribe of Sioux on the warpath. As for the final journey from Liverpool to London, that could be done in six hours or less and the story ends, inevitably, with Phileas Fogg winning his bet to the very minute. The whole epic journey began at the Reform Club where a member had remarked that the world is a big place, which led Mr Fogg to respond, 'It used to be.' The journey ended at the Reform Club with Fogg's point sufficiently made.

The romance of the railway has tended to centre upon the passenger coaches, the *wagon-lits* of the Blue Train or the Orient Express. For the business man the goods train can be more important and the mail van more vital still. Some reference has been made to the mail coaches in England, inaugurated and made obsolete within a lifetime. The mails were first entrusted to the railway in 1830, the service being merely between Manchester and Liverpool. Between London and Birmingham the mails went by train from 1838 and the change from then was rapid. The improvement in the speed of delivery was accompanied, moreover, by changes of policy. The Post Office had been earlier expected to make a profit, serving in effect as an instrument of taxation. A committee was now appointed to report upon this policy, and upon the Post Office generally, in 1837. Prominent in this committee was Sir Rowland Hill, whose view was finally accepted that the Post Office should be but was not 'an institution of ready and universal access, distributing equally to all and with an open hand the blessings of commerce and civilization'. This view was accepted by Parliament and an Act of 1840 was passed 'establishing penny postage for the United Kingdom, permitting the use of stamped paper or cover and imposing rates on foreign and colonial letters according to weight and distance conveyed.'[9] From that date the aim of the Post Office has been merely to recover its expenses. The effect of the lowering of postal rates was to more than double the number of letters sent in the following year. The 82,000,000 letters delivered in 1839 had become 2,323,000,000 by the beginning of the next century, this increase being at once the measure and a cause of social change. Postcards were introduced in 1870 and these were delivered for a halfpenny.

It had not been usual for England to lag behind the continent in the adoption of new postal ideas. Such was the case, however, with reference to the adoption of the convenient post card and the no less useful parcel post. In 1880 the question of the establishment of an international parcel post was discussed in Paris and an agreement was reached for the transmission throughout nearly the whole of Europe of parcels not exceeding three kilogrammes in weight. It was impossible for Great Britain to sign, as she had no inland parcel post at the time and found it difficult to establish one as an agreement with the railways was necessary. A movement was at once begun for one and it was started three years later. The first despatch of foreign and colonial parcels took place in 1885, and at the beginning of the following year arrangements were completed for the exchange of parcels with twenty-seven different countries, including some of the colonies, India and Egypt.[10]

Until 1870 all newspapers had to carry an official stamp costing two pence. There was some consolation for readers, however, in the fact that newspapers properly stamped could be posted free within the United Kingdom except those posted and delivered within the same town (which cost a penny). After the impressed newspaper stamp was abolished the rate on prepaid newspapers was reduced to a halfpenny each. Printed books were similarly privileged, being conveyed at a special rate of a penny for two ounces. Patterns and samples were also favoured, the view being taken that trade was to be encouraged. Post Office revenue fell off sharply in 1840 but then slowly improved, the net product of 1874 exceeding, for the first time, that of 1839. It yielded a modest profit to government for the rest of the century.

There were a number of nineteenth-century improvements in the postal system, one of the most useful being the 'travelling post office' a mail sorting office in a railway carriage fitted for the purpose. This was tried experimentally in 1838 on a Grand Junction Railway between Birmingham and Liverpool. The plan was for the mail to be sorted in advance for the stations reached first and for the train staff to sort the remainder as the journey proceeded, dropping the mailbags at each station. All this was done at night and some ingenious equipment was devised for dropping and picking up mail without stopping the train. When this service was first introduced a press comment called attention to 'a specimen of the exhaustless ingenuity which bids fair to annihilate time and space'.[11] This might now seem an overstatement as applied to a train which travelled at a little over twenty-five miles an hour but speeds were soon to improve. It became the Post Office boast that letters posted up to 7.30pm in inner London would be delivered early next morning at every major city in England and Wales. So far as speed goes in British railway history it is a curious fact that some of the highest speeds were reached at a relatively early period, one engine being credited with a maximum speed of 82 mph in 1887 and another exceeding 100 mph in 1904. With average scheduled speeds of over 60 mph on some routes in 1900, the mails certainly went 'post-haste' in the days of steam.

One development in the postal service is not very generally known today and that is the GPO's underground railway:

Traffic congestion is an ever-present cause of delay in London, and the increasing density of the ordinary street traffic made it necessary to endeavour to find some easier and quicker method of crossing the city than the horse-driven mail-van and, later, the motor mail-van. Mailbags arriving from the west country, for instance, at Paddington have to reach the GPO or other points such as the Western Central Office or Mount Pleasant, as rapidly as possible and even the best drivers in the greatest hurry are helpless in the press of vehicles and the crowded roads between.

In 1909 a Departmental Committee was set up to consider the problem. After exhaustive enquiry, it suggested that an underground tube railway should be constructed through which electrically-driven trains, automatically controlled, could run in both directions. The first section to be built should connect the West and East Ends of London, with eight stations situated at Paddington, Western Parcels Office, Western District Office, West Central District Office, Mount Pleasant, King Edward's Building, Liverpool Street Station and the Eastern District Office. The committee's recommendation was accepted and in 1913 powers to proceed were granted by Parliament.[12]

Owing to the outbreak of World War 1 this underground railway was not open to traffic until 1927. It is quite distinct from London's passenger underground railway. This began with the Metropolitan line (1863) and the District line in 1868, which both employed steam locomotives. The Inner Circle was completed in 1884. Electrification began with the construction of the deep-level 'tube' railways in 1890, the Inner Circle going over to electricity in 1905. The Post Office underground was of course electrified from the outset and the trains were driven automatically. There was no automation in the passenger underground until the first section of the new Victoria Line was opened in 1968. In this and in some other developments the British Post Office may be said to have led the way. It is notably more efficient than the Post Office in the USA.

The improvement of postal facilities was the result of changed social conditions but it was also the consequence of changes in the process of paper manufacture. While paper was hand-made the volume of correspondence was likely to be small, nor would the material be easily available for the wrapping of parcels. To the development of administration, whether public or business, however, the availability of cheap paper was as essential as the invention of printing. The story of machine-made paper begins with an invention of Nicholas-Louis Robert while he was in the employ of a manufacturer called Didot at Essonnes in France. Robert applied to the Minister of the Interior for a patent in 1798 and was given both the patent and a reward. The machine had no immediate success in France but Didot bought the patent from Robert for 25,000 francs and made contact with his brother-in-law, John Gamble, owner of an English paper mill. The two countries were then at war but the Peace of Amiens came at a timely moment and allowed Gamble to patent the invention in Britain. The £60,000 capital required to develop the invention came from two London stationers, Henry and Sealy Fourdrinier. Under their direction Bryan Dorkin made the first commercially successful machine at Frogmore Mill, Two Waters, Hertfordshire. Unfortunately for the Fourdriniers there was a flaw in their patent which enabled other manufacturers to copy their machine without paying any royalty: which many of them had done by 1807. Use of these machines spread to other countries, Russia being one, where they were brought into use at the imperial paper mills at Peterhof. Paper manufactured by this new process was made to the width of the machine (e.g. sixty inches) and in a roll of indefinite length. It was still made from rag stock, however, which was soon in short supply, the problem being to replace it by some fibre which would be more readily available:

What is generally considered to be the first paper-machine of Fourdrinier design to be erected in this country (i.e. the USA) was imported by Henry Barclay of Sangerties, New York. The machine, which was sixty inches in width, was built in England by Bryan Dorkin. It was put into operation on 24 October 1827, in a mill owned by Beach, Honnerken and Kearney....

The second Fourdrinier paper-machine installed in America had been made in France to the order of the Pickering paper mill, North Windham, Connecticut. The huge Fourdrinier packed in many crates and boxes arrived at an American port in December 1827.[13]

This second machine was assembled and erected in 1828 by George Spafford, who decided that he could build similar machines for himself. Entering into a partnership with James Phelps, he set up in business in South Windham, Connecticut. There they made the first American-built machine which they sold to Amos H. Hubbard of Norwich Falls. The shift of the industry to the USA was important because timber was plentiful there and this, in the form of wood-pulp, was to be the new material from which paper was made. It was not, however, until 1854 that Hugh Burgess and Charles Watt patented their process of manufacturing paper from wood fibre. Experiment until then had been mostly concentrated on esparto grass from Spain and North Africa. Nor was the paper first produced from wood pulp wholly successful, for it contained resin and other impurities. It was not until 1873 that the process began of boiling wood chips in soda or sulphate solutions. From about that time paper was produced in bulk and its purposes were differentiated – newsprint, stationery and wrapping paper. Art paper was also invented for use with illustrations, the paper being treated with gypsum or china clay. Another novelty was toilet paper in roll form, patented by the American Seth Wheeler in 1875 and widely distributed by the end of the century. Paper had been used for this purpose in ancient China, as Arab travellers had noted in the year AD 875, but it took exactly a thousand years for the idea to reach Europe. From about 1875 the age of cheap and plentiful paper begins.

With the paper came the typewriter and the typist. The first practical machine was devised in 1867 by three citizens of Milwaukee, Wisconsin: Christopher Latham Sholes, Carlos Glidden and Samuel W. Soulé. Soulé soon retired but C. S. Sholes, a printer by trade, built nearly thirty models before patenting the last and best of them in 1868. He may have been inspired by an earlier machine invented by a Marseilles printer in 1833 but his was a great improvement on that or any other model. He had solved, moreover, the main practical problem which arose from the clashing and jarring of type-bars when two adjacent keys were touched in quick succession. He so arranged the keyboard that letters frequently used in combination were placed well apart and his plan is virtually that which is still in use. Fortified by his patent, Sholes made a contract with E. Remington & Sons under which they would manufacture machines to his design, and the first of these were actually placed on the market in 1874. The Remington Company had been a gunsmith's firm, founded by Eliphalet Remington of Suffield, Connecticut. An established gunsmith in 1828, he moved to New York State, setting up in business at Ilion, in the area traversed by the new Erie Canal. There he manufactured rifles and carbines and brought out his own design of revolver in 1859, following on the success of the Colt revolver, patented by Samuel Colt in 1836. Remington did good business during the Civil War, as his weapons had a high reputation, but he died in 1861, leaving his three sons to carry on the business. They evidently decided to diversify their production, making not only type-writers but sewing machines too. The Remington typing machines were successful, especially after some improvements had been made. The shift-key mechanism, introduced in 1878, made the machine more compact and certainly more suitable for touchtyping which was developed between 1890 and 1900. Some early typists were men but it was soon agreed that women should do this work, an idea probably based upon an analogy with playing the piano. By about 1880 type-writers and typists were available to the less conservative business men.

To make the best use of the new machine it was soon evident that the typist would have to know shorthand. There had been systems of shorthand from an early period of history, one of them, for example, published by Thomas Shelton in 1630. This was the system used by Samuel Pepys, one fairly well known in his day. Then Samuel Taylor published his *Universal System of Stenography* (London, 1786) which was improved in later editions. It was this form of shorthand that was adopted in France, Germany and in Europe generally. Next came Isaac Pitman's *Stenographic Sound Hand* of 1837, republished in Boston (1844), the point of which was that the symbols used related to the sound and not to the sense of the original. Born in 1813, Pitman was a schoolmaster who eventually had his own school at Bath. Having learnt Samuel Taylor's shorthand he resolved to improve on it and did so, his system tending to replace all others in use. He was knighted in 1894 and his disciples were numerous enough to form the National Shorthand Reporters Association. His rival was John Robert Gregg, who published his *Light-Line Phonography* in 1888. For some reason his system was found especially acceptable in the United States where it became, and has remained, the shorthand most widely used. It is not easy to establish the exact date by which any businessman of consequence was likely to have a stenographer but there must have been many of them by 1880 and a majority perhaps by 1890. One of the first to appear on the stage was Flossie, shorthand-typist to a progressive clergyman in George Bernard Shaw's play *Candida*. That play was first published in 1895 and Flossie's part in it was evidently thought plausible at the time. The typist, Miss Proserpine Garnett, is a brisk little woman of about thirty, of the lower middle class, neatly but cheaply dressed in a black merino skirt and a blouse, notably pert and quick of speech. . . . She is clattering away busily at her machine whilst Morell opens the last of his morning's letters (Act 1). Several social changes resulted from the typewriter's coming into use, one being the entry of women into office work, another the disappearance of the copying clerk who had previously worked (standing) at a high desk. With the typewriter came the carbon paper with which duplicates could be made and with the duplicates a filing system instead of the older letter book. The new paper was not nearly as durable as the old had been and the new typescript tended to fade and become illegible after about twenty years, a fact which has since posed a problem for archivists. From the point of view of business, however, the typewriter represented an important stage in the process by which head-office control could be maintained over a large and complex organization.

Office equipment has developed a great deal since 1900. There has been, for example, the appearance of the dictaphone, the adding machine and the reprographic devices which can copy anything exactly and at once. It cannot be said, however, that these are more than refinements, doing more effectively and quickly what could have been done in any case. For purposes of communication the tools all existed at head office from about 1880. There are other inventions upon which comment could well be made, the changes in artificial lighting, for example, from candles to gaslight and from that to electricity. Although these changes were undoubtedly important, however, they probably made nothing possible in business that had been impossible before. This would not be true of the computer, but that subject is dealt with later in the book for the sufficient reason that automation is a Big Business in itself. In the USA at least the same could be said of the telegraph and telephone but these services, nationalized in most countries, are treated in this book as aids to business rather than as industries. The general effect of the inventions so far described has been to make for a closer relationship between the different parts of an organization, and especially between the centre and the periphery. More than that, it could be said that the growing size of organizations has been a reflection of what has become technically possible from about 1870 onwards. Other and later inventions, like aircraft, have made for a still closer system of control and a correspondingly diminished autonomy in the more distant branches. If this is characteristic of business in the twentieth century, the trend was manifest before the last century came to its close.

5 Telegraph, Telephone, Radio

When Richard Parker, the mutineer, was hanged on board the flagship at the Nore on 30 June 1797, the news was received at the Admiralty in a matter of minutes. It was transmitted from Sheerness by telegraph, using a system invented by the Reverend Mr John Gamble, fellow of Pembroke College, Cambridge, and chaplain-general to the forces, but since improved by Lord George Murray. Gamble was not, in fact, the first telegraphist for a type of semaphore had been invented in 1767 by Richard Lovell Edgeworth as a means, it is said, of obtaining racing results from Newmarket. It was a further development of Edgeworth's system which the Admiralty adopted, as described by Gamble in his book of 1795. The first line of telegraph stations, using a shutter system of signals sent from one hilltop to the next, ran from the Admiralty to Dover via Sheerness. There followed a line to Portsmouth, which could transmit a priority message in thirty-one seconds, but the system developed slowly in Britain and there was no line to Plymouth until years afterwards. So when the schooner *Pickle* came into Falmouth on 4 November 1805, bringing the news of the Battle of Trafalgar and of Lord Nelson's death, nothing was known of it in London until Lieutenant Lapenotière had arrived at the Admiralty by post-chaise in the small hours of 6 November. The telegraph system was not in fact perfected until 1816, after the war was over, when Sir Home Popham introduced a simpler mechanism with two arms pivoted on an upright post. This more nearly resembled the French telegraph, first approved in 1792, for which the lines of communication had been laid in the first instance from Paris to Lille, and afterwards from the capital to Calais, to Strasbourg, to Toulon, to Brest and (furthest of all) to Bayonne. These early telegraph systems were of great value in time of war but were costly to maintain, the French having 519 stations in all, manned day and night. The British lines of telegraphic communication were probably less useful than the French, for Britain was and is more liable to fog and mist, which reduced visibility to zero and sometimes even cut off a message already begun, with a consequent risk of confusion. It was experience with these early systems, commemorated today by the common place name 'Telegraph Hill', which stimulated the search for something better. Electricity, which was to solve the problem of tele-graphic communication, was demonstrated by Count Alessander Volta before the French Academy of Science in 1801. The Italian physicist had invented the electric battery, which was acclaimed at once by Napoleon as a major discovery. A scheme for constructing a 'voltaic telegraph' was put forward, moreover, by Soemmering at Munich, as early as 1811. His contrivance was a failure but it occasioned further discussion and experiment and the technical problem he had set out to solve was solved, in fact, in 1836. The inventor was Professor Muncke of Heidelberg, whose electro-telegraphic device could carry a signal from one room to another. Michael Faraday had discovered magneto-electricity five years before but it was Muncke, apparently, who applied it to this particular purpose.

Granted that signals could now be sent over a longer distance, some system would be needed for conveying an actual message. Such a system was devised in 1832 by an American artist, Samuel F. B. Morse, whose dots and dashes still form the Morse Code. While Morse was trying, without success, to gain support for his experiments in the USA, William Fothergill Cooke (formerly of the Indian Army) saw Muncke's device at Heidelberg and explained it to Faraday. He then discovered, rather to his dismay, that Professor Charles Wheatstone, of King's College, London, was working on the same project. They agreed, however, to collaborate in an experiment on a line set up between Euston Station and Camden Town. The experiment was a success and they formed a partnership in 1837. Their first line was set up in 1838, alongside the Great Western Railway between Paddington and West Drayton. The line was extended the next year to Harwell. Paddington

Station became one of the sights of London, and people paid a shilling to watch the telegraph functioning. Others paid the same sum to be admitted to Telegraph Cottage at Slough. The era of electric telegraphy had dawned.

The first, or nearly the first, example was afforded by the Blackwall Railway, opened in 1840. In the four miles from the Minories to Blackwall, there were intermediate stations at Shadwell, Limehouse, West India Docks, and Poplar. The trains were drawn, not by locomotives but by rope traction, with the aid of fixed steam-engines. The trains started every quarter of an hour in each direction. The announcement of departures, of stoppages, of the number of carriages attached to the wire-rope, of accidents or causes of delay, were regularly transmitted by electro-telegraphic apparatus placed at all the stations. . . .
Circumstances led the Blackwall Company to substitute locomotive for fixed power; but the value of the electric telegraph had been rendered too manifest to permit of its abandonment. Many of the railway companies deemed themselves justified in laying down a single instead of a double line of rails, owing to the safeguards which the telegraph afforded. By the year 1842, the system had been adopted on the London and North-Western, South-Western, South-Eastern and Eastern Counties lines. . . .[1]

The telegraph was thus first accepted as an ancillary to the railway, a safety device and a means of economizing over the track. The railways afforded space for the telegraph posts along the existing lines, and stations were readymade points for transmission and acceptance of messages. It was soon realized, however, that telegraphy could serve a wider public. Proof of this was offered by the case of John Tawell. This gentleman travelled down to Slough on New Year's Day, 1845, with the object of poisoning his discarded mistress who lived at Salthill. The murder took place very much as planned, the poison unnoticed (at first) in a glass of stout. The lady's subsequent screams attracted attention, however, and Tawell was seen leaving the cottage as he ran off to catch his train back to Paddington, congratulating himself on a job well done. Unluckily for him, a witness to his flight from Salthill came to the station at Slough. The result was the transmission of the following telegram:

A murder has just been committed at salthill and the suspected murderer was seen to take a first-class ticket for London by the train which left slough at 7.42 pm. he is in the garb of a kwaker with a brown greatcoat on which reaches nearly down to his feet. he is in the last compartment of the second first-class carriage.

There was some momentary doubt about the word 'kwaker' – 'Q' was not then in telegraphic usage – but the description was more than adequate. On arrival at Paddington the murderer was recognized by a sergeant (in plain clothes) of the railway company's police. When Tawell caught an omnibus to the Bank the sergeant did the same. When he visited one or two public houses he was still shadowed, and when he finally returned to his lodgings in Scotts Yard, off Cannon Street, the sergeant was careful to make note of the address. Next morning Mr Tawell was arrested and charged. It was only a question of time before he was tried and hanged. There was nothing very sensational about the crime as such but headlines were made by the process of his arrest. There was magic indeed in the device which could flash the news of the murder ahead of the fleeing criminal. If the railway aided a murderer's escape from the scene of his crime, the telegraph ensured that the police would be waiting at the other end. The future of the telegraph was now secure.

The Electric Telegraph Company was founded in 1846 by John Lewis Ricardo MP and William Fothergill Cooke, with its head office in Founders Court, Lothbury. The wires were laid in tubes buried below street level, connecting Lothbury with all the railway stations, with the Post Office, with Scotland Yard, with the Admiralty, with the recently constructed Houses of Parliament and with Buckingham Palace.

... There were established in Edinburgh, Manchester, Liverpool, Glasgow, Hull, Newcastle, and other towns, subscription newsrooms, for the accomodation of the mercantile and professional interests, to which was transmitted by electric telegraph the latest intelligence, including domestic and foreign news; shipping news; the stock, share, corn and other markets; parliamentary intelligence; London Gazette; state of the wind and weather from numerous places in England; and the earliest possible notices of all important occurrences.[2]

Use of the electric telegraph spread rapidly, an early development taking place in London itself. This was the Overhouse Telegraph founded by Messrs Waterlow & Co., a network connecting the different parts of the capital city. This London District Company, formed in 1858, worked over a four-mile radius from Charing Cross, carrying their lines over the rooftops and charging from fourpence to sixpence per message delivered to the door. The same system was quickly introduced in Paris, Brussels, New York and elsewhere.

The Electric Telegraph Company was nationalized by an Act of 1868 which took effect in 1870 and was made part of the Post Office, its nerve-centre being moved in 1874 to a new headquarters on the corner of Newgate Street and St Martin's-le-Grand. Into the Post Office were thus absorbed both the Electric and International Company and the British & Irish Magnetic, controlling between them, even in 1855, about 8,500 miles of line. By the time at which they and other companies were taken over there were 16,000 miles of line and some 2,040 offices from which telegrams could be sent. One explanation for the policy of nationalization was that negotiations had begun for a telegraphic agreement with the other European powers, a treaty being actually signed in 1875 under which official telegrams would have priority throughout the Continent. An interesting sequel to nationalization was that the number of telegraph employees doubled between 1870 and 1873.[3] The new department under the control of the postmaster-general was connected with different post offices by a system of pneumatic tubes through which the telegrams were blown, some for as far as three miles. The system continued to expand and elaborate, reaching its peak of popularity in 1899, the year in which ninety million Telegrams were exchanged. Two-thirds of the traffic related to business, with a high percentage of telegrams relating to fish, meat and fruit. Betting telegrams were next in frequency and social telegrams constituted about a third of the traffic. Perhaps the biggest improvement in telegraphy was the introduction of the 'Direct Printer'. The effect of this was to enable the message typed at one end to be typed again automatically at the other, with a loss of no more than six seconds between London and Melbourne. It was soon realized that the electric telegraph could be of importance in time of war. The man to make this discovery was Sir Garnet (afterwards Field-Marshal and Viscount) Wolseley (1833–1913). It was for him that men of the Royal Engineers constructed a telegraph line in the field, much to the confusion, no doubt, of his African opponents. The consequent ease of communications may have assisted him in the Zulu War of 1879; it did even more, perhaps, to establish his reputation for innovation and reform.

While the telegraph network spread over Britain, a similar system was being developed in the United States, where Samuel Morse shared the credit indeed for the first invention. He had secured his first American patent by 1840 but it was not until March 1843 that Congress voted $30,000 for testing and improving his invention. As a result a line was set up between Washington and Baltimore and it was completed one day before the Democratic Convention met in the latter city to elect its Presidential candidate. There could have been no better advertisement than such an achievement, the news of which marked the beginning in the USA of commercial telegraphy. It developed quickly 11,000 miles of cable being laid by 1850, 20,000 by 1853.

A large measure of amalgamation had been going on between the several American telegraph companies. After a period of intense competition and small profits, two of the New York companies combined; this proving successful four others joined them and formed together the *Western Union Company*, which has turned out well for them and for the public . . . a great feat was performed . . . in 1865, when a telegram was sent direct from New York to San Francisco, a distance of 4,000 miles. To the credit of the Americans, they were the first to introduce the wonderful system of newspaper telegrams. Several newspapers clubbed together and contracted with telegraphic agents for the supply of news from every part of the Union, the news being available to all the papers alike . . .[4]

As in Britain, the American telegraph system was closely associated with the railways, and it was found essential to rationalize or integrate the many telegraph companies that were formed. But while the British Parliament made telegraphy a public monopoly under the postmaster-general, the Americans saw the companies group themselves together to form the Western Union. There was parallel progress in Europe. The first German telegraph was completed in 1849 by Werner von Siemens and there was a general realization that, in telegraphy, only the biggest organizations can be effective.

Once the individual countries had a telegraphic system there were, inevitably, proposals for linking them together. Between countries with a land frontier there was no particular difficulty in connecting one capital city with another. It was quite a different problem where there was a sea to be crossed, as between England and France.

That submarine telegraphy could be achieved had already been proved. An experimental line, its wire enclosed in split cane wrapped round with tarred yarn, had transmitted signals across the river Hooghly in 1838. In 1840 Wheatstone put before a parliamentary committee proposals for a line across the Straits of Dover. Two years later, Morse laid a wire protected by indiarubber across New York harbour, and in 1845 a cable of two similarly insulated wires enclosed on a leaden pipe was laid in the Hudson River, which worked well for some months until damaged by ice. Signals were exchanged by wire from a boat to the shore in Portsmouth harbour in 1846.

The chief trouble was the imperfect insulation. No substance could be depended upon to resist the attack of seawater and the unknown dangers of the ocean bed. The whole aspect of submarine telegraphy was altered, however, by the introduction of gutta-percha as an insulating material by Dr Werner Siemens in 1847. In 1849 C. V. Walker, FRS, electrical engineer to the South-Eastern Railway, exchanged telegrams with London from a vessel two miles off the coast, the underwater cable being thus insulated and the land portion of the line following the route of the railway from Folkestone.[5]

Gutta-percha is the solidified milky juice or latex of certain evergreen trees which are native to Malaya, and especially that of the *Palaquium gutta*. It is a type of plastic which can be moulded when hot, is non-elastic and insoluble in water. The first European to describe gutta-percha was Dr William Montgomerie, a surgeon on the government establishment at Singapore. His account, with samples, went to the Society of Arts in 1843. In London the following year, Dr Montgomerie left a sample with Mr Samuel Matthews in the Strand, Matthews being an agent of Charles Mackintosh, the waterproof-clothing manufacturer. At Matthews's shop the sample was seen by Thomas Hancock, whose brother Charles concluded that it would be useful in the manufacture of soda-water bottle-stoppers and took out a patent for that purpose. In 1845 he formed a partnership with a Dublin chemist called Henry Bewley for exploiting the discovery, and a factory was set up next year at Stratford in Essex. There were many quarrels between the directors of the Gutta-Percha Company and its first products – tubing, suction pipes, machinery belts and acid-tank linings – had only a limited market. But Michael Faraday remarked to William Siemens that gutta-percha might prove useful as an insulator of electric current. The idea was taken up and there was a successful experiment in 1849 when messages were exchanged over two miles of insulated cable laid between the shore and a vessel called *Princess Clementine*. In the meantime two brothers, Jacob and John Watkins Brett, had obtained a concession from the two governments concerned to lay a cable between France and England. In a hurry to lay the cable before their concession expired, the Bretts ordered from the Gutta-Percha Company 'twenty-five nautical miles of No. 14 Birmingham gauge copper wire covered with great care in gutta-percha to half an inch diameter'.[6] On 28 August 1850 the cable was actually laid between Dover and Gris Nez. A few more or less intelligible signals passed before the line broke, accidentally hooked up by a French trawler. This was just enough to save the concession and encourage Mr Thomas Russell Crampton to finance another attempt with a stronger cable. The methods used were still primitive but the new cable was at least more substantial, sheathed as it was with galvanized iron wire. The cable was laid, not without difficulty, on 25 September 1851, and communication was actually established between London and Paris. One result of this success was the founding of Newall's 'Submarine Cable Works' at Sunderland. Another was the subsequent laying of a temporary cable between Varna and Balaclava during the Crimean War, a device which worked well for a year and pointed the way to further achievement.

The attempt to lay a cable across the Atlantic began with the formation of the Atlantic Telegraph Company on 20 October 1856. The moving spirit was Cyrus W. Field, a retired American business man. The expert knowledge was provided by John Brett, Charles Bright and Professor William Thomson (afterwards Lord Kelvin) of the University of Glasgow. Capital was raised in Britain, especially in Liverpool, Manchester and Glasgow, and an order placed for 2,500 nautical miles of heavy insulated cable. The difficulties were immense and the setbacks repeated but the cable was finally laid (1858) and some hundreds of messages passed, the first between Queen Victoria and the President of the United States. Then the line went dead, overloaded with excessive voltage. It had been shown, nevertheless, that the feat was possible and double the capital was now subscribed for another attempt in 1865. One difficulty encountered in 1858 arose from the fact that no existing ship could carry the whole cable. The plan had been for two ships to meet in mid-Atlantic from opposite directions, and splice their cables together. The cable broke repeatedly. By 1865 there had come into existence a remarkable ship capable of loading the whole cable. This was the *Great Eastern*, Brunel's masterpiece and, at 18,900 tons, the biggest ship in the world. Oceanic cables were now laid, the first from Brest to Newfoundland, another from Malta to Alexandria and a third, using the *Great Eastern* again, from Suez to Bombay. From about 1880 cables were laid by ships designed for the purpose, as telegraphic communication covering the earth was established. The last major task was to span the Pacific, a distance of 8,300 nautical miles. This was undertaken by the Telegraph Construction and Maintenance Company in about 1900, using a ship specially built to carry nearly 8,000 tons of cable from British Columbia to Queensland. As from the beginning of the present century, therefore, all the major countries of the world and all the chief commercial centres have been linked by telegraph. For the transaction of Big Business one further prerequisite had been supplied.

It was inevitable that inventors should study the possibility of transmitting speech over a cable, as opposed to the tapping of the Morse code. Various attempts were made but much of the credit for the final success must belong to Alexander Graham Bell. The son of a teacher of elocution and the inventor of phonetics, Alexander was born in Edinburgh (1847) but moved with his parents to Canada in 1870. He was not an electrician but a teacher in schools for the deaf, his first interest being in the human ear itself. Working on the transmission of sound by an electric current, he and his friend, Thomas Watson, had produced and patented a more or less workable telephone by 1876. It was exhibited at Philadelphia and Sir William Thomson brought a telephone back to Britain. The device was still, however, in the experimental stage and was not a commercial proposition until after the invention of the microphone in 1878. This was the achievement of Thomas Alva Edison, an American who went on to invent electric light and the cinematic sound projector. Edison's patent was taken up by Western Union, which formed a subsidiary called the American Speaking Telephone Company. The result was a legal battle with the Bell Telephone Company which ended in victory for the latter in 1879. Western Union withdrew from the fray, well compensated, and the Bell Telephone Company was left in possession of the field.

Once invented, the telephone spread over the face of the world with remarkable speed. It was of such universal value and so simple to use (a contemporary advertisement remarked 'Its employment necessitates no skilled labour, no technical education . . .') that there can be few inventions in history which came into everyday use so swiftly. Within ten years there were well over a hundred thousand telephones in the United States alone; within twenty-five years there were a million, and when Bell was buried (1922) thirteen million instruments were silenced.

The adoption of the telephone was, of course, immensely assisted by the fact that the telegraph, using very similar techniques and equipment, had been in use for thirty years, and it was relatively simple to work the telephone over many of the existing lines. . . .[7]

The United States had thus an impressive telephone system by 1890 and one which helped shape the pattern of American industry and life. Use of the telephone spread quickly to other countries, beginning with Britain, in which both the Bell and Edison companies were soon registered. Here, however, they were confronted by the postmaster-general's monopoly and a court decision of 1880 made it clear that a telephone was a telegraphic instrument in the eyes of the law. The result was that the two companies were required to hand over the country's telephones to the Post Office which was mainly interested in defending its telegraph department against this unfair competition. Some telephone companies, like the London & Globe, were allowed to operate under licence and the United Telephone Company was allowed to manufacture the equipment, but the situation was, and remained, an unhappy one. The Post Office had something like a telephone monopoly by 1912 but it is a question whether the public could not have been better served by private enterprise. Be that as it may, the use of the telephone was widespread by 1890 and was yet another factor in the move to centralize. Its use in Britain was more tentative than in the USA and there was a tendency at first to place the telephone in the butler's pantry rather than in the morning room or library. The Savoy Hotel, opened in 1889, had speaking tubes, not telephones, to connect the guests with room service, and there were only two public telephones in 1905. As recently as 1923 there was no telephone at Lord Curzon's country house so that a summons to London, consequent upon Mr Bonar Law's resignation, was sent as a telegram and delivered to Lord Curzon by a policeman on a bicycle. The telephone was not a normal stage property until surprisingly late in history, not perhaps until about 1930. There were in Britain only 6.5 telephones per hundred of the population on the eve of World War II. It would seem, in retrospect, that telephones in Britain were rather tolerated than welcomed.

In the USA, by contrast, telephones almost instantly became a part of the American way of life. More than that, the provision of this service became Big Business in itself, By about 1938 there were over 19,450,000 telephones in the United States and there were 15.3 telephones for each hundred inhabitants. At that period the American Telephone and Telegraph Company had the biggest capital assets of any company in the world: $16,000,000,000. It remains to this day a giant organization, as does the Western Electric Company, which manufactures most of the telephone equipment. The A. T. & T. sponsors, among other satellite activities, the Bell Laboratories, dedicated to research in the communications field. Big Business in this area is not the subject of this present study but we do well to note that the telephone has become the tool of business and one which has tended to overshadow all others.

There is, to begin with, the internal system connecting the different parts of the same organization. There are the direct lines between head office and the different plants. There are, finally, the outside lines which give access to the rest of the world. It is by means of these telephones that co-ordination is maintained between the different and distant parts of a complex organization. The countries best supplied with telephones are, after the USA, Sweden, Canada and Denmark, while those ill-supplied include France and Italy. The main improvement in telephony since it was introduced has been the automatic exchange, invented before 1897 but mainly developed since 1912. This has led to (eventual) improvements in service and reductions in cost. There was a time when the importance of a top executive might be measured by the number of telephone receivers on his desk. There was a later period when his importance might be emphasized by the receiver which the restaurant waiter would place at his elbow while he was ordering luncheon for his guests. By now there may be some indication of status in the radio link which makes it possible for him to telephone from his car or indeed from the company's executive jet aircraft. One way and another, the telephone is inseparable from Big Business and it could even be argued that Big Business without the telephone would be impossible.

Wireless telegraphy is an important extension of the facilities already described. The complex story of its development is bound up, of necessity, with that of electrical engineering in general. In so far, however, as one can simplify the story, it seems to begin with Professor D. E. Hughes's practical experiment of 1879. This first radio transmission took place in London and was witnessed by Mr W. H. Preece, later engineer-in-chief to the Post Office, and by a number of scientists. Professor Rudolf Hertz later proved by experiment that electromagnetic waves could be created and measured. Then came the moment, in February 1892, when Sir William Crooks wrote an article for the *Fortnightly* in which he pointed to the future with these words:

Rays of light will not pierce through a wall, nor, as we know only too well, through a London fog; but electrical vibrations of a yard or more in wavelength will easily pierce such media, which to them will be transparent. Here is revealed the bewildering possibility of telegraphy without wires, posts, cables, or any of our present costly appliances. Granted a few reasonable postulates, the whole thing comes well within the realms of possible fulfilment. . . .[8]

So far as short-range transmission went the problem had been, at least theoretically, solved. To long-range transmission there seemed, however, to be a final and insuperable obstacle in the curvature of the earth. It remained for Oliver Heaviside, a nephew of Sir Charles Wheatstone, to prove that there is a reflectory layer in the upper atmosphere which compels electro-magnetic waves to follow the earth's curvature. Sir Oliver Lodge gave a demonstration of wireless telegraphy in 1894 and then, two years later, there came to London a man who had bridged the gap between practice and theory: the young Guglielmo Marconi of Bologna, a graduate of Leghorn and a student of physics, whose claims were embodied in the British patent for which he applied in 1896.[9]

Marconi (born 1874) was welcomed by Sir William Preece, who invited him to demonstrate his equipment at the GPO in St Martin's-le-Grand, the place from which the mail-coaches used to take their departure for the provinces (see page 38).

Marconi reported for his interview with his two trunks and proudly unpacked their contents on to Preece's desk. Preece was amazed by the weird assortment of rods, wire, brass knobs and bottles of metal filings. The collection looked so gimcrack – just so much junk – that it seemed inconceivable that the apparatus would work. However, Preece reserved judgement and requested Marconi to assemble his equipment and proceed with his demonstration.[10]

The immediate result of this meeting was a first signal in Morse code sent from the GPO roof to the roof of another building some three hundred yards away. The success of this led to a second demonstration, this time before senior army and navy officers on Salisbury Plain. His signals carried over four miles but the naval men promptly asked whether they would carry over water. There followed another triumphant demonstration, this time across the Bristol Channel, and Marconi's further success was assured. He formed a company in 1897, with its research laboratory and workshops at Chelmsford (where they remain in use), and worked towards his next goal which was nothing less than sending a wireless message across the Atlantic. For this purpose he led a small team to St John's, Newfoundland, at which place, on 12 December 1901, he received a signal from the station he had set up at Poldhu in Cornwall. The battle for worldwide wireless communications had been won.

From a business point of view there was little that wireless could do on land that was not already possible by telegraph. Where wireless was of immediate and obvious use was at sea. It was no doubt his appreciation of this fact which led Marconi to offer his invention to the British rather than the Italian government, Britain being then the leading naval power in the world. The first permanent wireless station was thus set up at the South Foreland in 1898 for communication with the East Goodwin Lightship. That was and is a notoriously dangerous area for shipping and the value of wireless was demonstrated within a matter of weeks, for a German steamship collided with the lightship itself and it was a radio message which brought the lifeboat out and prevented any actual loss of life. From that beginning other wireless stations followed, at first along the British coast and later along the coasts of France, Belgium and Germany. Ships were also equipped with wireless, over two hundred of them by 1901. The Royal Navy began to equip its ships with wireless from 1907, the year in which the radio installation first appeared on the Admiralty roof, and Admiral Lord Fisher wrote in 1912[11] that 'Wireless is the pith and marrow of war', a fact illustrated by the Germans when they went out of their way to raid the wireless station in the Cocos-Keeling Islands. There had been, however, a still more dramatic use of wireless as early as 1910. This arose from the murder of Mrs Crippen, whose mutilated body was found in the cellar of her home in Camden Town. Suspicion centred upon her husband, Dr Crippen, who had disappeared in the company of his secretary, Ethel le Neve. The hunt for the suspected murderer and his possible accomplice failed for the sufficient reason that he had, not unwisely, left the country. Shaving off his moustache and discarding his spectacles, he had made Ethel dress as a boy. With his 'son' at heel he had then boarded the steamship *Montrose*, bound for Quebec. With no special originality he had assumed the name of Robinson but he spoilt the effect by a demonstrative affection towards his companion for which their official relationship could scarcely account. Captain Kendall's suspicions were aroused further by a glimpse of Ethel's underwear and he presently convinced himself that the suspected murderer was indeed on board his ship. He sent the following radio signal to Scotland Yard: ... Have strong suspicions that Crippen, London cellar murderer, and accomplice are amongst saloon passengers. Moustache taken off, growing beard. Accomplice dressed as a boy. Voice, manner and build undoubtedly a girl. ...' The result was that Inspector Dew sailed at once in another and faster ship and was already there when the *Montrose* entered the St Lawrence River. He boarded the ship, cunningly disguised as a pilot (a needlessly dramatic touch), and made the arrest with the efficiency for which Scotland Yard is famous. That the captain's signal left him open to a libel action is clear – he should have said the *alleged* murderer and his *suspected* accomplice – but Crippen was hanged and Miss le Neve, who was acquitted, brought no action against the captain or his wireless operator, possibly because the signal was no part of the evidence used at the trial. Like telegraphy itself (see page 86) the new technique of wireless telegraphy had an early and useful advertisement from its use in the punishment of crime.

It should be emphasized that the developments so far described were in wireless telegraphy alone, the radio transmission of messages in Morse code. Wireless telephony came later. In the meanwhile, in April 1912, came the loss of the White Star liner *Titanic*. The biggest ship afloat at 46,000 tons, she was on her maiden voyage when she struck an iceberg and began to sink. Her wireless operator managed to transmit a distress signal to the Cunard liner *Carpathia*, and to other ships in the vicinity. The result was that 735 of the 2,370 people on board were rescued while the wireless operator died at his post. All this was but the curtain-raiser to the naval conflicts of World War I in which, for the first time, wireless signals played a significant part. It is interesting to note that the Japanese were using wireless at sea in 1905, their signals being intercepted by their Russian opponents on the eve of the Battle of Tsu-Shima. Captain Vladimir Semenoff, a witness of the action, begins the second chapter of his narrative with the following comments:

Fate had apparently been kind to us, as up to the present we had not been discovered. The sending of telegrams in the fleet was forbidden, so we were able to intercept Japanese messages, and our torpedo officers made every effort to fix the directions from which they emanated. On the morning of 26 May and later on the same day, a conversation between two installations had begun, or perhaps more correctly speaking it was the reports of one ahead and nearer to us to which the other, more distant and on the port side, was replying. The messages were not in cypher, and although our telegraphists were unaccustomed to the strange alphabet, and notwithstanding the gaps in the sentences by the time we received them, it was still possible to pick out separate words, and even sentences. . . .

Towards evening we took in a conversation between other installations, which at night had increased to seven. The messages were in cypher, but by their brevity and uniformity and by the fact that they commenced and ceased at fixed times, we were able to calculate with tolerable accuracy that these were not reports, but merely messages exchanged between the scouts. It was clear that we had not been discovered.[12]

In the history of radio communications the Battle of Tsu-Shima is an early landmark, an action in which both sides were equipped with wireless, one of them already familiar with the need for wireless silence in a given situation and the other already sending messages in code. There is no indication, however, that wireless affected the outcome of the engagement. Granted, incidentally, that the Japanese owed something to the British navy – a phase of history which accounts for those Edwardian sailor suits still worn by Japanese schoolchildren – it would seem that the navy of Japan was radio-conscious at a very early date. By 1914, however, wireless had become every tactician's familiar tool and technical interest had begun to centre upon the advent of radio telephony, the transmission of the spoken word. What had been thought merely desirable became essential as soon as warfare took to the air:

The system was used for the first time during the First World War (1914–18) to give instructions to pilots of aircraft engaged in the war in Europe. Many an air battle against the Germans was fought and won with the help of wireless telephony. Great secrecy was maintained, and probably very few people outside government and military circles and the manufacturers of the equipment were aware that wireless telephony had reached this advanced stage, yet wireless was soon to transform the home life of millions of people all over the world.[13]

The wireless operator who had to be pilot, gunner, navigator and observer – because he flew alone – had no leisure for decoding the signals he received. He could only respond to the human voice. Short-range telephony was feasible and post-war research went into its further and longer-range development. By 1919 it was found possible to transmit the human voice between Ireland and Nova Scotia. Marconi took to the sea in that year, living and working aboard his steam yacht *Elettra* (RYS) so as to escape the publicity by which he was otherwise surrounded. It was from this vessel in the Atlantic that he made verbal contact (at over three hundred miles) with a friend at Monsanto near Lisbon. He also managed to transmit the music played by his gramophone.

Nearly a year after this Portuguese experiment, music from the *Elettra* caused great excitement at Cowes, where the *Elettra* was anchored during Cowes Week. In fact, on one occasion dance music played by the Savoy Orpheans in London was coming through so powerfully that representations were tactfully made by neighbouring yachts suggesting that the force of the music might be reduced – which of course it was. The strains of the band on that occasion, it was reported later, could be heard inland on the Isle of Wight.[14]

As this little story suggests, radio telephony led at once to broadcast entertainment. The first broadcasts went out from Chelmsford in 1920–21 but it was soon decided to give the monopoly to a publicly owned organization, to which was assigned the wave length 2 LO.

The British Broadcasting Company – later the BBC – was created (in 1922), and its first programme featured dance music from the Savoy. This was rendered by the Savoy Orpheans, led by 'Bill' Debroy Somers, of whom Arnold Bennett admitted 'They play bad music well.'

'Dance Music from the Savoy Hotel in London' quickly pulled up rugs all over the world. Millions tickled their crystal sets six nights a week to listen to the Orpheans and the Havana Band. Their music was relayed to places like Cowes where couples danced by moonlight on their yachts, and ham operators picked up the syncopated beat as far away as Long Island. Marconi reported that a French force in North Africa, while besieged by the Riffs, had tuned in to the Savoy and those not on duty danced together to kill the *Cafard*. Soon afterwards half an hour's truce was called every night so that both armies could enjoy the dance music in peace.

Towards the end of 1923, radio history was made by an exchange of messages between the BBC and the United States. . . .[15]

Whereas broadcasting in Britain and in some other countries constituted a public service, the expenses of which were met by licence fees, the American sound waves were left to private enterprise. The result was an industry in itself, parallel with that of the cinema and primarily devoted to advertising. This has had its economic importance, especially in building up a mass market for consumer goods. It has also had political importance throughout the world, giving the more dictatorial governments a new and powerful means of moulding public opinion. That is not our present concern. For purposes of business, the invention of wireless has extended and perfected the system of prompt communication which was introduced by the telegraph and telephone. Through a radio link telephone contact can now be made with ships at sea, with automobiles and aircraft. The main effect has been to centralize authority and weaken the initiative of subordinates everywhere. This was nothing new in itself, however, but merely a new emphasis given to an existing trend. What was revolutionary was the telegraph and no subsequent change has had a comparable importance.

Television had been the logical sequel to radio and this, too, has had far-reaching, though mainly social, consequences. The first experiments took place in 1929 and were rather unimpressive, there being no correlation between the picture and the sound track. In a speech, however, delivered at Trento in 1930, the Marchese Marconi foretold that these and other difficulties would be overcome:

> I am certain that the progress recently obtained in the stabilization of frequencies and in the transmission and reception of beam waves will tend towards surmounting the difficulties which still stand in the way of the practical realization of long-distance television. The great conquests already made allow us to assert now with certainty that by means of electro waves mankind not only has available a new and powerful means of scientific research, but it is conquering a new force and utilizing a new arm of civilization and progress which knows no frontiers, and can even push out into infinite spaces where never before has the feeling of any manifestation of the activity and thought of man been able to penetrate.[16]

This development followed, in fact, quite swiftly. After the BBC moved to its new headquarters in Portland Place in 1932, a tentative television programme was launched from a room in the basement. It was timed for midnight, after the radio programmes had closed down, and was received by a possible audience of about a hundred – that being the number of television sets then in existence. The programmes improved, the means of transmission developed and the viewers multiplied. Then came a single event which transformed a private hobby into a worldwide institution.

On 12 May 1937 the Coronation of King George VI and Queen Elizabeth was televized. Although it was drizzling with rain and visibility was poor this first outside television broadcast (other than those from the grounds of Alexandra Palace) was a triumph. About 10,000 people watched this historic event, the Coronation, on television, and the broadcast made a great impact.

During the next two years the number of viewers began to mount steadily, until by the summer of 1939 more than 20,000 people in Britain owned television sets, as compared with a mere 300 three years previously. But then in September 1939 the Second World War broke out – and there were no television transmissions in Britain for seven long years.[17]

Not at first much affected by World War II, the United States now went ahead in television and gained a technical lead in some respects. A new and important industry came into existence, supplementing and supplanting the influence hitherto established by the radio networks. On life in general the impact of television has been tremendous and, in some respects, catastrophic. On Big Business the effect has been less marked. It might be argued, however, that the tendency of television has been to turn the limelight on people thought to be picturesque or hypnotic and so lessen public interest in leaders of industry, who are usually less colourful even than politicians. On the other hand there is a limited future in closed-circuit television as a means of control in industry, the same system as that already used to a small extent in the detection of crime. Writing in the early days of British television (1949), George Orwell suggested that the television set would eventually become a camera as well as a screen, ensuring that the viewer can also be seen by those responsible for the programme. Whether this is technically possible it is for experts to say but the effect of Orwell's *Nineteen Eighty-Four* may have been to delay or even prevent the invention of any such two-way machine. His concept of and warning about 'Big Brother' has not been without influence and his may be one of the few prophecies which have forestalled a predicted event. The fact remains, however, that the technical trend of the twentieth century had been to strengthen the men at the centre of any organization and weaken the men on its periphery. This is the result, above all, of improved communications which have at once provided the means of control and lessened the need for initiative. In the growth of Big Business there are many important factors to consider but of these the chief is probably the ease and speed of communication which has characterized the century in which we live. Behind the annals of large-scale industry there are the older histories of landownership, commerce and finance. But the tale is also one of improved and improving means of communication. Without these the captains of industry could never have established their kingdoms and empires. It is at least of symbolic significance that Andrew Carnegie began work as a telegraphist and went on from there to become a railway official. Without swift communication and transport the multi-millionaire's career would hardly have been possible. Without the telegraph he would not have known where to begin.

6   American Railroads

British railways never became Big Business. The boom period of 1845 produced George Hudson (see pages 69–73), but he went bankrupt as soon as the boom ended. There were no great railroad proprietors after his time, only general managers who usually contrived to pay a little over 5 per cent to a staid and respectable body of shareholders. There was, indeed, another boom in 1865 and a further extension of the system, largely financed by the existing companies, but the heroes of that age were essentially the contractors. These were not always successful and at least one of them, Sir Morton Peto, went bankrupt during the financial crisis which followed the collapse of the Overend, Gurney Bank in 1866. But one pre-eminent contractor emerged as a millionaire and this was Thomas Brassey, whose career is certainly worthy of comment. Of Cheshire yeoman stock, Brassey is first heard of as a contractor for the Grand Junction Railway in 1835. From there he went on to the London and Southampton Railway, the Chester and Crewe Railway, the Glasgow, Paisley & Greenock and so to the Sheffield and Manchester in 1839. He was then in France for a time, building the lines between Paris and Rouen, Orleans and Bordeaux, Rouen and Le Havre. After 1843 he had simultaneous contracts abroad and at home, seeming to be everywhere at once. His more notable works included the sixty-mile railway from Turin to Novara (1850–53), 'completed for about the same money as was spent in obtaining the Bill for the railway from London to York'; the Grand Trunk Railway of Canada (1852–9); and the Crimean Railway (1854) which served the armies in the field as seventeen locomotives operated over nearly forty miles of track. Of this last effort it was remarked that seven miles of track were laid in twelve days from landing the material; it was also recorded that the chief agent in the Crimea had no sleep for three weeks after landing and died within four weeks of his return. For Brassey years of activity were to follow, his interests extending to Italy, India, Jutland, Mauritius, Argentina, Australia and Poland.

Thomas Brassey was a man of great energy and ability, as famous for his integrity as for his kindness, loved by his staff and respected by his clients. In the words of his biographer:

It were much to be wished that the intelligence and skill shown by the contractors for the making of railways, and notably by Mr Brassey as the most eminent of them, could have been shown in the management of railways after they had been made. . . . In fact, there has been a deplorable want of organization in all railway affairs, with the sole exception of the skill exhibited in their construction. . . .[1]

These are harsh words which the later history of the British railways was to refute. At the time it was arguable, and Brassey himself believed, that the French system, with its greater measure of state control, was preferable. In so far as this was true the credit must go to Napoleon III, for whom Brassey did very good work indeed. Nor did he fail to provide for himself and his family, working as he did up to the day of his death in 1870.

Out of all these activities, but chiefly out of his work in constructing railways, Brassey amassed an enormous fortune. His will was proved in 1871 at £3,200,000 in respect of his property in Great Britain alone (attracting death duties of £48,000). It was one of the largest English fortunes of the century, probably the largest ever made in his line of business. He had given away much in his lifetime, privately and quietly – some £200,000 it was said. . . .[2]

Brassey left a son, another Thomas, MP (1836–1918), who sailed round the world in his yacht *Sunbeam*, published *Brassey's Naval Annual*, held public office, became Governor of Victoria and achieved an earldom in 1911.

In the story of British railways Brassey's example is not cited as typical. He was the exception, and partly for the reason that his work was largely overseas. Totally contrasted is the epic of the men who developed the railroads of the United States. Theirs was a wilder scene and it is with them that the story of Big Business may be said to have begun. That their opportunity was different in kind was due to three main factors. In the first place, the distances involved were immense and the capital invested was vast in proportion. In the second place, the American railroads were to cross an almost uninhabited continent, creating the cities they were to serve and raising the land values as they progressed. 'Let the country make the railroads,' George Stephenson had said, 'and the railroads will make the country.' He was referring to Britain, however, a country already highly developed. The same principle applied tenfold to the United States. In the third place, American railroads were aided by a political corruption for which Europe, by whatever effort, could offer no parallel. If our task was to name the first Big Businessman of modern history, excluding land-owners and bankers, our choice might well fall (after some hesitation) on Cornelius Vanderbilt. If we had further to fix on an exact period and place during which Big Business first appeared, we would have to select the United States of 1865–75. One cause of the Civil War had been the annexation of Texas (1845) and the cession of New Mexico and California which followed the war with Mexico of 1848. The consequent strengthening of the southern 'slave states' was alarming in itself and foreshadowed the likelihood of California's joining the southern group. The discovery of gold in California (1848) gave added urgency to the efforts which were made to connect California by rail with the northern States; efforts redoubled when the war was over. A further effect of the Civil War (1861–5) had been to check the ex-pansion of trade and yet encourage some forms of industry. With the end of the war there came a sudden burst of economic activity, a wave of investment and a new wave of immigration. While the war was still in progress the United States Congress passed legislation to en-courage the construction of railroads and especially those which would eventually cross the continent. Intent on saving the Union by victory in war the northern politicians were as eager to strengthen the federal unity by a less belligerent campaign of comparable importance. This campaign was launched in 1862.

Before this point in history there had been two earlier phases in American railway development. During the first decade (1830–40) there had been a piecemeal construction of local lines, all radiating from the Atlantic seaports and the more important centred upon Philadelphia. This was followed by the multiplication of local lines throughout New England, with one line extending down to Washington, to Richmond and beyond. The second phase began in 1850 when Congress gave to Illinois, Alabama and Mississippi some 4,000,000 acres of land from the public domain to be used in aiding the construction of the Illinois Central and the Mobile and Ohio lines, the route which would connect Chicago with New Orleans. This work was largely completed by 1854 and Chicago's rail connection with the Atlantic seaboard had been finished the year before. Without much further elaboration these railway lines provided much of the framework for northern strategy during the Civil War. It is true that supplies still went by river in some campaigns but there was early recognition of the importance to the Confederacy of the Memphis-Chattanooga railroad. General Grant was once injured – nearly killed – when his horse was frightened by a locomotive's whistle. There was a moment, indeed, when Chattanooga was almost captured by a railway train, stolen near Marietta but overtaken by a Confederate train in the 'Great Locomotive Chase'. There followed a serious crisis for the Union in 1862 when General Lee set out to invade Maryland and Pennsylvania. He had shown President Davis that the capture of Harrisburg would cut the federal rail communication between the eastern and western States. The attempt failed at the Battle of Sharpsburg (17 September 1862) and Lee was compelled to recross the Potomac and withdraw into Virginia. Sherman's campaign, which is remembered by the song about 'marching through Georgia' was only made possible by a single line of railway which his opponents never managed to cut for more than a few days. Had they risen in 1850 the southern States would have gained their independence, for the railways did not then exist which were to sustain the decisive offensives staged by the Union armies in Tennessee and down the Mississippi. Railways were thus of vital importance throughout the war and there is a symbolic significance in that final scene when 'President Davis slipped away from Richmond in a special train ahead of the Union troops on 2 April, together with several members of his cabinet and about $500,000 in specie.'[3] Not until 1918 did the moment come when the armistice ending a major war would be signed in a railway carriage – and one destined to be used again for the same purpose.

The methods by which American railways were financed has attracted a great deal of criticism.

The whole system of subsidies and lands, granted at the instance of crooked politicians by State Assemblies or by Congress, made the American railway companies enormously wealthy and powerful corporations. They received vast and fabulously rich tracts of forest and swamplands underlaid by minerals. They were allowed to run through the open streets as the beneficiaries of the most outrageous franchises. They were permitted to help themselves to stone and timber in the public domain. ... From 1850 to 1872 Congress gave not less than 155,504,999.59 acres of the public domain either direct to railroad corporations or to the various States, to be transferred to those corporations. From 1850 the National Government had granted subsidies to more than fifty railroads ... and ... had made a cash appropriation to those six [transcontinental] railroads of not less than £140,000,000.[4]

If we concede that the history of railways in the United States is a story of rugged individualism, we do well to remember that both the states and the Union had some part in it and that the encouragement offered to investors was sometimes more than generous. As against that, the tasks attempted were vast in scale, daunting in concept and hazardous in their detailed execution. There were penalties, moreover, for failure which matched the rewards which would follow success.

The man who made the biggest fortune from railways was the gruff and tough Cornelius Vanderbilt (born 1794) who came to New York in 1829. His early business was in coastal shipping, at first under sail and later in steam, with a special interest in, and an eventual monopoly of, the Staten Island ferries. With the California gold rush of 1849 he launched a complex scheme by which those bound for California could go by steamship to San Juan del Norte, cross Nicaragua and so reach San Francisco by another Vanderbilt steamship. The scheme was successful for a time and the Commodore (as he was called) became a wealthy man, with real estate in Coney Island and elsewhere and an income of $100,000 a month from his steamboats alone. He started buying railway stock in 1863, acquiring over 55,000 shares in the New York and Harlem Railroad. He soon had complete control of it and planned an amalgamation with the Hudson River Railroad. This required state permission, which meant bribing the politicians at Albany. They refused, however, to observe their promises, having been bribed again by the Commodore's enemy Daniel Drew. The legislators then sold the shares short, wanting to force the price down and make their fortunes.

But a cornered Commodore was an even tougher customer than an ascendant one. The Commodore bought. He mortgaged his other holdings, he sold other properties, he endangered the very foundation of his fortune. But he bought. His brokers bought. His friends bought.

In the end Vanderbilt had purchased 137,000 shares of Harlem stock – 27,000 more than existed: he owned every share available in Wall Street. To deliver on their promises . . . the short sellers would have to come to Vanderbilt for stock, for there was no other source in the open market. Vanderbilt alone controlled the price and the short sellers had to have stock.

How much would he take per share?

One thousand dollars per share, said the Commodore.

Wall Street gasped. Half the houses on the Street had bet against Vanderbilt and sold short. Those houses would be forced into bankruptcy. Wall Street, in brief, would be ruined as a financial centre.[5]

Vanderbilt was eventually persuaded by Leonard Jerome (Sir Winston Churchill's grandfather) to relent over the price. He agreed to accept $285 per share from speculators who had counted on the price falling to $50!

From the second Harlem crisis Vanderbilt made $25,000,000, on paper. Actually, his profit turned out to be somewhat less because many of the legislators went bankrupt . . . (but) he had the pleasure of breaking up one of the most dishonest legislative bodies that ever graced the halls of Albany's capital. Even those who questioned his methods and his aims had to admit that.[6]

Vanderbilt's next major operation was to amalgamate the New York Central with the Hudson River Railroad. That done he declared that the combined railroad company was worth $45,000,000 more than the railroads had been worth singly, so he issued $45,000,000 more in stock to himself. Even with stock so watered the new line was made to pay 8 or 10 per cent, and railroad dividends were exempt from income tax! The Commodore then extended his empire to include the Michigan Central and the Lake Shore Line in Illinois, both routes, in fact, to Chicago. He finally crowned the whole edifice by establishing the New York Central Station on the site which it still occupies on Forty-Second Street and Park Avenue. When he died in 1877 he was the richest man in the United States. His son, William Henry Vanderbilt, inherited $105,000,000 (or so it was said) and went on to extend his father's empire until (by 1885) it reached Minneapolis, Detroit and St Louis. 'I am the richest man in the world,' William Henry remarked diffidently. 'I am worth one hundred and ninety-four million dollars.' That he was the wealthiest man in terms of income is a generally accepted fact, provided we exclude royalty. In capital assets he was not quite the equal of the Duke of Westminster but his position was nevertheless unique. Of the world's really great business men the old Commodore had been almost certainly the first.

Cornelius Vanderbilt had consolidated the railroad system between New York and Chicago, helped by the wave of investment which followed the end of the Civil War. There followed the still greater effort to build a railroad between the Missouri River and the Pacific. This great work had been delayed by the rivalry between northern and southern states but the Civil War ended the need to worry about southern opinion. The first railroad across the continent would roughly follow the 41st parallel, and that was that. It was then decided in 1862 that the Union Pacific should construct a railroad from Omaha to Ogden, receiving a grant of twelve million acres, and that the Central Pacific, in return for eight million acres, should lay the track between Sacramento and Ogden. The men who launched this colossal enterprise from the California side were: Leland Stanford, a grocer; Charles Crocker, a drygoods merchant; Mark Hopkins, a hardware dealer; and Collis P. Huntington, who was Hopkins's partner. The founders of the Union Pacific included men who were better known: Thomas Clark Durant, August Belmont, Erastus Corning, Leonard W. Jerome and Moses Taylor. A principal shareholder (not a director) was Brigham Young, head of the Mormon Chruch, who supposed – wrongly – that the line would pass through Salt Lake City. Considered as characters in the tale of Big Business the Big Four of the Central Pacific are more interesting than their counterparts of the Union Pacific.

Stanford tended political fences and was the railroad's suave front man in the home territory, where his reputation and connections as ex-Governor were most useful. Charles Crocker's great energy, easy working relationship with his men, geniality and persistence combined to make him an ideal leader of the construction work. Huntington, the wily trader, bold, supremely self-confident, nerveless, was the perfect member of this extraordinary team to do the major purchasing and arrange the financing. . . . Hopkins was the dedicated guardian of the corporate purse . . . (who) . . . even went around picking up nails and bolts that careless workmen had dropped or tossed aside. . . .[7]

That these men – with the addition at times of E. B. Crocker, the lawyer – made a formidable team is evident. What is still more interesting, however, is that they were the builders of modern California. Stanford (US Senator 1885–93) was the founder of Stanford University. Charles Crocker's bank is still well known and important. No visitor to San Francisco fails to see the Mark Hopkins Building and no wise visitor to Pasadena will omit a visit to the Huntington Library and Art Gallery. To rule the Central Pacific was once to rule the Pacific coast from Oakland to San Diego. This is a land where, more than elsewhere, Big Business has left its mark. Nor was its influence confined to California for the Central Pacific's activities were to stretch far eastwards. To take an example, plans provided for a railroad station at a place called Lake's Crossing on the Donner Pass route. Charles Crocker had obtained there a grant of forty acres which he laid out as a town in 1868, giving it the name of Reno. 'Reno sprang to life in a dazzling hurry. Its lots went on public sale May 9th, and at the auction some of them brought as much as $1000 apiece. . . .' There is reason to suppose that many of these lots might cost even more than that today.

Railways brought with them a tremendous opportunity in land speculation. Those, however, which crossed the continent presented appalling difficulties to the contractor and engineer. There were plains completely lacking in timber, mountains beyond which was a sterile plateau, the bleak and bitter desert and then the Sierra Nevada itself. There were no roads and almost the only inhabitants likely to be encountered were hostile Indians, resentful of this intrusion on their hunting territory. It was a motley collection of men who did the actual work, 'a predominantly Irish force of former Union and Confederate soldiers, mule-skinners, disillusioned miners, adventurers, newly arrived immigrants, runaway sons from Eastern families, fed-up farmers, gamblers and problem drinkers.' Ahead of the tracklayers went the construction force, using at one time as many as ten thousand horses.

Ahead of the construction force went the surveyors and ahead of them again an escort of cavalry. When the Irish graders and tracklayers on the Pacific side demanded more money, they were replaced by Chinese. Somehow the work went on, the contractors' main advantage lying in the fact that the railroad they were building was itself their line of communication. The two lines eventually met at Promontory Summit on 11 May 1869. As the time approached for the actual ceremony a reporter saw and described the arrival of Wells Fargo's Overland Stage No. 2 with its last load of mail for the West Coast. The old nags were worn and jaded, the coach shabby and 'with that dusty, dilapidated coach and team, the old order of things passed away forever.' Finally the moment came when the American flag was hoisted on a telegraph pole. Stanford stood beside the one rail, Durant by the other and, at a given signal, both tapped in their respective spikes – Stanford's being so contrived that it also fired a gun at San Francisco which would tell the world that the work was done. The fact may remind us that if the two railroad companies were Big Business, the Western Union Telegraph Company was never far behind.

In later years there were critics who described as an 'octupus' the form of control exercised by the railroad magnates in California. Governors, senators, judges, congressmen, police commissioners and even the harbour police were all nominated (it was said) by Leland Stanford. He and his colleagues had taken great risks and had suffered some anxious moments:

. . . But year by year as millions of people of the Great West paid toll to the quartet who controlled the price of their lands, who raised tariffs upon their crops with deadly effect in good seasons, the crushing debts of the system were fully redeemed. Hopkins and Crocker, who died earlier, left some twenty millions to their heirs; Stanford bequeathed thirty millions to found Stanford University in memory of his son; while Huntington's fortune was variously estimated at between fifty and ninety millions. Huntington and Stanford owned enormous vineyards in California – 100,000 acres – and in the East constructed palaces after their own fancy; Huntington's home being the vast and melancholy pile which long stood at Fifth Avenue and Fifty-Seventh Street, New York, as a Gothic monument to the new peerage of America. So extensive were Huntington's interests that at his death in 1900 only the Standard Oil family, acting through the ambitious Harriman, possessed the resources to buy them from his widow.[9]

Railway construction in the USA was rapid between 1868 and 1873, when 28,000 miles of track were laid. There was a pause after that due to a shortage of capital, and then a tremendous burst of activity between 1880 and 1890, raising the total mileage from 93,296 to 163,597 – 70,000 miles in a decade, more than the three leading European countries had built in fifty years. The main needs having been met, the subsequent progress was less hectic, but by 1906 there were 222,000 miles of track in the United States out of 562,000 miles in the world as a whole.[10] It was by any standard a colossal investment and one which was enormously profitable to some (though not to all) of the investors.

American railways covered longer distances and encountered greater dangers than did the railways of Europe. It was these conditions which produced the Pullman car and the Westinghouse air brake, each to be the basis for an important business. George M. Pullman built the first real sleeping-car in 1864.[11] This was the 'Pioneer', specially sprung and decorated and furnished, costing $18,000 as compared with the maximum of $5,000 hitherto spent on any railroad coach. It was also of exceptional width and height, too big for the existing platforms and bridges. This circumstance might have prevented the 'Pioneer' from being used but everyone agreed that the 'Pioneer' should be attached to the funeral train which conveyed the body of President Lincoln from Chicago to Springfield. That one line was adapted to suit the 'Pioneer'; others began to follow suit. There were at first some competitors in the sleeping-car business but these were bought out by the Pullman Company between 1867 and 1900. The same company came to operate in Europe and elsewhere, providing not only sleepers but also dining- and drawing-room cars. A natural sequel to the Pullman coach was the vogue for the private car; a suite of compartments for the use of a single individual or family. What was the prerogative of royalty in Europe became, for a time, the status symbol of millionaires in the USA. And whereas a privately owned car might belong to any man of sufficient wealth, the railway magnate had additional privileges. These are well described by Rudyard Kipling in his novel *Captains Courageous*, in which Mr Cheyne's car 'Constance', with the way cleared by telegraphed instructions, covers 2,350 miles, crossing the continent from tidewater to tidewater in 87 hours and 35 minutes. Cheyne's career had covered the building of three railroads and the deliberate wreck of a fourth. These and other interests had left him with thirty million dollars. Harvey, his son, had inadvertently spent a season in a fishing schooner out of Gloucester and shows the car to the men who have been his shipmates:

. . . Harvey laid the glories of the 'Constance' before them without a word. They took them in an equal silence – stamped leather, silver door handles and rails, cut velvet, plate-glass, nickel, bronze, hammered iron and the rare woods of the continent inlaid.[12]

The other great American invention was the Westinghouse air brake. The invention of George Westinghouse (then aged twenty-one) these compressed air brakes were first tried on the Pennsylvania Railroad in 1869. They proved infinitely superior to any other system in use. American freight trains originally had brakesmen who walked along the roof and applied the brakes by hand when not using their clubs to brush off hoboes who had hitched a ride. Hand-brakes so operated were too slow, of course, for use in an emergency. The next step was to install brakes applied by compressed air to every wheel in the train. The drawback in this system was that a break in the pipe made the whole system useless. George Westinghouse then devised a different system by which each car had an air reservoir with a pressure of 70 or 100 lbs per square inch, all the reservoirs being connected by a pipe in which the pressure was the same. When pressure in the pipe was reduced by the engine driver the air in each reservoir applied the brakes. Adopted in the USA from 1875, this invention was quickly copied in some other countries but not, unfortunately, in Britain where there was already a vacuum brake devised by a British inventor. A British railway historian points out that as no vacuum can exceed 14.7 lbs per square inch, 'any vacuum-powered mechanism is a low-pressure system, inevitably either feeble, sluggish or both, and always bulky.'[13] To this one technical error, and its paralysing effect on freight trains, this author attributes many of the subsequent troubles to which British railways have been liable. In the USA, by contrast, the Westinghouse Company went on from strength to strength and we shall have occasion to refer to its later history and current importance, due not entirely to compressed air brakes, but to the fact that George Westinghouse had also an interest in electricity and its application especially in AC as opposed to DC.

The great days of American railroads may be said to have lasted from 1862 until about 1916. For much of that time the railroads represented Big Business. There were other industries of comparable importance, some created by the railways themselves, and there were also some influential men whose concern was with finance rather than industry or transport. One such man was Jay Cooke, the financier of the Civil War. He was essentially a banker but it was he who inspired the construction of the second transcontinental railway. This was the Northern Pacific, chartered in 1864 but constructed from 1870, connecting Duluth and St Paul, Minnesota, with Seattle and Portland, Oregon. It received a colossal land grant but had both technical and financial troubles and was still far from complete in 1880. This effort had its parallel far to the south in the Santa Fe Railroad which began in Kansas and reached Santa Fe, the capital of New Mexico, in 1880, stretching then over to Phoenix, Arizona and the southern California coast. The Santa Fe thus did for Los Angeles what the Central Pacific did for San Francisco and the Northern Pacific for Seattle. Jay Cooke it was who financed the election of Grant to the presidency in 1872 and went bankrupt the following year.

... His mansion outside of Philadelphia, 'Cooke's Castle', as Justice Chase called it, had fifty-two rooms; its walls were decorated with frescoes, and further ornamented with three hundred paintings. ... It contained a theater, fountains, conservatories and finally an Italian garden, 'facing a wall built to resemble the ruined castle of some ancient nobleman'. ...[14]

That Jay Cooke should have gone bankrupt is not altogether surprising, but he made at least a partial recovery:

... He somehow managed to repay all his creditors, and though never a financial power again, he got back some of his money, and left, unlike Morris and Girard, a family in Philadelphia. His descendants, now safely integrated, still flourish in Penllyn, alongside the Ingersolls, Foxes and Coxes.[15]

Although Huntington and Stanford were among the great railway magnates of their day, and while even Jay Cooke counted for a time as one of them, the pre-eminent railway king was still Cornelius Vanderbilt, whose son succeeded to his kingdom in 1877. The sequel to this succession was that the son, William Henry, decided three years later, to sell a part of his interest in the New York Central. For this delicate transaction William Henry Vanderbilt approached Pierpont Morgan, well known as a banker for his handling of a part of the federal government's bond issue of 1877. Pierpont was also important as the New York representative of his father, Julius Morgan, head of the firm in London.

On November 26 (1880), at two forty-five in the afternoon, the press was on hand when a large group of bankers and railroad officials emerged from the white marble Drexel, Morgan Building at the corner of Broad and Wall. Then the news was revealed . . . The bankers had bought 150,000 shares of New York Central stock at 120, which gave William Henry Vanderbilt $18,000,000. At that moment the stock stood at 135 on the New York Stock Exchange, which meant the bankers had a possible profit of $2,250,000. They also held an option on another 100,000 shares . . . at the same price.

. . . Most of this stock had been placed by the J. S. Morgan Company in England. . . .

In 1880 then, Pierpont Morgan became vitally interested in American railroads. That year he headed a syndicate which bought and sold $40,000,000 in the 6 per cent gold bonds of the Northern Pacific Railroad . . . (He saw) that by extending it to the Pacific as planned, the railroad could enjoy a prosperous future. So it was done, and with the enormous prestige of the Morgan banking firm the issue was sold out.[16]

Pierpont Morgan's immediate achievement was to place the New York Central stock without the market breaking. In the long term, he had started a new era in railroad finance, one in which banking firms would take the place of individual dynasts. The process was gradual, however, and some of the railway kings died hard. Three names are especially worth recording. First, there was Jay Gould (1836–92) who controlled four of the western railroads and whose son, George J. Gould, did not sell out until 1918. In 1909 George is said to have spent $200,000 on the coming-out of his daughter Marjory, soon to be Mrs Drexel. Then there was Edward Henry Harriman (1848–1909) of the Illinois Central and other mid-western lines, whose son, William Averell Harriman, is well known as politician and one-time US Ambassador to the USSR. Last, and perhaps the greatest, was James Jerome Hill (1838–1916) of the Northern Pacific, whose extension of the St Paul & Pacific Railway to Seattle has been described as probably the greatest feat of railway construction in the history of the United States. He formed the Great Northern Railway in 1890 and was sufficiently active in 1901 to join with J. P. Morgan in defeating Harriman in the battle for the Chicago, Burlington & Quincy Railroad. The railway boom was not finished even then, for another 40,000 miles of track were laid during the decade from 1900 to 1910. At its peak, in 1916, the American railway system covered 254,250 miles of track. By then, however, it was no longer a very profitable investment. There was growing competition from road traffic. The railway companies tried to meet the new situation by mergers designed to reduce the overheads and by discounting service on the less profitable routes. The mergers were resisted in the courts as tending to establish monopolies, but the abandonment of unremunerative lines continued after World War II and was hastened, indeed, by growing competition from airlines. Seventeen railways discontinued passenger services entirely between 1945 and 1962[17] and the process has not been reversed. Except for a few limited purposes, the railways seem to have had their day.

For our present purpose we have followed, in outline, the history of American railways and can appreciate their importance in the development of heavy industry. They created a demand for iron, steel and coal and they aided the economic growth of the regions to which they supplied access. Apart from this, however, they were Big Business in themselves. From 1865 to about 1905 they were the concern of the biggest financiers and provided the basis for some of the biggest fortunes. Neither in the USA, however, nor in the rest of the world, did they provide the sort of organization which would remain prosperous during the present century. To twentieth-century Big Business they provide a part of the background, a transport system which has not yet outlived its usefulness. They have also provided the wealth which has enabled some families, still of importance, to establish themselves in the realm of high finance and even higher fashion. This last and significant process had its most dramatic moment in 1883 when Mrs Astor went to call upon Mrs W. K. Vanderbilt. The occasion was on the eve of the Vanderbilt's fancy-dress ball of 26 March – the preparations for which were so elaborate, so stunning, that the highest circles of the older establishment were reduced to something like panic.

Up to this moment, we must recall, Mrs William Astor had never called upon any of the Vanderbilts, and none of the Astors were invited to the coming ball. The court of society's queen was therefore convulsed in a great social crisis. No one knew what should be done. Then at last, the queen saw that there was no escape from the dilemma. Amid a general sensation throughout the plutocratic world, as the historians of the affair report, 'Mrs Astor unbent her stateliness, went to call upon Mrs Vanderbilt, and in a very ladylike manner made the *amende honorable!*'[18]

We better understand the nature of this crisis when we realise that this was the period when 'society in New York became concentrated and centralized like the railroads or the slaughterhouse system.' Mrs Astor was the acknowledged leader of all who were thought to be solid and respectable as well as rich. At her elbow, however, was Mr Ward McAllister, and it was he who invented the mystic 'Four Hundred' on the occasion of the famous Centennial Ball of 1876. It is doubtful whether the Four Hundred were ever more than a myth but the idea prevailed of a society more or less closed to people of low connections who were still in trade. On this subject it would be fair to remark that the Astors themselves were of no very noble birth and could have been snubbed by the Stuyvesants, descendants of the Dutch Governor of New York in 1647–64. John Jacob Astor, founder of the family had been an uncouth German immigrant and his son, William Backhouse, who doubled the fortune he inherited, was almost equally taciturn and unsocial. It was William Backhouse Astor, Jr who altered the family's position by marrying Caroline Webster Schermerhorn – the legendary Mrs Astor.

In the days of these early millionaires and multi-millionaires one symbol of their acceptance was to be found in the town of Newport, Rhode Island, an historic seaport which had once been a centre for the African slave trade and which had later figured in the War of American Independence. A symbolic moment in its history had been the landing there of Victor Marie du Pont and his brother in 1800, a family which came from near Nemours in France. The great days of Newport as a fashionable resort came later, however, and it might be difficult to fix the exact period at which they dawned. The process may have begun after the Civil War and was certainly well advanced by 1880. Among the earlier summer residents were Mrs Schermerhorn, Mrs

William Astor, Mrs John Jacob Astor, Mrs Belmont and Mrs Paran Stevens. These were the hostesses, married to husbands who did not figure to the same extent in the leadership of society. Central to the group was Mrs William Astor – *the* Mrs Astor as she preferred to be known. She was fortunate in that two other possible claimants to the title had removed themselves. The appointment of John Jacob Astor III as Minister to Italy in 1882 had removed one Mrs Astor, and a Philadelphian at that. Then there was the migration to England of William Waldorf Astor, which removed yet another possible rival to the throne. So Mrs Astor reigned supreme and felt entitled to regard Cornelius Vanderbilt and his family as upstarts.

It is true that the old Commodore was profane and coarse but he was the owner in 1853 of the finest steam yacht in the world.

. . . His *North Star*, costing half a million dollars – an incredible sum for those days – ushered in, in style, the Golden Days of the Private Yacht. Over 270 feet in length and (of) 2,300 tons . . . she had a ballroom running half the length of her deck, and every one of her saloons was furnished either in rosewood upholstered in green plush or in Commodore Vanderbilt's idea of the period of Louis XIV; her dining room was decorated in ligneous marble adorned with medallions of Washington, Franklin, Webster and Clay . . . For this cruise the Commodore buried the hatchet with his family, taking all of them with him, even his in-laws. He also took along a minister, the Rev. J. O. Choules, for grace and evening prayers. 'There never was any disagreement,' the Rev. Mr Choules reported. 'The Commodore did the swearing and I did the praying.'[19]

Even with such a yacht, he remained socially unacceptable in the more exclusive circles. It was William Kissam Vanderbilt, William Henry's son, whose wife Mrs Astor had finally to recognize socially. This wife was Alva Smith, daughter of an Alabama cotton planter and it was her party (6 March 1883), the most elaborate fancy-dress ball in American history, which compelled Mrs Astor to pay her celebrated call. The citadel had been breached and from this time the Vanderbilts stood second to the Astors. Their position came to be represented by at least two houses in Newport. First, there was 'Rough Point' which belonged to Frederick W. Vanderbilt but later passed to Doris Duke, whose father was head of the American Tobacco Company. Then there was a house called 'The Breakers' where a last member of the family was still resident on the top floor in 1960. The Vanderbilts' status was further confirmed when William Kissam's daughter, Consuelo, married the Ninth Duke of Marlborough, her two sons being respectively the Marquis of Blandford and Lord Ivor Charles Spencer Churchill. With that event, or possibly with the marriage at Newport of Gertrude Vanderbilt with Harry Payne Whitney (1896), the railway age in the USA had reached its climax and all that could follow was decline. This did not, of course, remove the Vanderbilts from the scene. With the Astors and the Whitneys they are to be classed among the great dynasties of the USA. The Whitneys, ranking third among families of social importance, also have their place in railway history but in a different context, for William Collins Whitney, who came to New York from Massachusetts in 1864, ended by owning the greater part of the city's streetcar business. Nor did he believe in hoarding all that he made:

When it came to houses and entertaining, Whitney put even the vaunted Four Hundred to shame. Purchasing the old Robert L. Stuart mansion at 871 Fifth Avenue, he turned it, in four years, into one of New York's most elaborate private residences. Bronze gates came from the Palazzo Doria in Rome, ball-room, banquet hall and drawing room came, respectively, from a castle in Bordeaux, a palace in Genoa, and a palazzo in Rome. One corridor came from a French monastery, everywhere were stained-glass windows taken from cathedrals, and one Flemish tapestry alone cost $100,000. . . .
And yet this house was only one of ten which Whitney owned. At the time of his death, in 1904, he owned some 36,000 acres and homes in no less than five States – including two houses on Long Island, two in the Berkshires, two in the Adirondacks, not to mention 'Blue Grass Farm' in Kentucky, 'Stony Ford Farm' in Goshen, New York, and down in Arken, South Carolina, a house, a farm, a race course, and 200 acres of hunting land.[20]

The great days at Newport were threatened by the death of Mrs Astor at 'Beechwood' in 1908, and threatened still more by the Sixteenth Amendment in 1913, which introduced the tax on income; but did not end until World War II. Eleanor Young had her debut at Newport in 1936 and there were many other occasions of the kind. With the war, however, Newport's decline became manifest. It is true that Perry Belmont 'Newport's No. 1 *bon vivant* and clubman' lived until 1947, but he was then aged ninety-seven, too old for much frivolity. The last historic party is said to have been that given by

Alexander Hamilton Rice on his eightieth birthday in 1955. All that remained after that was the Society for the Preservation of Newport Antiquities and the clumps of hydrangeas which look so unnatural, as some people think, along the once majestic Bellevue Avenue.

It would be quite wrong, of course, to think that the dynasts of the railway age were the only wealthy men of their time. There were other millionaires whose money came from mining, from commerce, from the growing of cotton or, later, from the breeding of cattle. It was the railways, however, which introduced wealth on a new and unprecedented scale. The Vanberbilts were a new phenomenon, the most successful men of their time – perhaps of any time. They were in Big Business as none before them had been. What they did not leave behind them was an established and developing industry. Although the investment in railways had been immense and although railway property must be of enormous value, the industry itself is on the decline, superseded by other forms of transport. It is overshadowed, moreover, by the subsequent growth of the industrial giants, by the great organizations based upon steel and oil, chemistry and rubber. But if a distinction is drawn between railways on the one hand and, say, oil on the other, we must never forget that the railways of the world, whatever their present state (nationalized or bankrupt or both) were essential to the development of industry as a whole. Without the basis of agriculture and landownership, without the provision of roads and harbours, without the establishment of banks and insurance offices, without the telegraph and without the railway, the Big Business we have to describe could never have come into existence.

Part II   THE DYNASTS

Part II   THE DYNASTS

1   Steel

The first metal in practical use was copper and it was first mined in the Caucasus, between the Caspian and the Black Sea. The use of gold and silver was older still but these metals, ideal for ornament or currency, were suitable for little else. The Caucasus had the metal ore, the fuel and the water, and it was there discovered that copper could be cast into shape, hardened with the hammer and sharpened so as to make an edged tool or weapon. This trade secret spread outwards to Persia, India, China and Egypt (5,000–2,000 BC) and finally reached Europe towards the end of that period. Copper is easy to reduce from the ore but the resulting metal, however hammered, is relatively soft. What is called the Bronze Age began with the probably accidental discovery that an alloy of copper and tin is harder than either metal used separately and can be either cast or wrought. This first lesson in metallurgy was of vital importance and led to an urgent search for tin which was, originally, scarce. The use of bronze spread quickly to Sumeria, Assyria, Babylon, Anatolia, Persia and Egypt. The Homeric period of Greek history and legend coincides with the later Bronze Age, bronze being the metal with which both Greeks and Trojans were armed. For some few purposes, like the casting of statues, bronze remains unsurpassed. For most other purposes it was superseded by iron.

There are two sources of iron. Some comes from outer space and the rest from iron ore which has to be mined. Meteorites were well known to peoples of ancient times, who knew perfectly well that they had fallen from the sky. Meteoric iron is remarkably pure although it contains a percentage (5 per cent to 26 per cent) of nickel, being really an iron-nickel alloy, and is far superior to iron of less celestial origin. There was so little of it, however, that it came to be fifteen or twenty times the price of copper, more valued, in fact, than silver or gold. In the languages of the ancient world it was 'metal from heaven' and prized accordingly. Its value reflected short supply and its wider use, outside royal tombs, depended upon progress in mining. Iron ore was first mined, it seems, in Chalybia, the southern slopes of the Caucasus mountain range, the Chalybes being mentioned as ironworkers by Herodotus and Aristotle. The first people to use iron extensively were the Hittites of Anatolia who had considerable military success before they were conquered and dispersed in about 1200 BC. They are thought to have invented the ironclad war chariot, used afterwards by the Philistines and Canaanites. There are bitter references to this device in the Old Testament, the Israelites of that period condemning the use of an armoured fighting vehicle as oppressive and unfair. By 1000 BC iron was in general use not only for weapons, including the bow, but also for axes, harrows and saws. The use of iron spread to India in the other direction, where it was used for surgical instruments, and to China, where it was used for making cast iron statues of Buddha. As for Europe, the Greek civilization of the sixth century BC was founded upon iron and the rise of the Roman Republic owed something to the iron ore of Tuscany and Elba. In later periods the Romans found better supplies in what we now call Styria and Carinthia and better yet in Catalonia. As from the Roman conquest of the Iberian peninsula (*c.* 140 BC) it was with Spanish iron that the legions were armed.

For commercial purposes iron can be either wrought or cast. The ore as it comes from the ground contains not only iron but such other elements as silicon, sulphur, manganese and phosphorus. Heated by charcoal, the iron begins to form a spongy, porous mass (at 2,190° Fahrenheit), absorbing carbon in the process. If removed from the furnace at this point and hammered on an anvil, the iron would shed its cinders and slag. Heated again in a charcoal forge and hammered again repeatedly, the iron would reach an almost pure state.

This was wrought iron, and contained generally from 0.02 to 0.08 per cent carbon. The minute amount of carbon in wrought iron is just enough to make the metal tough and malleable. In the improbable event that the temperature in this type of furnace approached 2400°F., the iron sponge would absorb from 3 to 4.5 per cent carbon and melt. This is cast iron. So high a proportion of carbon makes iron hard and somewhat brittle. It is liable to crack or shatter under a heavy blow and cannot be forged at any temperature.[1]

Wrought iron was and is used in many ways, for tools and implements, for door furniture and gates. Cast iron was widely used in medieval Europe for church bells, which were as often cast in bronze or an alloy, but bellfounding technique was also used in the manufacture of iron cannon and there are other purposes for which cast iron is still useful even in the twentieth century. There is a description, however, of Charlemagne's entry into Paria in 773 in which that ruler is called the Iron King, armoured and armed in iron with iron helmet and lance, his shield of plain iron without any device and his men as nearly like him as they could fashion themselves, 'so iron filled the fields and the ways, and the sun's rays were from every quarter reflected from iron'. There was iron everywhere, as the Italians complained, and if that metal were ever accorded its apotheosis, this might be it.[2]

Distinct from iron, whether wrought or cast, is the product we call steel. In current use the word is applied to a number of hard, strong, durable and malleable alloys of iron and carbon, usually containing between 0.2 and 1.5 per cent carbon and often with the addition of manganese, chromium, nickel or tungsten. For iron to gain this higher carbon content it must be brought into contact with charcoal and sealed off, in a furnace, from contact with the air. If this is not done the carbon will unite with the oxygen of the atmosphere, producing not steel but carbon monoxide. This process was discovered in India and was described by Aristotle in 384 BC. Iron bars mixed with wood shavings were sealed into clay crucibles. These were placed in the furnace until the metal became fluid and then allowed to cool slowly. After the iron had been reheated and hammered, removing excess carbon, it became a high-carbon steel and fit for use. 'Wootz' steel, as this product was called, was shipped to Damascus in Syria where it was made into sword blades, the process involving both hardening and tempering. The blade was hardened by being plunged, while red hot, into cold water. It was tempered, after grinding, by heating to the appropriate colour (e.g. blue) and by quenching again in water. It was finally ground, sharpened and polished. There were two tests for quality, one being to bend the blade from tip to hilt, the other to cut off an expendable slave's head with a single stroke. The Persians used a rather similar technique, achieving even better results, and the theory has been put forward that the Spartans were also in the secret and owed to it such success as they had against the other Greeks. To produce the highest quality steel it only remained to add tungsten, manganese and nickel, a technique which was developed at Toledo in Spain. Toledo military swords were used by the Romans, were famous in the Middle Ages and are still made today, although perhaps for a dwindling market.

In centuries before the nineteenth, the chief use of high-grade steel was always for sword making and it is important to realize what technical progress predated industrialization. Particular interest centres upon India and Persia, Scandinavia and Japan, countries in which the steel-bladed sword was, even more than elsewhere, a symbol of rank and privilege. To take India first, as the country in which steel was most probably invented:

For centuries the prestige of the Persian blade had been immense, and in Persia the manufacture and export of blades had been highly organized. Many Mughal swords were mounted with Persian blades, but as the seventeenth century progressed Indian craftsmen became competent to fulfil even the most exigent wants, so that the direct purchase of Persian blades fell into abeyance. . . .
The majority of Persian blades that have been preserved are 'damascened'. That is to say that by means of burnishing and washing with a dilute acid a pattern of strands of light and dark metal has been made visible on the surface of the blade . . . (There were four categories of damascened blade) . . . and fourth, the least esteemed, is the 'Sham', meaning Syrian. . . . These old Persian damascened patterns were produced by a method which is referred to in the present study as Mechanical Damask, also sometimes called Pattern Welding. It consisted of building the blade out of a billet composed of alternate high- and low-carbon content steels, and submitting it to a complex forging process in which cutting and rearranging, folding, twisting, chiselling, punching, and grinding played a part. This method was also used by both Celtic and Japanese swordsmiths. (Many blades were signed by the artist who made them, the most famous smith being the probably sixteenth century Assadullah of Isfahan.)
The aesthetic qualities of the Indian sword reached the highest point they ever attained in the weapons of the Mughal period. . . . Since the fundamental appeal of the sword to its owner is primarily phallic, and the weapon is regarded as the repository of his power of energetic action, in the aesthetic appreciation of

the *Talwar* curved sword of Mongol origin a Platonic conception of beauty as the visual embodiment of perfect adaptation to purpose is of prime importance. The elegance of a fine *Talwar* blade has much in common with the elegance of formulation admired by the mathematician and the engineer, but is more profoundly rooted in emotional significance. The purpose, the action which lies at the base of the weapon's appeal, is not a mere function, but an activity of deep personal significance to the user; conflict, killing, personal prestige, and power all lend their emotional force to the aesthetic effect of the fine sword blade, and at no time were these more firmly wedded in their expression to a science of swordsmanship than in the Mughal period. . . .[3]

Whatever its personal significance to the owner, the *Talwar* was also an instrument for the propagation of the Faith and scientifically designed so that the angle of incidence is first established at the blade's centre of percussion. A great deal of thought, as well as a great deal of art, went into the making of the sword blades which used to support the truth of Islamic doctrine.

In Scandinavia, where Sweden has always been a source of iron ore and mining expertise, the sword plays a large part in legend and has the further significance that each notable sword has its individual name and is given in the Norse Sagas its own personality – as, for example, when it is reluctant to leave the scabbard.

Most of these swords were fashioned in a complicated and wonderful way. Their blades were made up of three separate parts . . . the two edges were forged separately, and the central part was made up of numerous narrow strips of iron. These strips were all twisted together, cold, in various patterns and then forged; then they were twisted again, and reforged on to the separate edges. Then the whole thing was with infinite care filed and burnished until the surfaces were totally smooth; the result of all this was that the central portions of such blades had intricate patterns, made up of regularly repeating designs wrought into the fabric of the iron. Most of these patterns are very similar to the markings on a snake's back . . . Many such blades have been cut into sections, and microscopic photographs have been taken and examination made, as well as X-ray photographs of the integral structure. . . .[4]

If the examination of these blades has been scientific, their original construction was not less so. Nor was their design a purely aesthetic matter. The twisted wire built into the blade was to combine elasticity with strength, and something of the same technique was used, even in this century, for making the barrels of the heaviest naval artillery.

All other swords, however, are as nothing when compared with the steel weapons of Japan. Iron ore is relatively scarce in that country and the historic emphasis has been on the perfect manufacture of weapons for the few. The classic age, from the swordsmith's point of view, was the period 1250–1350 and Gorō Masamune of Sagami is generally regarded as the greatest swordsmith of all time. Different methods were used by different experts but the following is apparently typical:

A piece of steel plate is welded on to an iron rod and beaten to = 5/20 mm thick × 30/60 × 150/200 long, then marked across with a chisel and folded in two, then beaten again to the same original size, the folding and rebeating process being repeated up to fifteen times. Then four such pieces are welded together and to a thicker plate, and again the cutting, folding and rebeating process is carried out five times. Thus he (G. Hütteroth) calculates that from two layers originally worked fifteen times (up to 32,768 in geometrical progression), the final total number of layers resulting from the refolding amounts to 4,194, 304, a figure which can readily be calculated as the sum of the terms of a geometrical progression in which the ratio is 2.[5]

Here then is a blade with over four million layers of steel. The process however, was more complex than that, for steels were blended with a differing carbon content and there was a final elaborate and ceremonial process by which the blade was hard-tempered and finally given a razor edge. The typical Japanese technique was to combine a soft iron core with a hard steel case or edge. The object of this was to make a sword which was strong and resilient as well as sharp, the back and the edge being of different metal. The sometimes elaborate design of the hilt perhaps reflected the fact that the wearing of jewellery in any form was forbidden by imperial edict. Different swords were worn with armour and with civilian dress but the Samurai always carried two, the second being a sort of dirk. Swords were tested at executions or on the bodies of those already executed. Other tests, on an old helmet or a bundle of straw, were thought less satisfactory.

Swashbucklers might hide themselves at the corner of a street and cut down a passer-by, merely to try the edge of a sword. The contempt of the Samurai class for the common people allowed such excesses, and so openly did the test murders take place, that they found their way into humorous stories. For instance, it is recorded that once a Juijitsu teacher saw a Samurai at the corner of a street suddenly drawing his sword to cut him down. He turned three somersaults, and on standing up at a safe distance from the astonished swash-buckler, put out his tongue at him, and went his way.[6]

Juijitsu was the answer of the unarmed peasant to the Samurai whose conduct might verge, at times, on the inconsiderate. But the Japanese sword, 'the pride of warriors and the theme of poets', did not leave too much scope for argument. It is said that the best of them could cut through the barrel of a musket. Civilian wearing of the sword was abolished in Japan by the imperial edict of 1877 but military swords were still worn and even used during World War II, some of them ancestral, others made in the traditional style. They represented a dying tradition in which, as in many other countries, the wearing of the sword was a mark of status. For ceremonial purposes this may still be so but steel, meanwhile, has passed into common use.

It was a revolution in human affairs when the mass production of steel was initiated. The story begins in the English midlands and was eventually to centre upon Sheffield. The earlier iron industry of England had flourished in the Sussex Weald where iron ore was found in close proximity to the woodlands which supplied the charcoal. But the Sussex ironmasters were chiefly famous for casting cannon, at first in iron and later in what came to be called gun-metal. English guns were in great demand during the Elizabethan period for, whereas cannon cast in brass or bronze might look more impressive (and were certainly more expensive), they heated up too much. Allowing time for the barrel to cool after each discharge slowed down the rate of fire. In this respect the iron guns were superior and those from Sussex were among the best. England had better supplies of iron ore in an area between Sheffield and Bewdley, extending from there into south Wales, but industrial development there was hindered by lack of charcoal which was bulkier to transport than the ore itself. What that area possessed was coal, used by the blacksmith but not, at that time, by the ironmaster. So the mid-land blacksmiths imported much of their iron, the best of it from Sweden. Sheffield was known for its cutlery in the Middle Ages and especially for the manufacture of 'the thwytel or whittle, a kind of knife anciently worn by the lower orders, who were not entitled to wear a sword'. The Miller of Chaucer's *Canterbury Tales* wore a 'sheffield thwytel' but there is reason to believe that arrow heads were produced at Sheffield in still greater numbers. Its growth was slow, however, and a survey of 1615 records that the inhabitants then numbered only 2,207. A few years later the Cutlers' Company was established by an Act of 1621, placing the trade under the authority of the master cutler, the wardens and searchers. Their authority was short-lived but their prestige has remained, the present Cutlers' Hall being built in 1832, the scene of the annual 'Cutlers' Feast, over which the master presides, and to which the local and neighbouring nobility and gentry are invited'. Birmingham was well known for its tools and nails from the reign of Henry VIII but developed its trade in small arms during the reign of William III. By the time of the French wars Birmingham could and did manufacture 14,500 muskets each week with bayonets to match. Wolverhampton industries were rather similar but with more emphasis on locks, files and screws. Other metal trades were developed at Dudley, Walsall and Stourbridge; nail-making was predominant but there was a considerable output also of horseshoes, bolts, chains and farming implements. Here in the English midlands were the centres of an iron trade which would eventually become a trade in steel.

We hear of steel conversion in Sussex as early as 1609 but the first major steelworks were around Newcastle-on-Tyne, the port at which the Swedish iron was landed. The first steelworkers were German but the enterprise was soon taken up by Ambrose Crowley and Isaac Cookson. The cementation process was used, the iron bars being enclosed in clay 'coffins', and the art in this form had reached Sheffield by 1709. Its practice still depended, however, upon the use of charcoal as fuel – upon charcoal imported expensively into a region where coal was plentiful and cheap. There were areas in the midlands, nevertheless, where there was timber as well as coal and one of them centred on Coalbrookdale in Shropshire where a small foundry existed in the seventeenth century. This was leased in 1708 by Abraham Darby (1676–1717), a Quaker from Dudley, who had learnt his trade as iron-master in Bristol. The foundry was well placed for expansion.

Timber was available, together with ironstone, clay, sand, limestone and, what is more important, coal, all at a short distance from the furnace. A little stream suitable for powering the furnace bellows, ran down the valley through the works to join the river Severn, and the latter river provided a useful highway for the dispatch of finished goods.[7]

Here was the classically perfect site for an eighteenth-century factory and here, in 1709, he began to smelt iron with coal, or rather with coke. Many others had failed in attempting to do this but they had used coal as it came from the pit. Coke, as used then in smelting, was made by baking the coal under a layer of wet ashes until the smoke and sulphur fumes had ceased to rise, leaving behind an almost pure carbon, not very different from charcoal. For the coking process, however, some coals are more suitable than others. Darby had been lucky with his coal supply but some of his imitators ran into trouble, with the result that charcoal was superseded only slowly over the next hundred years. The Darby family flourished, nevertheless, under successive owners, all called Abraham. It was Abraham Darby III (1750–89) who built the world's first iron bridge at a point on the river Severn since called Ironbridge – a work of art put together without rivets or bolts. The Darby works are still in existence under the ownership of Allied Iron-founders Ltd and the museum at Coalbrookdale is a place of pilgrimage for all students of industrial archaeology.

The discovery that coke could be used for smelting iron was of crucial importance to a country which would soon exhaust its supplies of charcoal. It did nothing in itself, however, to improve the supply of steel. The next important step was taken by Benjamin Huntsman (1704–76), a clockmaker of Doncaster, who was dissatisfied with the quality of the steel he used for springs and pendulums. Huntsman moved to Handsworth on the outskirts of Sheffield in 1740 or 1742 and there developed the art of purifying steel in a clay crucible. Using coke as fuel he managed to eliminate the slag and produce, in small quantities, what came to be called crucible steel, an expensive metal used only for special purposes, such as the making of surgical instruments and chronometers. Huntsman thus founded the reputation of Sheffield as a world supplier of high-grade steel. Technically, he had made a useful contribution. Financially, the greater rewards went to the ironmasters who cast the guns with which the allies fought against Napoleon. Cadell, Roebuck and Garbett set up the Carron Works in 1760 with £12,000 capital already worth £150,000 by 1773. John Wilkinson (1728–1808) of Bradley in Staffordshire devised a better method of boring cast-iron cannon in 1774, his guns gaining a reputation which made him a fortune. It is doubtful whether English swords were ever as famous as English cannon, the early swordsmiths at Hounslow and at Shotley Bridge (near Newcastle) being German. The Wilkinson Sword Company was founded, however, in 1772 and flourishes to this day, able to turn out some 15,000 swords a year but possibly doing an even better business in safety razor blades. There were other successful ironmasters like the Crawshays and Foleys but the two families which established themselves most solidly were both based on south Wales: the Vivians of Swansea and the Guests of Dowlais and Merthyr Tydfil. First ironmaster of this dynasty was John Guest, whose eventual successor was Sir Josiah John Guest, Bt (1785–1852), FRS and MP, whose descendants became successively barons (1880) and viscounts. Even the Guests did not exactly represent Big Business in their day but they did represent industrial wealth. They had proved at least that there was money to be made in iron.

The iron and steel industries were revolutionized by the process which cheapened the production of steel. Henry Cort (1740–1800) had done much for the iron industry by his invention of the puddling process and the grooved roller. More was done by the introduction of the steam engine from 1790. But the really dramatic change was brought about by Henry Bessemer (1813–98) who was not an ironmaster but 'a self-taught genius' whose mind flew from one invention to the next. After inventing plate glass (a dubious blessing in Victorian architecture) he turned his attention to iron. What he invented was a new method of converting molten pig-iron into steel. Carbon and silicon could be removed by a blast of air blown through the molten metal, its place taken by ferro-manganese or spiegeleisen. His converter, patented beforehand, was explained to the British Association in 1856. With its aid he could produce cheaply and quickly, what he called semi-steel 'being in hardness about midway between ordinary cast steel and soft malleable iron'.[8] Mild steel, as it came to be called, was capable of mass production and could be used for a variety of purposes, especially in shipbuilding.

A number of the larger ironmasters were ready to give the Bessemer process a trial, even if others remained suspicious, and several licenses were taken out within a few days of the reading of the celebrated paper. Among the first works to set up Bessemer converters were the large Dowlais and Ebbw Vale Ironworks, in south Wales and Monmouthshire respectively. Foreign firms also took out licenses. Apparatus was set up very quickly, the licensees made metal according to the inventor's instructions, and in every case the results were a failure. Bessemer had made perfectly good iron at Baxter House but all the licensees could do was to produce a brittle metal resembling the worst possible puddled iron.[9]

It transpired, after much further experiment, that Bessemer's first success had been with a pig-iron from Monmouthshire which was almost free from phosphorus. With phosphoric pig-iron, as at Dowlais and Ebbw Vale, the results were different, the iron being cold-short. The remedy was to find other and non-phosphoric sources of iron ore, at first in Lancashire and Cumberland. After Bessemer set up his own company at Sheffield in 1858 the example was followed by John Brown in 1860 and by Charles Cannell in 1861. All these were Sheffield firms but it was eventually discovered to be better to use iron ore from Sweden or Spain, a discovery which led to the establishment of new tidewater factories, especially on the north-east coast.

Whatever the difficulties, however, and whatever changes there had to be in the raw material, the Age of Steel had arrived. And the demand for steel centred upon the railways. The first Bessemer steel rails were laid at Crewe Station in 1863 and were so successful that the London North-Western Railway set up its own steelworks in 1865. It had become obvious that all the existing iron rails would have to be replaced. The metal used might not have been recognized as steel by the old craftsmen of Damascus, Toledo or Japan but it was the basis now for technical progress. In point of fact the Bessemer process did not hold the field for long. On the heels of Bessemer came the scientifically trained German, C. W. Siemens (1825–83), who assumed British nationality and was knighted in 1882. Sir William was the second of three famous brothers, the eldest, Werner, the electrical engineer and the youngest, Karl, was also an engineer of note. Sir William, who died childless, left a fortune of nearly £400,000. William's energies were directed towards improved furnace design with a view to fuel economy. He was the inventor of the open hearth furnace, patented in 1867, which he first tried out at a small factory in Birmingham. Then he founded the Ladnore Siemens Steel Company with its works at Swansea. The essence of his system was to use the waste gases from the furnace to heat the air that was pumped into it, thus saving up to 70 or 80 per cent in fuel costs. Over the years his regenerative system came into general use and did not lose its pre-eminence until fairly recent years.

Bessemer and Siemens transformed the British steel industry but it mostly remained in the hands of fairly small firms. There were exceptions, however, and these were concerned particularly with the supply of arms and armaments. The leading engineer of Victorian England was a Newcastle man, Sir William Armstrong (1810–1900), knighted in 1859 and raised to the peerage in 1887. He joined with Sir Joseph Whitworth (1803–87) to establish what was to become the firm of Armstrong-Whitworth. Twenty small firms in Birmingham amalgamated with the intention of supplying small arms for the campaign in the Crimea of 1854–6. They eventually formed the Birmingham Small Arms Company (BSA) which went on to produce rifles for the American Civil War. This company's production of 142,819 rifles in 1861 was raised to 388, 264 in 1862, the weapons going impartially, it appears, to either side.[10] This was business on an impressive scale but it was not steel production. Nearer to the steel industry proper was Sir John Brown (1816–96) who opened the Atlas Steel Works, Sheffield, in 1856. But he, too, went into the armament business, originating the use of rolled steel for naval armour plating. The fact would seem to be that there was more money in engineering than in steel production. This may help to explain how the British steel industry came later to be nationalized.

In the United States the story was entirely different, mainly because of the enormous demands made by the American railways. Central to this transatlantic story was Andrew Carnegie (1835–1919), a Scottish immigrant brought to iron-working Pittsburgh by his parents, whose first employment was as a telegraphist, his second on the Pennsylvanian Railroad. When the great railways boom began with the conclusion of the Civil War in 1865, Carnegie saw that the whole vast campaign must depend upon iron for the rails and iron (eventually) for the bridges. His first company was the Keystone Bridge Company, which soon had all the work it could handle, but he quickly had to turn his attention to the actual production of iron. He formed the Freedom Iron Company in 1861 and obtained a controlling interest in Union Mills. He soon realized, however, that the future lay not with iron but with steel. Bessemer had announced his discovery of mild steel in 1856 and steel rails were laid at Crewe in 1863 with an immense projected saving on the maintenance of the track. The importation of steel rails from Britain had begun and it was clear that if Bessemer could overcome his difficulties with phosphorus, the American ironmasters would have to make their own steel by the Bessemer process or, eventually, go out of business. Pennsylvania ores had a high phosphorus content and were unsuitable for the Bessemer converter, and there was fierce litigation over patent rights between the Bessemer agents and those acting for William Kelly of Kentucky, who claimed to have made the same discovery nine years before. Hoping to overcome these geological and legal obstacles, Carnegie reorganized his Freedom Company in 1866 and turned it into a steel plant. He did so in the nick of time for that was the year when the opposing lawyers reached a settlement for pooling the patent rights in the Bessemer process.

Of even greater importance for the practical use of the Bessemer process in the United States was the opening of iron ore fields in the upper peninsula of Michigan. These fields were not only the richest yet found on the North American continent; the ore there was almost entirely free of phosphorus. Here was a vast treasure house of ore, beyond the wildest hopes of Henry Bessemer. The United States now had the potential for becoming the greatest steel producer in the world.[11]

The Michigan iron ore had been located by William Burt, a government surveyor, in 1841. On his map he had indicated the presence of iron along the southern shores of Lake Superior at what came to be called Iron Mountain. His discovery was confirmed by prospectors in 1845. The difficulty was to bring the ore to the furnaces of Pittsburgh and Bethlehem. This obstacle was overcome in 1855 when the Federal government built a canal to bypass the rapids of Sault Ste Marie and when a small railway line was constructed between the Iron Mountain and the town of Marquette on Lake Superior. From there the ore could travel by lake, river and canal to the railroad terminals of Ohio, Pennsylvania and New York. Its superior qualities were not known until the first tests were made in 1868, nor were supplies in bulk available until after 1870. By 1872, however, when Carnegie went to England, the problem of the ore supply had been solved.

... After viewing the great converters in Sheffield and Birmingham and hearing the plant managers discuss their plans for future development, Carnegie realized that only by building on a scale comparable to that of the British mills could he hope to compete in the Age of Steel. What he needed was not a converted plant of limited facilities but an entirely new mill with the most up-to-date equipment available. As he watched the silver-white stream of steel pour out of the great pear-shaped vessel, his plans for the future expanded with the heat that engulfed him. It was a prospectus for new worlds to conquer that he was to carry back to his doubting partners in the Union Mills.[12]

It was this 'prospectus for a new world' which brought together Andrew Carnegie and Alexander L. Holley, one of the more improbable figures to appear in American economic history. Although a poet, journalist, novelist and orator, his final loyalty was to steel. Having met Bessemer and undergone the engineering equivalent of a religious conversion, he had obtained a contract for the exclusive use of the Bessemer process in the USA. It was now to him that Carnegie had to turn and the result of their collaboration was the Edgar Thomson Steel Works with capacity sufficient to produce 30,000 tons of steel rails a year. Steel rails had averaged $110 a ton, with $97.50 their lowest price. Holley estimated that the Edgar Thomson plant could produce rails at a cost of $69 a ton, leaving the owners with a minimum profit of $855,000 a year. Work began in August 1875, and the fuel used was coke, a product of the Pennsylvania coalfield and notably of the Connellsville area in which the coking coal belonged to Henry Clay Frick, who had organized the business from 1871. Carnegie now acquired a considerable interest in Frick's company, giving him permanent access to this essential fuel. When the new Carnegie Company was formed in 1899 with a capital of £60,000,000, Frick's company became part of the combine. He also acquired a controlling interest in the Pittsburgh Limestone Company, another source of raw material. It remained to secure his supply of iron ore as the Marquette Range ores became depleted. But the whole ore problem had been altered by the ingenuity of Sidney Gilchrist Thomas, who discovered in 1878 how to extract phosphorus from iron. He found that phosphorus at 2,500°F. will quit iron and attach itself to lime, being thereafter removable as slag. He solved the technical problems in 1879 and so ended the world's search for phosphorus-free iron ore. As from that date any iron ore could be fed into the converter, the main consideration being the cost of transport. In the light of these changed circumstances, Carnegie agreed to lease the mines of Mesabi, west of Duluth, 'the most valuable iron deposit ever to be discovered on the entire North American continent'. The mines were the property of the Consolidated Mining Company which belonged, in turn to J. D. Rockefeller.

If we exclude Vanderbilt, whose railway empire was to lose its importance, Andrew Carnegie was the first, perhaps, of the true industrial dynasts. His career set the pattern, moreover, for others. Seeing the possibilities of a new process, he had made the most of them, establishing himself as monarch of a key industry. That done, his later efforts went into vertical integration – the acquisition of control over supplies and outlets. For the mere safety of his empire he had to gain control of his raw meterials – iron ore, coal and limestone. For security again he had to control his communications – railways and shipping. He had finally to control his market, which was rapidly changing. His first millions came from railway lines and bridges, his steel replacing timber and iron. The railway construction boom had practically ended by 1895 and Carnegie moved at once into structural steel, making the parts, for example, for the Brooklyn Bridge. From steel manufacture his group moved, inevitably, into engineering and into a myriad other activities which centred upon steel. This line of development has become normal in Big Business. Normal again, among the dynasts, were the two problems which faced him in his later years: how to retire and what to do with the money? In answer to the first he abruptly sold out in 1901. It was a deal such as only J. P. Morgan & Company could arrange (see pages 60-1) and its first effect was to establish the United States Steel Corporation, with a capital of $867,550,394 and comprising ten companies in all, the most important being the Carnegie Company, the National Steel Company, the American Steel & Wire Company and the American Tin Plate Company. Its second effect was for the new corporation to buy out Carnegie's interest for $492,006,160, payable in preferred and common stock and in bonds secured by a mortgage on the corporation's property.[13] In this way Carnegie provided, not inadequately, for his childless old age. But, what could he or anyone do with such a fortune? He could increase it of course, by wise investment and it was bound, anyway, to swell by its own momentum. But what then? Carnegie's answer was to give it away. Such vast benefactions went to Carnegie Hall and the public libraries of the world – over $350,000,000 by one estimate – that he had only $30,000,000 when he died in 1919. This sum sufficed to take care of his relatives and provide pensions, incongruously, for David Lloyd George, John Morley and former President Taft, for Mrs Theodore Roosevelt and Grover Cleveland's widow.

The mark that Carnegie left on the industry will never be wiped out. In his late days he set the pace for all to follow, and it was a fast one. Although pitiless to his competitors, he had the gift of drawing to him men of high ability; he was a wonderful judge of men, and to his intimates he was generous and open. A born commander, a Napoleon of industry, he built up an organization that had no equal in its day, one that was at the same time extremely efficient and utterly loyal.[14]

The architect of US Steel was Charles M. Schwab, Carnegie's chief associate. It was he who sold the idea to the New York bankers and it was he who became first President of the new group. He resigned, however, in 1903, and went over to Bethlehem Steel, which was soon to stand second in the list of steel producers. His place was then taken by the Illinois lawyer Elbert H. Gary (1846–1927), who now ruled the group from his position as chairman of the board. He lacked the more picturesque qualities which had brought success to Carnegie, Frick and Schwab and was rather apt to propound the copybook maxims which apply to organizations already well established: 'If we succeed as businessmen,' he would announce, 'we must do it on principles that are honest, fair, lawful and just.' He realized, nevertheless, that there was a world market for steel and that it was shared at this time between Great Britain, Germany and Belgium. He moved into the export business, basing his operations on a steel production which was 52 per cent of the US total by 1907. His policy more than justified itself during World War 1 when Germany was blockaded and when British and French industry was totally committed to the war. It was only then that American manufacturers discovered the existence of a world market for manufactured goods. 'Without mass quantities of steel at economical prices, no nation can rise to industrial greatness.'[15] This is a twentieth-century fact; it was underlined, however, in time of war when steel production has helped to ensure not so much greatness as mere survival.

If steel brought Big Business to the USA, it did no less for Germany, where the Bessemer process was introduced by Alfred Krupp (1812–87) in 1862. The Krupp family had been settled in Essen since the sixteenth century and their foundry had been started by Alfred's father, Friedrich, in 1819. The firm specialized in cannon from an early period, subsisting on foreign orders, especially from Russia (1863), but later from Prussia. The Krupp guns played an important part in the Franco–Prussian War of 1870, the sequel to which was the German acquisition of the iron-ore mines of Lorraine. The Krupp firm, which had six employees in 1826, was of major importance by the time of Alfred's death in 1887. It was stated at that time in the *Kölnische Nachrichten* that '. . . some 13,500 workmen are employed. Office workers number 740, watchmen 170. A permanent fire-brigade of 70 persons is maintained by the firm. The members of the establishment are served by co-operative stores, a hotel, three beer-halls, a mineral water factory and a bakery . . . There is a private hospital attached to the establishment with 100 beds and an infirmary for infectious cases with 120 (beds) . . .'[16] The Krupp paternalism was almost unique but the growth of its business was a feature of the period. Alfred, 'the cannon king', was succeeded by his son Friedrich Alfred, who died in 1902, leaving an only daughter who married Gustav von Bohlen und Halbach (1870–1950). He controlled the firm during World War I and was succeeded by his son, Alfred Krupp von Bohlen und Halbach, who was the proprietor during and after World War II.

Krupp soon had rivals in steel production. In 1871 August Thyssen (1842–1926) established his works at Mulheim in the Ruhr, not far from Essen. K. F. von Stumm-Halberg (1836–1901) did the same in the Saar and Prince G. H. von Donnersmack (1830–1926) in Silesia and the Rhineland.

In 1871 Germany produced no less than a quarter of the pig-iron of the United Kingdom: in 1910 it was producing not only as much but nearly half as much again. This gigantic expansion had no parallel anywhere in the world, and it poured into railways, ships, and above all, armaments.[17]

August Thyssen was not yet thirty when he helped to found the works at Mulheim, soon to be improved by the construction of a port at Alsum on the River Emscher, a tributary of the Rhine. Using the Siemens-Martin open-hearth process and taking his coal from the firm of Hamborn, which was to be absorbed by Thyssens in 1891, he built up a firm of great importance. Also important was the firm of R. and M.

Mannesmann which specialized in manufacturing steel tubing. In the development of steel, Germany stood next to Britain and USA.

Elsewhere in Europe the steel industry was established wherever the raw materials for it existed. In France the Schneider brothers produced nickel steel at their Le Creusot factory, in quantities they could market, from 1888 onwards. What is now the giant ARBED organization was founded in three modest Luxembourg foundries, established respectively in 1847, 1856, and 1882. In 1823 John Cockerill (1790–1840) set up his engineering works, since named Cockerill-Ougrée-Providence, at Seraing near Liège. This was before Belgium existed as a country but the firm had become a key industry by 1900. Sweden had produced iron ore from an early period and two component companies of the present Svenska Metal Group – Skultuna and Granefors Kopper – had been in the steel trade since the seventeenth century. Other steel products came from Bahco of Eukoping, founded in 1889 to manufacture – among other things – the ubiquitous primus stove. There were other centres of the steel industry in Spain and Italy but these were late in developing their industrial potential and those in Italy shared the fate of those in Britain, being nationalized in recent years.

Steel became Big Business in two other countries, Australia and Japan. In New South Wales the Broken Hill Proprietary Company began mining silver ore in 1885 and made its peak profit from silver in 1892. As silver prices fell, however, the company switched to iron ore, encouraged by the discovery of vast deposits – 'a very mountain of ore' – at Iron Knob. Steelworks were planned at Newcastle, with a seaport at False Bay, renamed Whyalia. The first object of the exercise was to provide steel for the state-owned Australian railways, built between 1870 and 1900 and extending, by the latter date, to 13,500 miles of track. The outbreak of World War I, however, changed the situation and interrupted the supply of steel from Europe. The Broken Hill Co., which produced 4,500 tons of steel rails in 1914, was producing 171,134 tons by 1916 and more than that when the war ended. There was a period of overproduction but Broken Hill survived and entered the shipbuilding business during World War II, going on to exploit the West Australian ore discovery of 1961. Some of the ore from Australia now goes to Japan where modern steel manufacture accompanied the modernization of the country which began in 1868.

The Kubota Iron and Machinery Workshops were founded in 1890 and Sumitomo Metal Industries went into production in 1897. Overshadowing these and other industrial groups are the two giant combines of Mitsui and Mitsubishi. These and other firms, as formidable in technology as in size, have made spectacular progress in recent years. The Mitsuis were originally shopkeepers at Yedo and Kyōto but went into banking in 1691, this side of their business becoming the Mitsui Ginko in 1876. They went on to acquire the Miike coal field in 1889 and later the Shibaura Iron Works, and their other interests extending to paper manufacture, celluloid and shipping. The Mitsuis are a numerous clan, with many interests centred upon the family holding company. By 1970 the Nippon Steel Corporation was ahead of US Steel in its scale of production. Seven of the world's largest blast furnaces are now in Japan. The Kanasaki Steel Corporation has replaced coking coal by oxygen and crude oil, or liquified natural gas, and Japanese capital, in partnership with Broken Hill, has been invested in the steel industry of Western Australia. Political boundaries are not always proof against molten steel.

8   The Armament Kings

We have seen that the production of steel became Big Business. We have also seen, however, that leaders of industry have a tendency to favour vertical integration. This urge is not so much aggressive in origin as defensive. The head of a big organization with thousands of men on the payroll has a responsibility to his employees as well as to his shareholders. He must keep his machinery in motion. But continuity of production depends upon raw materials and trade outlets. What if his suppliers prefer to sell elsewhere? What if the wholesale merchants choose to buy from someone else? His instinct is to gain security by buying out both suppliers and wholesalers, and sometimes by seeking to control the retailers as well. Carnegie did exactly this, and later steel producers have done the same, moving rapidly into other and probably more profitable fields: the manufacture of rails, tubes, wire and plates; the construction of engines, vehicles, factories and ships. It thus becomes almost impossible to distinguish between steel production and manufacture. The story of mechanical engineering is, perhaps, the bridge between the two. No story could be more fascinating, but much of it falls outside the theme of this book. Industrial Big Business may be said to begin with Andrew Carnegie but it soon becomes the story of the armament kings. For while there were a thousand uses for steel, the tradition of the swordsmith was still very much alive. The skill that had made the sword blade was soon applied to guns and to armour, to warships and tanks. Nor can we question the fact that the biggest business, where steel was concerned, was the business of armament.

While the swords might be turned into ploughshares or safety razor blades in peace, we can be sure at least that the swords were of first importance.

To the drama of the big armaments the story of mechanical engineering is the essential preliminary. It begins with a small group of men, a group to which Henry Maudslay (1771–1831) was central. Maudslay first made his reputation by making a tumbler lock for Joseph Bramah (1748–1814), the locksmith who invented the water closet. The lock, to Bramah's design, was displayed in 1804 in his shop window in Piccadilly, with a notice offering a reward of £200 to anyone who could pick it.

For forty-seven years it resisted all efforts. It was not until 1851 that an American named Hobbs, armed with a set of elaborate instruments, succeeded in opening it after sixteen days of effort.[1]

Maudslay had proved himself a superb craftsman and was encouraged to start his own business in about 1800. It was in Margaret Street, Westminster, that he met with Marc Isambard Brunel, who had patented machinery for the mass production of ships' blocks and who now, with Maudslay's help, obtained an Admiralty contract for setting up a block-making plant at Portsmouth dockyard. He owed this contract to General Sir Samuel Bentham, Inspector-General of Navy Works from 1795 to 1807 – the brother of Jeremy Bentham – who was himself a noted engineer and shipwright. The work took six years but the results justified the effort:

The machines proved capable of an output of 160,000 ships' blocks a year with only ten operatives as compared with the 110 men who had previously been employed on block making. They were the first example in the world of a fully mechanized production line and as soon as they were set running they became an object of pilgrimage. . . .[2]

While setting up this famous plant Maudslay attracted Joshua Field into his employment and later into partnership. Field had been a dockyard draughtsman working in General Bentham's office and his gifts were perfectly complementary to those of Maudslay. As Maudslay became better known he moved his business to a larger site at Lambeth where it remained, as Maudslay, Sons and Field, until 1900. From Lambeth came the best of British marine engines from 1814 to 1840 and nearly all those supplied to the navy. Maudslay himself invented two machines of crucial importance: the screw-cutting lathe and a micrometer capable of measuring 1/10,000th of an inch. He was even more important, however, because of the inspiration he gave to others. Field was a Fellow of the Royal Society and President of the Institution of Civil Engineers. Joseph Whitworth was his pupil and James Nasmyth his personal assistant. Richard Roberts had worked for him and so had Joseph Clement, A. C. Kirk and Charles Brown. His career illustrates the story of British engineering from Joseph Bramah to the younger Brunel. It was a fourth generation Maudslay, moreover, who founded the Maudslay Motor Co. of 1903. For a later period the most remarkable career might be that of R. E. Crompton, the engineer who could remember the trenches before Sebastopol but lived to see the beginning of World War II. His career and that of Bramah form the overture, as it were, to the story of the armament kings.

Nineteenth-century competition in arms development can be traced to Napoleon III, 'the patron saint of inventors, promoters and traders in projects from all over the world, especially in the field of mechanical warfare'.[3] Napoleon III was a gunnery enthusiast and the author, indeed, of an artillery manual which was widely used. Behind him, however, stood Joseph-Charles-Paul Bonaparte, the son of Jerome Bonaparte (1822–91), whose interests were naval. As a result of the prince's influence France had in his day the best navy seen there since the time of Colbert. There were eventually four hundred men-of-war, forty of them being of the line and all of them with auxiliary engines. British alarm at this unwelcome situation was expressed by Hans Busk, of Trinity College, Cambridge, who pointed out that Britain's position had become relatively weaker.[4] There was some reaction to the danger to which he and others called attention but the course of events brought France and Britain into alliance against Russia. In the Crimean campaign the allied forces became aware of some new developments in the art of war. In the first place the Russians, who had used shellfire to destroy a Turkish squadron at the Battle of Sinope in 1855 – a feat which had taken about twenty minutes – were using similar ammunition against their English and French opponents. What soon became apparent was that the cannon on either side were primitive compared with the small arms. The evident need was for better guns and more high-powered explosives. But these developments, which could be fairly expected, suggested in turn the need for protection – the need, that is to say, for armour. The effect of shellfire on a wooden ship was established as early as 1824, two years after the French general Paixhans had first proposed the replacement of shot by shell. It was, however, the attack on the Russian fort at Kinburn (17 October 1855) which proved the value of armour. On that occasion the three French armoured vessels, *Dévastation*, *Lave* and *Tonnante*, came under heavy fire but sustained little damage. 'The results of the action have been momentous. On that day was developed the theory that a small number of guns protected by armour are more effective than a greater number without armour; that to protect yourself is more important than to destroy the enemy. . . .'[5]

There had begun a period of competitive development as between guns and armour, the experts too often tending to forget that fire power is itself a form of protection. Whatever the fallacies involved, however, the successive fashions were highly profitable to the armament firms. Palmer Brothers of Jarrow were founded in 1851 and built HMS *Terror* in 1854. Firths turned to armaments in 1852. The Swedish inventor, Alfred Nobel, was producing high explosives for Russia; Du Pont was doing the same for the USA. The vital step, however, was taken by William Armstrong of Newcastle, a lawyer by training who founded an engineering firm in 1847. His factory was at Elswick on Tyneside, two miles from Newcastle, and his first speciality was the construction of hydraulic cranes. When the news came of the Battle of Inkerman (1854) Armstrong was shocked to hear that a hundred and fifty men spent three hours in manhandling two cannon into action. Each 18-pounder weighed over two tons and they had to cover a distance of a mile and a half. Could not a lighter and better gun be evolved from the rifle that was already in use? Armstrong resolved to make a rifled breech-loader with a reduced recoil, able to fire a self-igniting cylindrical shell. His gun was tested and accepted in 1859, fairly beginning the era of the steel-lined Armstrong cannon. In the same year the French arms factory at Le Creusot was founded, and the French produced their armoured warship *La Gloire*, with four and a half inches of wrought iron backed by eighteen inches of teak. To this the British replied with the *Warrior* of 1860. Other ironclads followed and their value was demonstrated in the American Civil War and especially in the duel between the *Monitor* and the *Merrimac*. This was a period of tension between Britain and France, with the Volunteer Movement (moustaches complete) much in evidence and fortifications more fashionable than before or since. The arms manufacturers were very prosperous indeed.

Anglo-French rivalry did much to assist the rise of Prussia, where Bismarck became Minister President to the recently crowned William I in 1862. His was a policy based, as he was the first to admit, on blood and iron: more precisely, perhaps, on manpower and steel. For the steel he turned to Alfred Krupp, of whose career we have already had a glimpse (pages 138–9), a rising industrialist who had so far specialized in railway wheels but had turned to casting steel cannon in about 1859. He provided the rifled breech-loaders which were fired at the Austrians in 1866. The breech mechanism was imperfect and Krupp guns, refused by Napoleon III, were momentarily out of favour. In the war of 1870, however, the Krupp guns, five hundred of them, were decisive in their accuracy, rapidity and range. The French infantry crumpled under artillery fire and so did the fortress of Metz. Paris fell in its turn, lacking the cannon which Napoleon III had refused. After the war Alfred Krupp was swamped with orders from all over the world, increasing his pay-roll from 7,000 to 10,000. 'Railways,' he declared, 'the greatness of Germany, the fall of France, belong to the Steel Age; the Bronze Age is past.'[6] Two facts lent emphasis to this claim. In the first place there was a tremendous demand for steel rails in the USA where the local steel industry had yet to be established. In the second place, the annexed territories of Alsace and Lorraine contained phosphorescent iron ore, now suddenly valuable because of Gilchrist Thomas's discovery of 1875. The Krupp business was more prosperous than ever, the work force numbering 20,000 by 1884. It was, beyond question, the biggest industrial complex in Europe. It had a rival in the firm founded by August Thyssen in 1871 but the importance of Thyssen was a thing of the future. When Alfred Krupp died in 1887 he was the sole proprietor and left his business to Fritz, his only son.

The fate of France should, in theory, have brought relief to Britain, where naval estimates were actually reduced in 1869–78, but the French recovered quickly. Nor had the French navy taken any active part in the war, having virtually no adversary and no role save in convoying French troops from Algeria. The French fleet remained intact, therefore, and might have Russian co-operation. Against such a possible alliance the British would need to arm themselves. One established firm, Palmer of Jarrow, was active from 1870. Other industrialists foresaw their opportunity, particularly those who founded the Naval Construction and Armament Company at Barrow-in-Furness. Headed by the Duke of Devonshire, this company received its first order in 1877. In 1880 the Wallsend shipbuilding firm of Swan, Hunter & Co. was founded. Armstrong & Co. acquired the Low Walker Shipbuilding Yard in 1882 and went on to found the Elswick Yard especially for warship construction. Vickers entered the armament business in 1888 and acquired the Maxim-Nordenfelt Co., parent of what would become the Vickers machine-gun.[7] On the one hand, efforts were being made to manufacture armour which would resist anything; on the other, the object was to produce projectiles which would pierce anything. It was Schneider of Le Creusot who made the first wrought-iron armour. It was no good, however, against the Armstrong cannon, and Schneider turned to steel, which was found to be too brittle. So two Sheffield companies, Cammell & Co. and John Brown & Co., made a compound armour, steel-faced iron, which was popular for some years but was superseded by a new type of steel produced by Schneider in 1881. The answer to this was the armour-piercing shell, developed almost simultaneously by Holtzer in France, by Firth and Vickers in Britain. To frustrate the new projectile came the nickel steel armour plate invented by the American engineer H. A. Harvey in 1891 and manufactured at the Bethlehem Iron and Steel Works. Harvey nickel steel was widely used until Krupps improved on it by a new process. This was also applied, however, to cannon which were thus enabled to use Nobel's new propellant with a picric acid base. Shells of a new design were penetrating armour again by 1894. The technical details are not to the present purpose but it is obvious, even from the barest outline, that the armament firms were in a very profitable business. Those in Britain were further encouraged by the jubilee naval review of 1887, by the Naval Defence Act of 1889 and the launch of the *Royal Sovereign* in 1890. Britannia was still intent on ruling the waves.

At this point British naval superiority was challenged, not by France but by Germany. The classic books on sea power, written by an American, Admiral Mahan, and published in 1890 and 1892, may not have influenced the USA but were to have a profound influence on Britain and, still more, on Germany. The first advocate for a powerful German navy had been old Alfred Krupp whose ideas were first outlined in 1885 stressing the value of gun-boats and smoke screens. He died soon afterwards but Fritz, his heir, was present when the Kiel Canal was opened by Kaiser Wilhelm II in 1895. By the following year Krupp had bought a shipyard at Kiel and was preparing to build the German navy. Its architect was Admiral Von Tirpitz whose appointment led to the Navy Bills of 1898 and 1900. From this time war was more or less inevitable. Britain replied by reaching agreement with Russia and, some years later, with France. Apart from these diplomatic moves there were huge naval estimates from 1896, backed by the vocal support of the Navy League. Armstrong amalgamated with Whitworth the following year and paid a 20 per cent dividend. Cammell paid $17\frac{1}{2}$ per cent and it was claimed, the year after, that armament was the world's most flourishing industry. 'Sheffield lives by the navy, more or less,' said Balfour in 1896. As for Newcastle, half its population of 200,000 was dependent on Armstrong Whitworth by 1897. It was calculated, moreover, that a million people had an interest in the building of warships and that each battleship on the slipway gave employment to two thousand men for from two to three years. The world market for battleships was dominated by the great armament firms of Armstrong, Schneider and Krupp.

Battleship fever was not confined to the great powers but spread to Turkey, to South America, to China and Japan. This was the period of the great arms-selling agents, headed by Sir Basil Zaharoff, inherited by Vickers from Maxim-Nordenfelt but a shareholder, it was said, in Le Creusot. His rivals included Sir Eustace Tennyson D'Eyncourt, cousin of the poet, who represented Armstrong's, and Friedrich Wilhelm von Bulow, ace salesman for Krupp. When agents were competing to supply arms to King Alfonso XII 'almost every Spanish officer above the rank of major was an employee of either Krupp or Vickers'.[8] The latest weapons were supplied to the more prosperous countries like Argentina, the obsolete were good enough for Mexico or China. The speed of build-up was intensified after 1903, as countries entered the arms race which culminated in World War I. This last phase began when France ceased to compete – partly because of the *entente* with Britain – and, more dramatically, with the dawn of the *Dreadnought* battleship. At the insistence of Admiral Sir John Fisher the keel-plate of the revolutionary HMS *Dreadnought* was laid at Portsmouth on 2 October 1905. She was launched on 10 February 1906, and completed in December of that year: a turbine-driven ship of unusual size, mounting ten 12-inch guns and capable of steaming at 21 knots. As every other battleship had become obsolete overnight, the arms race was one for superiority in capital ships, and Britain had a substantial lead at the outset. The armament firms were to be busy as never before.

As for warships, these were supplied by Armstrong's Elswick Yard to Japan, China, the USA, Brazil, Argentine, Chile, Norway, Portugal, Italy, Rumania and Spain. The biggest battleship in the world was ordered from Armstrong's by Brazil. She passed to Turkey before completion but ended as HMS *Agincourt* and was one of Admiral Jellicoe's fleet at the Battle of Jutland.

Battleships were Big Business – but how big? The leading firms were clearly Armstrong and Krupp, followed at a distance by Schneider and Whitworth. Armstrong employed 16,500 men in 1886, over 20,000 by the turn of the century. His reputation rose with the success of his ships and guns in the Russo-Japanese War. His own financial success was at least symbolized by his country house in Northumberland, his philanthropy and the fortune he left when he died. Cragside, as his house was called, took fourteen years to build and was surrounded by 1,700 acres planted with seven million trees. It was the first private residence in Britain to have electricity, a place of high-pitched gables and twisted chimney stacks, adorned internally with oak panelling and pictures by Turner and Millais. To Newcastle he gave his estate of Jesmond Dene and to the city's Royal Infirmary a bequest of £100,000. The local College of Science received such help from him that it was renamed Armstrong College in his memory. He finally bought Bamburgh Castle and transformed it into a well-equipped and endowed convalescent home. There were those who deplored the fact that his keen intelligence was devoted to the science of destruction but they could not deny the facts which proved his generosity. When he died in December 1900, he left a fortune of two millions, proof of his success and proof, too, that his interests had always been more scientific than financial.[9]

Armstrong's works on Tyneside represented the power of Big Business but they were overshadowed by the Krupp complex at Essen. There were two main reasons for this. In the first place he had more competitors in Britain than Krupp had in Germany, his company not being merged with Vickers until 1927. In the second place, old Alfred Krupp had managed to establish the principle that while he could sell arms outside Germany the German government could buy arms only from German factories. So close was the alliance, in fact, between the Hohenzollern and Krupp dynasties that the emperor was thought to be a shareholder in the cannon king's firm. This rumour would seem to have been unfounded, each reigning Krupp being the sole proprietor until the group was broken up in 1968, but the relationship was like nothing known in Britain. To an almost incredible extent the Krupps were allowed a monopoly. Fritz, the heir to Alfred's empire, began with an income of 7,000,000 marks but it rose in time to 21,000,000. By the time of his suicide in 1902 his firm had 63,000 employees. His successor was Bertha Krupp who presently married Gustav von Bohlen und Halbach who headed the group during the dismal period which followed World War I. Shielded by a bewildering complexity of ownership, the Krupp interests shifted to Holland and Sweden, acquiring the Bofors plant in the latter country and three ship-building yards in the former. After open rearmament began the Krupp Konzern's assets rose from 72,962,000 to 237,316,093 marks in value, sales reaching their peak in 1943. Without attempting to follow the Krupp fortunes under Adolf Hitler and in World War II, suffice it to say that Gustav's son, Alfred Krupp von Bohlen, was imprisoned (1948) after conviction at the Nuremberg trials – he was accused of employing slave labour – but was released in 1953 and lived to complete Germany's first nuclear plant. When the European Economic Community was formed in 1959, Krupp seemed destined to play a central role:

Alfred Krupp entered the Common Market as its richest individual and most powerful single industrialist. His Konzern was one of seven member firms in the great customs union with a four-billion-mark turnover, and the only one which was privately owned. He and his satellite Scholtbarone produced half the coal used by the Six, and in theory he could, with a crisp order to Beitz, halt three out of every four ships entering and leaving Rotterdam. . . .[10]

At the peak of his career Alfred was said to be worth $1,120,000,000; nearly a billion and a quarter dollars. He controlled a hundred and twenty factory towns with annual sales of over a billion dollars and he had interests throughout the world. His empire seemed to be the most solidly based and most powerful organization in Europe. Its finances collapsed, nevertheless, in 1967 and he himself died, the last of a dynasty, leaving the vast and ugly Villa Hügel, near Essen, as a monument to what had been the ruling family of the Ruhr.

Over the monuments to the armament kings, over Cragside and the Villa Hügel, over the graves of Schneider and Whitworth, there remains a question mark. Had these men a share in causing the wars from which they profited? Suspicions of this sort were often voiced between 1900 and 1914, France being controlled, it was whispered, by Schneider and Japan by Mitsui. But, as Manchester rightly observes, the rivalries were more sophisticated than that'. They were indeed, Vickers alone having subsidiary or allied companies in Holland, Spain, Italy, Switzerland, Rumania and Turkey. The question of sinister pressure was raised again after World War I and the following words came to be enshrined in the Covenant of the League of Nations (Article VIII): 'The Members of the League agree that the manufacture by private enterprise of munitions and implements of war is open to grave objections.'

This solemn concept led in Britain to the appointment of a Royal Commission in 1935–6, the task of which was to investigate the allegations made on the subject of undue influence and bribery. Attacks were made on the armament firms by Dr Addison and Mr Noel Baker, but the case for the prosecution was finally destroyed by Sir Maurice Hankey. If peacetime arms production were confined to government establishments, how would production be expanded in time of war? That ended the immediate argument but a quantity of literature remained, one book, for example, *Merchants of Death*, being published in London in 1934. The authors, Engelbrecht and Hanighen, had no difficulty in showing that the Du Pont Company controlled the state of Delaware; that the real victor at Omdurman was Sir Hiram

Maxim; that it was Zaharoff who planned the Russian artillery works in the Donetz basin; that Joseph Eugene Schneider was worth 100,000,000 francs at the conclusion of the Franco-Prussian War, and that Britain was the biggest exporter of arms in 1930 with 30.8 per cent of a market to which France contributed only 12.9 per cent and the USA only 11.7 per cent. There is a mass of literature on this topic. What does it prove? It shows that arms manufacturers are as responsible for war as sleeping-tablet vendors are responsible for suicide. The real causes of each war are perfectly well known as are the names of the politicians who fail to prevent it. That armament kings had or have much political influence has yet to be proved. They have always profited from war but what evidence we have shows that they have often regarded its actual outbreak with some dismay. In 1915, for example, the chairman of Armstrong-Vickers bewailed: 'We become a government arsenal under government control.'[11] As for arms manufacturers gaining political power the Chamberlain family seem to provide us with the chief if not the only example. They controlled and represented the Birmingham (of BSA) over a long period and at one time they owned shares in Kynoch to the value of £250,000. But the picture we remember is that of Neville Chamberlain, a ludicrous figure, umbrella in hand, pleading desperately for peace. He may not seem particularly impressive as a national leader – he might seem, rather, at first sight, to provide an appalling example of ineptitude and ignorance. One cannot, however, see him in the guise of a warmonger: whatever the other charges against him, we can at least acquit him of that.

9   Petroleum

The use of oil is at least as old as civilization. From ancient times it has been needed for both lighting and lubrication. There were vegetable oils – olive oil, for example, being used in cooking and cosmetics, linseed oil being used in varnish and paint; there were animal oils – grease for the cart axle and later for the cartridge, wax for the candle and tallow for the lamp. Towards the end of the seventeenth century came train oil, derived from whale blubber and used for carriage lamps and soap making. These oils were all too expensive to use as fuel and they were replaced, as illuminants, by coal gas. From about 1820 onwards city offices, houses and streets were increasingly gaslit and so remained for the rest of the century. Piped supplies from a gas company's plant provided the answer to many urban problems but were of no help to remote townships and farms, least of all in North America where the distance could be immense. It was appropriate, therefore, that the process of distilling oil from coal or shale was discovered in Canada. This product was called kerosene and sold, from 1846, at a dollar per gallon. There was a parallel development in the more remote parts of the British Isles where Dr James Young (1811–83) sold much the same product under the name of paraffin. This was commercially available in Scotland from 1856, some of the profits going to pay for Livingstone's exploration of Africa. The lighting of paraffin lamps was the first step towards the general use of mineral oils.

Kerosene is derived from coal but there are places in the world where mineral oil can be found in liquid form. There are even places where it

comes to the surface providing the raw material for Nebuchadnezzar'
fiery furnace, furnishing an essential element in the Greek Fire c
Byzantium. Mineral oil which thus reaches the surface is scarce an
often (incidentally) unwelcome, an annoyance to folk who are diggin;
for water or salt. The main supplies, however, are deep in the earth an
far beyond the reach of classical or medieval engineers. Granted tha
they could sink a well, they had no engine which could operate a dril
It is natural to ask at this point how the oil comes to be where it is founc
There is no certainty about this but the commonly accepted theory i
that marine plants and animal life collected on the prehistoric sea be
and were there covered by silt and clay, the organic matter being the
transformed by bacteria into petroleum and gas. As the earth's crus
buckled, forming mountains and fissures, some oil accumulations wer
trapped in porous material under cucumber-shaped domes of impervi
ous rock. The early oil discoveries were the result of seepage but promis
ing geological formations can now be located by geophysical method
Certain characteristics of the dome or anticline are vital to the process c
tapping the contents. First, the trapped oil and gas deposits are usuall
under pressure, their expansion prevented by impervious rock. Whe
released, the petroleum will escape with the initial force of the explos
ion. Second, the anticline which holds petroleum may also, at differen
levels, hold both water and gas. Third, the oil and gas can move under
ground so that the well sunk at location A can draw off the oil whic
lies, untapped, below location B. It is also worth remembering that o
deposits are widespread throughout the world, few of them wort
developing except perhaps in time of war. Where the find is of majc
importance it is because the supply is likely to last for some years. It i
finally worth noting that no oilfield, however valuable, will last fo
ever. Each well is thus a wasting asset with a life to be measured i
years rather than in decades. The vendors of petroleum are thus con
stantly looking for new sources of supply, each tending to be le
accessible than the last.

The first oil well, it is generally agreed, was sunk by Edwin Drake a
Titusville, Pennsylvania in 1859. He struck oil at about 70 feet, the we
producing twenty-five barrels a day, selling at $20 a barrel. There wa
a rush of speculators, who sank wells for miles round, four-fifths c
which were dry, although some were wildly profitable.

All the rushes that occurred in the United States, before and since, gold and silver together, were small change compared to the riches that piled up in western Pennsylvania from oil after 1860. Thus the Egbert brothers ... from a thirty-nine acre farm leased in 1859 shared a profit between $8 and $10 million by the mid-sixties. ...

In 1861 came the spectacular development of the 'flowing' wells, gushers geysering above the derricks: driven by subterranean gas. The Empire Well flowed at 2,500 barrels daily; the Davis and Wheelock Well at 1,500 barrels daily, and the Maple Shade Well at 1,000 barrels daily. Production of oil, which was only 650,000 barrels in 1860, rose to 3,056,000 barrels in 1862.[1]

As the oil began to flow, two things became apparent. First, there was much to be done before the oil could be sold to the public. The immediate difficulty was to find the barrels, which simply did not exist, but that was just one aspect of the transportation problem. Then the crude oil had to be distilled – converted, that is to say, into a marketable form. After this had been done it had to be moved again from the oil refinery to the main centres of distribution. The final problem was to sell it for defined purposes, creating a market where there was none, and preventing any disastrous fall in the selling price. Second, it was discovered by research and analysis that crude oil could be broken down into a variety of products, refined petroleum being only one of them, and that (originally) of the least value. The main derivatives of mineral oil include carbon black, methane, ethane, propane, butane, benzene, xylenes and naphthalene – the basic elements in a vast diversity of products such as detergents, plastics, fertilizers, weed killers and nylons. These uses developed slowly and there are, no doubt, many still to come. In the early days, by contrast, the market was merely for kerosene and even for that the demand was not unlimited. During 1860 the price fell to $2 a barrel and then fluctuated so wildly that many investors (including Andrew Carnegie) came to regard oil shares as too speculative an investment. Of the men who drilled for oil more were impoverished than were enriched. More solid were the fortunes of the oil refiners whose factories were established in Pittsburgh, Cleveland and Buffalo. Leader in this group was John D. Rockefeller of Cleveland (1839–1937), whose oil refinery was established in 1863 and became the Standard Oil Company in 1870.

Rockefeller was a Baptist book-keeper whose gifts included a genius for choosing subordinates, selling by-products, reducing costs and raising capital. His aim was to absorb most of the oil refineries into one organization, a company large enough to keep prices steady and drive a hard bargain with the railways. Highly favourable to this plan was the economic depression of 1873 which drove many refineries out of business. Rockefeller bought up one plant after another, gaining a strong position in the industry. This brought him into conflict with the Empire Transportation Company which had acquired (1873) two of the pipeline networks which carried the crude product from the oil-fields to the nearest point on the railway. The war ended with a giant take-over, Standard acquiring all the Empire oil refineries, pipelines and tank cars for $3.4 million. Another war followed, this time with the Tidewater Pipe Company which had established a six-inch pipeline, 100 miles long, between the oilfields and the coast, crossing the Allegheny Mountains at a height of 2,600 feet. When peace was made in 1883, Tidewater had become another Standard subsidiary and Rockefeller's position was now unassailable. By 1879 the Standard Oil Company produced 90 per cent of America's petroleum and three-quarters, in fact, of the world's supply. At the age of fifty John D. Rockefeller was said to be the richest man in the world. In 1916 the *New York Times* stated that he was America's first billionaire and that his oil holdings alone were worth $500,000,000. Even that gives a misleading impression of Standard Oil and Esso, for his associates were also millionaires and much of Rockefeller's money had already been spent on philanthropic projects ranging from higher education to medical research.

Rockefeller got to his position by an almost fanatical sense of mission, by utter ruthlessness in pursuit and by extreme competence in the operation of transport, refining and combining. ... To describe him in the words of his official biographer, Allan Nevins, he was 'careful, patient, cautious, methodical, quick to observe and to learn, grave, pious, aloof, secretive, reticent, inscrutable and taciturn'. The piety is the point. As Rockefeller saw it, the Almighty had chosen him, and nobody else, to be His agent to impose upon mankind the immeasurable benefits of this miraculous new mineral substance which He had put under the earth for the lightening of darkness.[2]

Even after John D. Rockefeller's death, Standard Oil and the Rockefeller Foundation were each to be a power in the land. Nor is

New York's Rockefeller Plaza an insignificant memorial to so tremendous a figure in the world of Big Business.

Standard Oil never had a world monopoly for in 1873 there were
founded the oilfields of Baku in the Caucasus. This area, known in
ancient times for the sacred fires which burnt eternally before Zoro-
astrian shrines, had been ceded to Russia by the Persians in 1813. Little
attempt was made to exploit the oil until the brothers Nobel appeared,
establishing a monopoly in the supply of Caucasus oil to the rest of
Russia. It travelled up the Volga and thereafter by rail. Rival businessmen proposed to build a railway to the Black Sea port of Batum, a
project which was financed by the Paris branch of the Rothschild
family.

With the completion of the railway in 1883 the growth of the Russian oil
industry was incredible, and by 1888 its production was over $2\frac{1}{2}$ million tons a
year. The entire field at Baku covered only a few square miles, instead of being
scattered over a wide area as in Pennsylvania, and the yield from its wells was
infinitely greater than those of the United States.

Some of the more spectacular 'spouters' as the most prolific wells were called,
could throw their oil more than 300 feet into the air, and one of the wells
belonging to the Nobels could produce more than a million gallons a day . . .
nothing could have stood in the way of American oil and Standard would have
dominated Europe as thoroughly as the United States if it had not been for the
arrival of Russian oil. In southern Europe, when a great oil port was established
at Trieste, it took over the lion's share of the market and even as far north as
Britain it sometimes accounted for 30 per cent or more of the country's annual
imports.[3]

For a moment it might have seemed that John D. Rockefeller's
commanding position in the USA would be matched by a Rothschild
dominance of Europe, but the situation altered dramatically in 1901. On
10 January of that year a hole drilled by Patillo Higgins and Anthony F.
Lucas struck oil at 1,160 feet at Spindletop near Beaumont in Texas.
Nothing like it had ever been seen before in the whole world. The oil
poured up in a straight column and with a stupendous roar. The
Hamil brothers, who were working on the derrick at the time, were
flung in the mud. Mrs Lucas, from her home in the town, saw the
column towering in the air twelve miles away. In the fields outside
Beaumont the terrified cattle bolted. . . .[4] As the hysteria gave way to

serious calculation it was discovered that, soberly and truly, Spindle
alone could produce as much oil as the whole of Pennsylvania
could account for half of the nation's total oil output. The Stand
monopoly was finished. In its first year, the original Spindletop v
produced as much oil as all the wells in the eastern states combined.
the following year there were 137 other wells at Spindletop, produc
more oil between them than came from all other sources in the wo:
The great days for Texas had begun, its rapid growth represented
the fact that its bank deposits, $84 million in 1884 (based on ca
raising) had become $246 million by 1914 and $2,500 million by 19
Part of this astonishing growth came from the natural gas deposit:
the Panhandle but the point to note is that the proud Texans kept tl
oil out of Rockefeller's grasp and ended with two giant organization
their own, Texaco and Gulf. Only a few months after oil was strucl
Texas there was a comparable oil boom in Oklahoma where Tulsa •
soon claiming to be the oil capital of the world. Later still came
opening of the Californian oilfields but here the story was different,
Rockefeller moved in, establishing the Standard Oil Company
California alongside the original Standard Oil Company of N
Jersey and the later Standard Oil Companies of Indiana, Ohio and N
York. But Standard was henceforward to have its rivals.

Until about 1900 the oil companies were selling fuel for oil lamps :
lubrication. Then came the invention of the internal combustion engi
the credit for which must be shared between Gottlieb Daimler, K
Benz and F. W. Lanchester. Petrol-driven engines were first patented
1885 and came into use over the following decade. With the inventi
of the motor engine the prospects of the oil industry were transform
Petroleum, originally the least valuable element in mineral oil, was n:
to be a source of power and profit. With oil mostly used, as it had be:
for domestic lighting, there would soon have been an excessive sup]
and a fall in price. The development of the motor car (see chap
fourteen) changed the whole situation, creating a limitless and insatia
market for petroleum or gasoline, petrol or (more simply) gas. 1
foundation of the Ford Motor Company in 1903 marked the beginni
of a new age and one to which an oil supply had become vital. Wh
British inventors played some part in the automobile revolution 1
British reaction to oil, considered as a source of power, was to t:

rather of its use at sea. Could oil supplant coal as the fuel by which warships might be driven? If so there would be a tremendous gain in refuelling time and an even more significant gain in operational range. With the armament race gaining in momentum these questions were bound to be asked. At the same time the comment was also inevitable that Britain herself had no source of supply.

British efforts to find oil began in 1901 when William Knox D'Arcy, an Australian millionaire, obtained a concession to drill for oil in Persia. The point chosen was Chinh Surkh on the road from Baghdad to Teheran, the engineer in charge, G. B. Reynolds. Oil was struck in January 1904 but the well ran dry again. Next year D'Arcy agreed to share the venture with the Burmah Oil Company. After failure on a second site Reynolds moved on to a third location and was on the point of giving up when oil was struck at a depth of 1,180 feet. 'The day was the 26th of May, 1908, and, though we may be sure that not a single schoolboy will find it in his history books, it was in fact one of the most significant dates in world history.'[5]

Reynolds and his crew had discovered the biggest oilfield then known to man. Further drillings confirmed the find and there was formed, in April 1909, the Anglo-Persian Oil Company with Lord Strathcona as chairman. The next task was to build a pipeline from the oilfield to the Persian Gulf, a distance of 130 miles. This was finished by 1911 and the next step was to construct the oil refinery at Abadan, which meant the planning of what would become a town. Finance was lacking to complete the system and by May 1914, the British government had bought a controlling interest in the Anglo-Persian Oil Company and appointed its own directors to represent Britain's interests.

Behind the negotiations which reached this logical conclusion were the potent influences of Lord Fisher and Mr Winston Churchill. Henceforward the Royal Navy would rely upon oil from the Middle East. As early as January 1901, Fisher had reached the conclusion that 'oil fuel will absolutely revolutionize naval strategy'.[6] So it did and this fact underlay the production of oil at Abadan. As Lord Curzon said after the conclusion of World War 1: 'The Allies floated to victory on a sea of oil.' The Turks, going to war on the German side, posed a serious threat to the Persian oilfields but the Persians stood firm and the oil supply was maintained.

Production from the Persian fields grew from 274,000 tons in 1914 to 1,385,000 in 1920. The staff and labour force of Persians (the vast majority), Indians and British increased with the scale of work. To Persia, and more immediately to the province of Khuzistan, the Company's activity brought an infusion of wealth and an example of progress without parallel in the country's history. . . .

In 1915, no less than fourteen anxious and arduous years after the granting of the Concession, the Company balanced its account for the first time and was able soon afterwards to declare a modest dividend.[7]

Essential to the Anglo-Persian Oil Company was its tanker fleet, developed during World War I and entrusted in 1915 to its subsidiary, the British Tanker Company. These early tankers were quite small, from 5,500 tons to 10,000 tons, but there were twenty-five of them by 1919. Under a new concession, agreed after much negotiation in 1933, the Company continued to export oil from Persia for another twenty years, much to the advantage of the Persian treasury.

Not all Middle East oil was to come from Persia and other developments were involved with the career of Marcus Samuel (1853–1927). Marcus's father, of the same name, was a Jewish shopkeeper whose home and place of business, from 1835, fronted on St Katherine's dock in London. His speciality was buying curios from the sailors who came ashore there, the sea shells he thus acquired being subsequently glued to Victorian trinket boxes and sold. Shell boxes, hideous as they may have been, were popular among Victorian ladies and the business prospered. The elder Samuel's business expanded and diversified and he established strong trading links with India, with China and (from 1868) with Japan. After his father's death the younger Marcus, having inherited the business, visited the Far East in 1873 and quickly widened the scope of the family's enterprise. In 1890, after a visit to Batum and Baku, Marcus planned a campaign for selling Caucasian oil in the Far East. The plan depended upon carrying the oil in specially built tankers, laden in bulk to cut the cost of loading and unloading and designed to be acceptable in the Suez Canal. After much argument the Canal authorities agreed to the specification of the bulk tanker *Murex* of 4,000 tons, soon to be followed by five more ships of similar design, all to be built at Sunderland or Newcastle. Bulk carriage of oil implied, however, bulk storage ashore. Standard Oil interests were supreme in the Far Eastern trade and Marcus was attempting to fight his way into what had been a closed market. The question of oil storage ashore gave his giant rivals the chance to oppose his entry in a dozen subtle ways, one being purchase of the suitable sites, another centring upon an appeal to fire regulations. The battle began at Singapore where Samuel's agents bought a site on Freshwater Island (Pulo Bukum) beyond the jurisdiction of the Singapore harbour authorities, a place, moreover, where there would be deep water beside the pier. There was another battle at Bangkok, a third at Batavia, and so the campaign went on to its later phases at Hong Kong, Shanghai and Kobe. All this feverish preparation led up to the first voyage of the *Murex*. She loaded oil at Batum, and passed through the Suez Canal on 24 August 1892. She and the other tankers following her were equipped to clean out their holds with steam and so load a return cargo of sugar, tapioca or rice. The success of this trade was immediate and business improved again when retail sales were made in red tins as contrasted with the Standard tins which were painted in the less popular colour of blue. It came to be realized that some peasants valued the tin more than the oil, the metal being used again to make bird cages, chamber pots, sampan awnings, incense-burners and cuspidors.

The next step in the career of Marcus Samuel was represented by the formation of the Shell Transport and Trading Company in October 1897. Because of the sea-shell business with which the Samuel family began, the tankers – *Murex, Conch, Clam, Volute* and others – all bore the name of a shell. They formed the Shell Line which now became the Shell Company. The emphasis was on transport but Marcus wanted to free his company from its dependence on Russian oil. There began, therefore, a search for oil in south-east Asia, especially in Sumatra and Borneo. Encouraged by a knighthood (August 1898), Sir Marcus pressed on with trial borings in Dutch Borneo. But Borneo was an area where the Dutch themselves were active, one of their companies being the Royal Dutch, managed by J. B. August Kessler whose sales manager, from 1896, was Henri Deterding. Early in 1898 came the dreadful news that the main Royal Dutch oilfield was producing salt water instead of oil. There was panic among the shareholders and Kessler saved the company, with difficulty, by purchasing enough oil from Russia to meet orders until a new supply was found.

At the time of this Royal Dutch crisis the Shell oilfield was productive and Sir Marcus, addressing the first annual general meeting of Shell on 17 August 1899, was optimistic about the future:

It is with great satisfaction that your directors are able to announce that there is every prospect, with reasonable distance, of the company being able to wean themselves from the Russian source of supply, and to obtain their requirements in a larger measure from their own fields in Kutei, where we have spent, up to date, a sum approaching £350,000 in developing the property and in construct-ing a refinery now fast approaching completion, and capable, in full working order, of dealing with about 1,000,000 tons of crude oil per annum.[8]

At the time of this first annual general meeting of Shell stockholders, the future of oil still seemed uncertain. The Royal Navy had not con-verted its ships to oil fuel and Sir John Fisher was alone in realizing that such a conversion must take place. Sir Marcus found consolation, however, in the public road trials held by the Automobile Club (now the AA) in June 1899. Of twenty-five horseless carriages leaving Whitehall Court, no less than eighteen reached Richmond, where the Hon. C. S. Rolls raced a motor-tricycle against a horse. Sir Marcus noticed that the motor spirit used came from Standard Oil tins. He resolved that Shell, which was better and cheaper but known only in Asia, should soon share what he knew to be a growing market. As for himself, Sir Marcus hated motor traffic and, although he had a Mercedes from 1904, he used his carriages for preference almost to the end of his life. Other people, as he realized, took to the automobile more readily.

Shell was still prospering in 1900, the £100 shares quoted at £300. Then, quite suddenly, the price of oil began to fall. The slump was general, stemming from a disastrous harvest in Russia, but Shell was in a peculiarly weak position, holding vast stocks which had been purchased at a relatively high price. As coal prices fell ships reverted to solid fuel and the position was made more serious by a suddenly increased production of oil from Burma. Sensing an opportunity, Standard Oil strengthened its monopoly of distribution in Britain. Royal Dutch suddenly struck a new source of supply in Sumatra, 200,000 gallons a day pouring by pipeline into the Achinese port of Perlak. At this point Kessler died and was succeeded by the energetic and ruthless Deterding. By now the Dutch were employing geologists to make oil drilling a scientific experiment rather than a gambling ven-

ure. Using these methods Deterding proceeded to capture the oil supplies of the Dutch East Indies. For Shell the situation was perilous but at
that instant the Spindletop gusher shot skywards near Beaumont in
Texas (see page 158). Sir Marcus saw his opportunity. Shell had so far
been supplying oil to the oriental world, excluded from the west by
existing monopolies. If this new supply could be directed to Europe in
Shell tankers, the world's shipowners – and above all the Royal Navy –
would turn to oil fuel with a confidence they had so far lacked. It
might be expected, at this juncture, that the Texas oil would be sold to
Standard. But the Texan legislature, with its intense local pride, would
never allow their industry to be captured by an organization based on
New York. The J. M. Guffey Petroleum Company, the Texan firm
which controlled the oilfield (with Mellon backing), reached agreement
with Shell, selling half their total production for the next twenty-one
years. This famous contract solved the problem of supply but not that
of price. To save the situation Sir Marcus had somehow to break into
the European market. He had also to defend himself generally against
Standard, between which organization and Shell there was now a
state of war. For Sir Marcus the year 1902 was shadowed by other
events: the failure of HMS *Agincourt*'s trials with liquid fuel – the result
of using obsolete vaporizers – and the news that the Spindletop gusher
had run dry. To make matters worse, Sir Marcus had become lord
mayor of London, a coveted honour but one which distracted his
attention from a business which was still run on a very personal basis.
The result was a series of complex negotiations which ended in 1904
with Shell virtually taken over by Royal Dutch. In fact both organizations were taken over by holding companies of which Sir Marcus was
chairman, but Royal Dutch held 60 per cent of the shares and Shell
only 40 per cent. Victor in the struggle was the new managing director
of the whole concern, Henri Deterding, a financial genius, though Sir
John Fisher still called Sir Marcus Samuel the Napoleon of oil. He
received a peerage, as Lord Bearsted, in 1921, and died a few years later
in 1927.

In the years which followed the amalgamation of Royal Dutch and
Shell the boom in petroleum was the result of the boom in automobiles.
There were more than a million cars on the roads of the United States
by 1912. Standard supplied American needs and exported largely from

American reserves of oil. Shell was an international concern, by contrast, and it was Deterding's policy to find new supplies in close proximity to new markets. He thus turned to Mexico and even to the USA, but his most important move was his purchase of exploration rights in Venezuela, which later (from 1922) became the largest single oil-exporting country in the world. All available oil was needed because the effect of World War 1 was to build up a tremendous demand. Oil fuel was needed for the Royal Navy, reluctantly converted to its use, and the army had 79,000 cars and trucks before the war came to an end. To these were added tanks and aircraft, all equally dependent upon petroleum. Among the German handicaps was a shortage of oil fuel, their only source being Rumania where the refinery plants had been destroyed before capture. When the war ended the USA was still the largest oil-producing country but world interest was beginning to centre upon the oil possibilities of Iraq. Standard Oil had been split up by legal process as a result of its being found to constitute a monopoly, but a scheme was put forward in 1921 by which the seven principal oil companies – Standard (New Jersey), Standard (New York), Gulf, Texas, Sinclair, Atlantic and Mexican – formed a syndicate for representing American oil interests in the Middle East. This was not an area in which the American companies expected to predominate. It was a field of enterprise in which they expected to share.

The Middle East included the Anglo-Persian oilfields round Abadan but also the potential of Mesopotamia or (nowadays) Iraq. One person particularly interested in that area was Mr Calouste Sarkis Gulbenkian, the clever son of an Armenian merchant in Constantinople, who had taken a degree in civil engineering at King's College in London. He presently became personal assistant to Alexander Mantashoff, a prominent figure in the Russian oil industry, through whose influence he came to London in 1897 as representative of several Russian oil companies. In this capacity he became known to Fred Lane, Marcus Samuel's closest associate, and to Henri Deterding. With Deterding, Shell and the Deutsche Bank, he set up the Turkish Petroleum Company in 1912. When the shares were allotted, following a conference in London, Shell and the Deutsche Bank took 25 per cent each, Anglo-Persian took 50 per cent and Gulbenkian, for his services in negotiation, was given 5 per cent, being thereafter known as Mr Five Per Cent.[9] The events of World War 1 then altered the balance of oil interests considerably. The Russian revolution closed the oilfields of Baku to international trade, cutting off 65 per cent of the world's oil supply. Oil prices had tripled, partly as a result of this, partly because there were now ten million cars and trucks on the roads of the USA. What had been Mesopotamia was now Iraq, and France, another of the victorious allies, had formed its own petroleum company and was anxious to share in the spoils of war. The final result of negotiations between the major companies was the Red Line Agreement of 1927 which assigned the whole Arabian Peninsula, together with Iraq, Syria, Jordan and Turkey, to a jointly-owned international organization which came to be called the Iraq Petroleum Company. On 27 October 1927, at Baba Gurgur near Kirkuk, oil was struck which burst out of the well at the astounding rate of 12,500 tons a day. The IPC was thus firmly established and with it the Gulbenkian fortunes. Oil was available in such plenty that the IPC showed no interest in proposals which were made for further drillings at Bahrain and Kuwait. Frank Holmes obtained the concession at Bahrain and induced Standard Oil of California to take up the option. Oil was struck there in 1932, encouraging Gulf to make a similar experiment at Kuwait. The Kuwait Oil Company was formed for the purpose and registered in London, the general belief being that Kuwait would be about as valuable as Bahrain. That belief was mistaken. Kuwait is all but floating in oil and contains about a sixth of the world's known reserves. A later development was the concession in Saudi Arabia of a favourable lease to the Pacific Western Company, owned by J. Paul Getty, another business man who lost nothing by the bargain.

The story of oil is nothing if not complex, and there is no space here for more than a bare outline of the more striking episodes. This may suffice to prove two essential facts: first, that oil is Big Business and arguably the biggest business of all; second that it is essential to our present civilization and way of life. This is obviously true of our motor-driven world, but oil means far more even than that. The crude oil breaks down to form a score of by-products and these are turned by the chemist into hundreds more. The simpler products range from high-octane aviation fuel to ordinary gasoline, from kerosene to lubricating oil. Production of these will leave behind, unused, such things as asphalt, wax and petroleum coke, substances from which many other products can be made. Oil is essential to industry and as vital to defence. In the light of these facts it is disquieting that the earth's supplies of oil are diminishing and that new discoveries of oil are hardly keeping pace with increasing consumption. It has been calculated that supplies may dwindle by about 1987. Be that as it may, the oil we burn now is at once Big Business in itself, and basic to all other Big Business with which we are concerned.

Chemicals

Chemistry developed late in history because such knowledge as the Greeks had of experimental science or *chimea* developed in second-century Alexandria, passed to Islam and became, by the acquisition of the arabic principle, *al-chimea* or alchemy. Some good work was done at the Baghdad Academy, founded by the caliph Al-Mansour, especially by a ninth-century scholar called Geber or Yeber, and by a later chemist, the great Razi or Rhazes; but the alchemists' main interest was in finding some magical recipe for prolonging life or for turning base metal into gold. When their teaching reached Europe, often in a bad translation, it was doubly suspect as coming from Islam and being obviously inspired by the powers of darkness. Those who indulged in chemical experiment were therefore accused, like Vincent de Beauvais, of sorcery or stoned, like Lulli, by an enraged populace. Early in the thirteenth century emerged such eminent chemists as Albertus Magnus, Roger Bacon and Arnaud de Villeneuve but they faced a mainly hostile environment and Villeneuve's works were burnt by the inquisitors. Paracelsus, born in 1493, fled from his native Basle and Henry Cornelius Agrippa of Nettesheim was imprisoned as a magician. It was a long time before chemistry could free itself from association with the occult and longer still before it came to be recognized by the universities as a subject for serious study. Some knowledge of drugs was needed by the physician but most practical discoveries were made by the craftsman and the industrialist. These, by the middle of the eighteenth century, had done much to improve the technology of textile production, glass-making and soap manufacture.

If any one man can be said to have founded the science, as opposed to the practice of chemistry it would be Robert Boyle (1627–91), who set up his laboratory at Oxford in 1654 and revealed the existence of the elements, forms of matter which cannot be resolved into any other substance. Then came the Frenchman, Antoine Lavoisier (1743–94), who published his most important work, a study of the theory of combustion, in 1777. This topic had baffled others in the past, including Voltaire, but Lavoisier proved that matter, while undergoing chemical changes such as combustion, is itself indestructible. The groundwork of chemical science was later completed by John Dalton (1766–1844), who discovered that each element consists of its own variety of atom, each compound of different atoms in a specific combination capable of definition by a specific formula. These were the basic theories upon which chemistry was to develop as an exact science. Dalton's career is of additional importance in that he became professor of New College, Manchester in 1793, giving 'natural philosophy' an academic status which it had hitherto lacked. The first American chair of chemistry was established at Princeton soon afterwards in 1795, the first incumbent being Dr John Maclean.

If Britain was first in the field, however, with Thomas Thomson's laboratory, founded at Glasgow in 1817, there was to be a more rapid and systematic development of the science in Germany. Justus von Liebig was professor of chemistry at Giessen from 1824 and his methods of instruction were copied by F. Wohler at Göttingen from 1836 and by R. W. Bunsen at Marburg from 1840. Bunsen immortalized himself by the invention of the burner which bears his name and which came to be used in the great laboratories of Berlin, Leipzig and Bonn. When the British College of Chemistry was founded in 1845 it was a German, A. W. Hofman, who planned the laboratories and was persuaded by the Prince Consort to accept the professorship. This institution became the Royal College of Chemistry in 1853. After amalgamation with the Royal School of Mines it became the Royal College of Science in 1890, the Imperial College of Science and Technology in 1907. Oxford and Cambridge lagged behind but Cambridge could boast that the millionaire Henry Cavendish (1731–1810) was at least in residence at Peterhouse and that it was he who analysed the composition of air and water. Cambridge even had a professor of chemistry from 1764 – Richard Watson who later became Bishop of Llandaff, but there is little reason to suppose that his chair was much more than a sinecure. Oxford could boast of Robert Boyle but he was no more of a teacher than Cavendish and as far from establishing any sort of school. There was later a professor of chemistry, Thomas Beddoes (1760–1808), but he disgraced himself by expressing his approval of the French Revolution. One of Germany's advantages at this period lay in the mere number of its thirty-nine universities, corresponding in some measure to the number of its major principalities. There may also have been some merit in the cross-fertilizing system which enabled the German student to begin his studies at one university and graduate finally from another. Whether for these or for some other reason, the German universities retained the lead until World War 1.

The first great step in the development of the chemical industry – as distinct from the science – lay in the synthetic production of alkali. Much of the alkali used came from Canada in the form of potash. It was the loss of Canada which made the French look for an alternative source of supply. Nicolas Leblanc solved the problem in 1791 by treating common salt with sulphuric acid. The resulting sodium sulphate was roasted with limestone and coal, producing soda which was extracted in water and dried by evaporation. The process was soon copied in Britain, notably by James Muspratt in Liverpool. But the production of synthetic alkali created a new demand for sulphuric acid, which came from Saxony and was already in short supply. It was found possible to manufacture the acid by burning a mixture of saltpetre and sulphur over water. The Leblanc process, meanwhile, gave out hydrochloric acid gas as a by-product. It was discovered, however, that chlorine, when passed through potash or over lime, became a bleaching powder, a product of great importance to the cotton industry. Textiles had always been bleached by treatment with buttermilk and exposure to the sun. As spinning and weaving came to be mechanized, however, it became apparent that the space for exposing all the cloth did not exist. Chemical bleaching was the alternative, offering the further advantage that it ruined the stuff, compelling the customer to come back for more. Without bleaching powder the industrial revolution in Britain would have been impossible. The man who provided it was the first big manufacturer of industrial chemicals, Charles Tennant of Glasgow

(1768-1838), who first made bleaching powder in 1799 and set up his factory at St Rollox in 1800. He began to manufacture sulphuric acid three years later and made soda by the Leblanc process from 1825. His works, covering a hundred acres and employing more than a thousand, was soon the largest chemical factory in Europe. The Leblanc process was replaced, however, by a new technique invented by two Belgian brothers, Ernest and Alfred Solvay, and patented in 1861. This led to the establishment of the Dombasle works in France, the works at Winnington, Cheshire, set up by Brunner, Mond & Co., and similar enterprises founded at Whylen in Germany and at Syracuse in the USA. Tennant's supremacy did not last long.

Next in importance to the supply of alkali was the production of dyestuffs. Vegetable dyes had been in general use since Roman times but the industry was revolutionized by the use of derivatives of coal-tar, a by-product of coal gas. From coal-tar comes benzine, nitrobenzine and, finally, aniline. From this W. H. Perkins (1838-1907) dyed silk with a new colour called mauve. This became so popular that other chemists hastened to see what else could be done with aniline, one colour, magenta, being so named in deference to Napoleon III, another, a brown, named, by contrast, after Bismarck. Other synthetic dyes followed, gradually driving the traditional dyes (like indigo and madder) out of the market. Dyeworks founded at this time were later to develop into major chemical factories. There was, for example, the Gillet Group of Lyons, founded in 1830. Then there was Alexander Clavel of Basle whose enterprise founded the firm afterwards known as CIBA. At another dyeworks established in 1863 at Barman, Wuppertal, in Germany, Friedrich Bayer did valuable work for an enterprise which was destined to become the Farbenfabriken Bayer Aktiengesellschaft. Despite the fact that many early discoveries were made in Britain and that important dyeworks were established there, particularly at St Helens, the biggest centres of production were in Germany and Switzerland. It was Adolph von Baeyer who discovered a substitute for indigo and founded, at Mannheim, the Badischs Anilen und Soda Fabrik (BASF) in 1865, which was to be the world's biggest dyestuff factory for the next fifty years. Research into dyestuffs soon developed into research on paint. It was research in this field which finally produced nylon at the Du Pont works in the USA, replacing rayon which had been the first substitute for silk. A parallel development was that of high explosives – originally a by-product of the soap industry – which placed on the market such substances as gun-cotton, lyddite (first effective at the Battle of Omdurman in 1898), and cordite, which became and has remained the standard propellant for use in small arms. High explosives are also important, however, in mining and civil engineering.

Earlier chemical discoveries began with alkali and went on to the uses of sulphuric acid. On the bases of these materials the German chemical industry grew. Its founder was Justus von Liebig (see page 168) who discovered, among other things, how to make beef extract. This was an expensive commodity in Europe but could be produced cheaply in South America where cattle were slaughtered merely for the sake of their hides. An engineer resident in Uruguay, George C. Giebert, studied Liebig's process and set up a factory at Fray Bentos on the Uruguay River, already a centre for the cattle trade. The success of this venture encouraged Giebert to set up a company in Britain (1863) which was to market the extract under the name Oxo. Meat extract was big business but it was, above all, in dyestuffs that the German chemists made themselves supreme. Central to the story was Friedrich Bayer who quickly extended his business to a branch at Albany, New York. From dyestuffs Bayer went on to pharmaceutical products, which meant, first and foremost, the production of aspirin. Next came inorganic pesticides in 1892 and eventually the organo-phosphates which provided some of the insecticides which are still in use. At Ludwigshafen there grew up the industrial complex known as BASF, already mentioned as a source of dyestuffs but destined to become a leading producer of artificial fertilizers. Until 1914 the supremacy of German chemists was generally acknowledged.

One effect of World War I (as we have seen) was to deprive Germany of oil. Another effect was to deprive the allies of dyestuffs and other chemical products. The result was the development of the chemical industries of Britain, the USA and France, ensuring that the Germans would never recover the markets they had lost. In each instance an industry already existed with an adequate supply of enterprise and skill. In each instance it proved capable of rapid expansion under war-time conditions. To take Britain first, the founder of the St Rollox works had eventually been succeeded by his grandson, another Charles Tennant. It was in his time that the amalgamation took place (1900) which established the United Alkali Company, of which Tennant became chairman. He had wide business interests, which extended to banking, and he acquired an important collection of paintings.

The dominant figure in Glasgow was Sir Charles Tennant, created a baronet by Gladstone in 1885, whom we have already met in connection with Nobel's affairs. He was head of the great firm based at St Rollox Works, which since its foundation in 1797 had been a pillar of the heavy chemical industry based on the Leblanc cycle. . . . He was a man of enormous vigour and commanding personality . . . (who) had had a daring and successful career in many fields beyond the range of his family firm, and more was yet to come, including becoming Asquith's father-in-law and begetting a child when he was past eighty.[1]

It was Tennant's daughter, Margot, who married Herbert Asquith in 1894 and assumed a central position in both society and politics. Of her father Margot was to write:

(He) was a man whose vitality, irritability, energy and impressionability amounted to genius. . . . He had a great character, a fine memory and all his instincts charged with almost superhuman vitality, but no one could argue with him. Had the foundation of his character been as unreasonable and unreliable as his temperament, he would have made neither friends nor money; but he was fundamentally sound, ultimately serene and high-minded.

Born a little quicker, more punctual and more alive than other people, he suffered fools not at all. . . .[2]

After the end of World War I the major British chemical firms were four in number: The United Alkali Co. Ltd, Nobel Industries Ltd, Brunner, Mond & Co. Ltd, and the British Dyestuffs Corporation Ltd. The United Alkali Company was the Tennant kingdom and Sir Charles was very much one of the dynasts – fit target for G. K. Chesterton's pen and his reference to the man 'whose host was a Guest but whose landlord was a Tennant'. Nobel Industries had been the British Dynamite Company, founded near Glasgow to exploit Alfred Nobel's patent, with Nobel's help as shareholder and adviser. The works had been established (with good reason) in the remote sandhills at Ardeer on the Forth of Clyde. There the main ingredients, sodium nitrate, glycerine and sulphuric acid, were blended to make what was at first a highly unstable compound. Production began in

1873 and 'blasting gelatine' was soon in demand among civil engineers, the factory becoming the largest of its kind in Europe. In the years before 1914 Nobel Industries had been secretly establishing a virtual monopoly in the supply of cordite. The firm had openly acquired Chilworth Gunpowder but went on to purchase the British Explosives Syndicate, the New Explosives Company and the Cotton Powder Company. The Admiralty and War Office were kept in ignorance of these transactions, which allowed them to think that they could play off one supplier against another, while they were dealing, in fact, mostly with subsidiaries of the same firm.

In the United Kingdom at the outbreak of the Great War Nobel's Explosives was the undisputed head of both branches of the explosives industry: civil and military. The company was aggressive, expansive, and prosperous, though technically not notably inventive. It controlled a group of subsidiaries which, through the Birmingham Metal and Munitions Company, brought it in touch with ... metal industries and ... light engineering.[3]

The story of Brunner, Mond runs parallel with that of Nobel Industries Ltd. John Tomlinson Brunner (1842–1919) was the son of a Swiss teacher who set up his school at Everton, Liverpool. Dr Ludwig Mond, son of a German-Jewish silk merchant of Cassell in Hesse, had learnt chemistry at Cassel Polytechnic but came to Widnes and went into the chemicals industry in 1860. It was the local supply of salt which made Cheshire attractive to industrial chemists; Widnes in Lancashire is close to the same source of supply. Mond and Brunner were both employed by John Hutchinson at his Widnes Alkali factory, where Brunner was chief clerk. Mond met Ernest Solvay (see page 170) in 1872 and acquired from him the British rights in his patent. Armed with this, Brunner and Mond went into partnership, borrowing the money with which to buy up most of the Winnington estate (1873) near Northwick in Cheshire, the destined site for their factory. The vendor was the eccentric Lord Stanley of Alderley, a fervent Muslim but at the same time a strong supporter of the Church of England – especially in Wales. Production at Winnington began in 1874 and the original partnership became Brunner, Mond & Co. Ltd, in 1881. The company's main product was caustic soda, sold mostly to soap manufacturers in Britain and the USA. Among the most important of these was William Hesketh Lever (1851–1925), who entered his father's grocery business at Preston, Lancashire, and was a partner in it by 18⁷ He turned from groceries to soap manufacture in 1885. He gave t trade name 'Sunlight' to a new product which differed from the ev smelling yellow soap which was all the ordinary housewife had ev known. In 1888 he set up his factory on a marshy and unpromising s: on the Cheshire side of the Mersey, a muddy creek which he renam Port Sunlight. His raw materials were palm nuts (turned into vegetal oil) and caustic soda. His success in manufacture, advertising and d tribution was so fantastic that it has become a legend. Having conquer the British market he looked for other markets overseas:

He invaded them like a missionary preaching salvation, with Sunlight soap his gospel. Soap was not merely a cleansing agent but an economic force. It w to William Lever what adventure was to Francis Drake, and salvation John Wesley. Unless we think of Lever in the symbols and language of t merchant adventurer and the religious enthusiast we shall never understand t peculiar mixture of fanaticism and daring which was the mark of this l Elizabethan.[4]

So colourful a character as William Lever was likely to ma enemies and this he did. His first and most spectacular quarrel was wi Lord Northcliffe whose newspaper, the *Daily Mail*, had accused Lev of establishing a monopoly against the public interest. The docume in the case were submitted to one of the most brilliant barristers of t day:

The bunch of documents was so formidable that Mr F. E. Smith fortifi himself with a bottle of champagne and two dozen oysters before sitting up night to measure the injury which Northcliffe had done. When morni dawned in the windows of the Temple, Mr F. E. Smith had made up his mir The laconic opinion he wrote on the brief has become famous: 'There is answer to this action and the damages must be enormous.'[5]

Battle was joined (1907) between Sir Edward Carson and Mr Ruf Isaacs and the result was to prove that F. E. Smith's opinion had be correct

Lever's next battle ended less decisively, his opponents bei Brunner, Mond & Co., his only suppliers of soda ash and caustic soc Brunner, Mond had Lever at a disadvantage in 1907 – the sales Sunlight soap having been reduced by Northcliffe's attack – and th drove a hard bargain, compelling Lever Brothers to take their enti supply from the one firm and preventing them from manufacturing the stuff themselves (as Lever had threatened to do). Although Brunner, Mond were similarly prevented from manufacturing soap the contract was unfavourable to Lever. By 1911, therefore, when his firm was in a stronger financial position (selling margarine as well as soap), he bought at Lymm, Cheshire, a salt-bearing property which would allow him to enter the alkali business as from the termination of the existing contract. Brunner, Mond promptly retaliated by their purchase of Joseph Crosfield & Sons, Ltd, an old-established soap-making firm. They went on to acquire another soap factory – William Gossage & Sons of Widnes – giving them a total output greater, probably, than that of Lever Brothers. There were in this situation all the makings of a trade war which could have been fatal to either protagonist (or both) but attempts were made to reach agreement, attempts which were still in progress when World War 1 began and which continued with growing bitterness until 1924.

Compared with the organizations so far described, the British Dyestuffs Corporation Ltd was the result of a wartime amalgamation. The British dye manufacturers had been of small importance when compared with their rivals in Germany, their annual output of 5,000 tons going only a small way towards providing what was needed in Britain. The Germans produced 135,000 tons a year and even Switzerland made twice as much as Britain. British dyeworks were small, conservative and tied to the needs of the textile industry. The most active firm had been set up in Manchester by Ivan Levinstein, a German Jew, who was succeeded by his son Herbert. Chief rival to Levinstein Ltd was the firm of Read Holliday & Sons Ltd of Huddersfield. These and other companies expanded their business in 1914 but the government decided to supplement their efforts by setting up a publicly-sponsored firm to be called British Dyes Ltd. This company then bought up Read Holliday and transformed it into an organization for producing high explosives, TNT and lyddite. Dye manufacture was thus largely left to Levinstein Ltd, which virtually took over British Dyes in 1918, becoming from this time the British Dyestuffs Corporation Ltd. One of the directors was Sir Harry McGowan who had joined the Levinstein board to represent Nobel's Explosives, who were important shareholders.

World War I did not lead to an immediate transformation of the British chemical industry, least of all in dyestuffs, but it did bring the leading firms into close association with each other under the Ministry of Munitions. Output had expanded – particularly, of course, in explosives – and the importance of the industry was at least symbolized by the career of Sir Alfred Mond who was politically prominent from 1916 to 1923. He came back to his own firm as chairman in 1926. He and others, notably McGowan (now chairman of Nobel Industries) became aware of a revived threat from Germany. The German plants like those on the allied side, had been expanded during the war and were undamaged at its conclusion. BASF had made a great discovery in the synthesis of ammonia and the dyestuff firms had entered a pooling association called IG (later) IG Farbenindustrie. So powerful and technically advanced was this new combination that the British industrialists were seriously alarmed, the more so when an actual merger took place in 1924, BASF taking over Bayer, Agfa and three other leading firms. (This combine was broken up after World War II and Farbenfabriken Bayer re-established in 1951 with 180 laboratories and 78,000 employees, of which total 2,000 can be counted as scientists.) It was McGowan who first suggested the formation of 'a British IG', the details of the final plan being agreed between him and Sir Alfred Mond on board the *Aquitania* during her passage (October 1926) from New York to Southampton. A merger between the four major British groups would create Imperial Chemical Industries Limited, since widely known as ICI, with Mond as chairman and McGowan as deputy. The new giant organization was to have an authorized capital of £65,000,000. Had this merger not taken place, one or other of the major British groups would certainly have made an alliance with IG. The policy actually pursued represented a belated move to exploit what unity remained in the British empire. While this is undoubtedly the fact, however, the British firms had all been exposed to German influence. As for Alfred Mond 'he had desperately sought Englishness, and Englishness had eluded him',[6] his accent remaining German to the end. A more significant aspect of this merger is the trend it illustrates towards forming larger and more impersonal combines to replace the kingdoms created by the earlier dynasts.

The American reaction to World War I was roughly parallel with the British so far as the chemical industry was concerned. But here was another and potent interest which was peculiar, at first, to the USA. The development of the American oil industry had brought in its wake an intensive study of the derivatives obtainable from petroleum or natural gas. Petrochemicals began as substitutes for products derived from more expensive fats and oils, whether animal or vegetable. It soon appeared, however, that petroleum could be turned into other substances: synthetic rubber, for example, resins, plastics and fibre. Much of the investment in these processes came, inevitably, from the oil companies themselves and notably from those based in the USA. Petrochemistry has since developed in other countries. In Britain, for instance, petrochemical plants at Carrington and Stanlow have been set up which are to produce polyethylene, polypropylene, polystyrene and benzene. These belong to Shell, but BP Chemicals has a similar project at Raglan Bay for the production of polyvinyl chloride, ethanol and vinyl acetate. ICI has developed similar plants at Wilton and North Tees. Other companies have set up plants at Grangemouth, Ellesmere Port and Fawley, their products to include butyl rubber and bakelite. Nearly all these recent developments trace their origin to the USA, where most of these petrochemical products were invented. There can be no doubt that the chemical industry has been transformed in many of its branches by the introduction of oil derivatives. It is also clear that this process was hastened by World War II, especially as a result of the Japanese occupation of territories which had been the world's chief source of natural rubber. The Germans were equally deprived of rubber, and from an earlier period, but they, unlike their opponents, had no oil to use as the raw material in synthetic rubber plants. They were ill-supplied for fighting a twentieth-century war.

The effect of both world wars was to exclude German chemicals from America, at first by the British blockade and later through the USA's entry into the war. It was during World War I that the sequel to this exclusion was most dramatic. There was immediate concern over the shortage of some pharmaceutical products like Salvarsan, used in the treatment of syphilis, and a vigorous effort followed to develop the US chemical industry. Output and profits began to soar and the sales revenue of one group, Abbott Laboratories, rose from $664,000 in 1916 to $904,000 in 1917, to $1,259,000 in 1918 and $1,468,000 in the following year.[7] A drastic reconstruction of the industry took place. By 1920 the field was led by two giant corporations, Allied Chemicals and the older Du Pont. Allied was formed in that year by a merger of five existing firms, one of them the Solvay Process Company. Its assets were given at that time as $282,743,047 – more than the capital of ICI when first formed – but Brunner, Mond, with 20 per cent of the shares, were, in fact, the largest shareholders. Du Pont's assets were valued at $253,359,871 and included, from 1918, a 25 per cent share in the capital of General Motors. The great expansion of Du Pont took place between 1901 and 1907, when some sixty other companies were absorbed. It was at this point that the corporation was taken to court for violation of the Sherman Anti-Trust Act. It took five years to find the corporation guilty and this was but one of a series of anti-trust suits against Du Pont, all more or less futile. The Du Ponts were a numerous and resolute tribe and were still deeply entrenched at the end of the campaign, having made millions, indeed, while it continued.

The manufacture of heavy chemicals can be very big business. Another business has grown up, however, that of the supply to the public of drugs, toiletries and cosmetics, which is on a scale too vast to be ignored. One firm in this field has already been mentioned, Lever Brothers, founded by Lord Leverhulme and now known as Unilever, which is firmly established in Britain and the Netherlands. Unilever comprises Lever Brothers, makers of soap and margarine, the Macfisheries retail chain, added by Lord Leverhulme in 1922, and Walls, a company which originally manufactured only sausages and pies but went into the icecream business at the time of the merger. When Lever Brothers merged with the Margarine Union in 1929 – the Union itself a merger of two Dutch firms, founded respectively by Anton Jurgens and Simon Van der Bergh – the combined group became Unilever Ltd of London and Unilever NV of Rotterdam. Other factories in the Unilever group manufacture such things as paper, plastics, detergents, adhesives and packaging.

Some firms have remained in the pharmaceutical business, Burroughs, Wellcome & Co, for example. Its founder was Henry Solomon Wellcome, born in Wisconsin in 1853. The company was established in 1880 and had immediate success, branches being opened throughout the world. The Wellcome Research Laboratories were set up in 1896

d the whole business ended as the property of the Wellcome Founda-
on. The Abbott Laboratories of North Chicago were established as a
isiness by Dr Wallace Calvin Abbott in 1888 and now ranks among
e larger concerns in the drug industry. The manufacture of medicines
not concentrated in the USA, however, among a few big combines
it is shared by well over a thousand companies. There is a greater
easure of concentration in Britain where Glaxo and the Beecham
roup represent very big business indeed.

Thomas Beecham (1820–1907) was the owner, from 1847, of a
iemist's shop in Wigan. In the same year he patented a laxative pill
hich he advertised under the slogan 'Worth a guinea a box'.
eecham's gospel as a business man concentrated upon the virtue of
xatives (a Victorian obsession), upon the need to advertise and upon,
1ally, the mechanization of the plant. He made a fortune of £86,000,
s pills reaching their widest market in about 1913. His son, Joseph,
as so interested in music that he bought the Royal Opera House at
'ovent Garden and his son, Sir Thomas Beecham, was interested in
othing else. The whole firm, Covent Garden included, was acquired
y Philip Hill in 1924 and began a rapid process of expansion. The
:quisition of Maclean's toothpaste in 1938 was followed by the pur-
1ase of Lucozade, Eno's Fruit Salts and Brylcream. Later purchases
lded Ribena to the group (1955), Horlicks – remedy for 'night
arvation' – in 1969, and the Fischer & Fischer products, Badedas foam
ath essence and UHU adhesive, in 1970. Although the big profits had
ome from toothpaste, Lucozade and Brylcream (the last sold widely
1 the USA) the group founded its own laboratories and began its
:search programme in 1943. This enabled Beecham's to play a part in
ie development of antibiotics and semi-synthetic penicillin. Much of
1e credit for this success story went to Leslie Lazell who set aside the
1oney for research and inspired the effort since put into analgesics,
1ti-depressants and tranquillizers. The parallel story in the USA is that
f Pfizer, founded by two German immigrants (Charles Pfizer and
:harles Erhart) in 1848. From keeping a chemist's shop in Brooklyn
1ey went on to manufacture iodine and citric acid. The business
ourished under John Anderson and the founders' descendents whose
ig opportunity came in 1941 with the discovery of penicillin. The
roblem was to produce it in quantity and this the Pfizer Laboratory

managed to solve in 1944. The same organization went on to produce Terramycin, using its own brand name throughout the world. By 1965 the group, with 32,000 employees, recorded a world sales total of $500 million.

It is difficult, in practice, for the most scientific firm to avoid having some side interest in cosmetics and other consumer products. Pfizer acquired Coty perfumes and even Unilever manufactures deodorants. In the same way the enterprise of Mr Jesse Boot did not stop at producing the goods a Pure Drug company might be expected to market. From a modest beginning in Nottingham the Boot retail chain spread over Britain, so diversifying its products that the pharmaceutical business now forms only one, and that not the largest, branch. At the height of his success Mr Boot sold his whole business to an American syndicate, eventually using much of the money to found the University of Nottingham. When the Stock Market collapsed in 1929, marking the beginning of the great trade depression, 'Boots the Chemist' was bought back by a British syndicate headed by Mr Reginald McKenna, a former chancellor of the exchequer. But Boots has only a share of the retail trade in cosmetics, since it is a competitive market in which many firms have an interest. Pond were the makers of vaseline, for example, the destined base for face creams and lotions, and the Pond Extract Company was thus given a lead in the cosmetic business which has since become a multi-million dollar industry. But the profits in the patent medicine business are not to be despised, nor for that matter those from the provision of 'ethical' (i.e. prescribed) remedies. The business centred, of course, in the USA where the pharmaceutical industry is seven times larger than the British and spends thirteen times as much on experiment and sales promotion. A chief result of setting up the National Health Service in 1948 was to swamp Britain with American drugs.

Every second bottle of medicine or packet of tablets or capsule of pills handed over the chemist's counter is American. Fifty per cent of the Health Service prescriptions are for American-owned drugs. Six of the top ten companies supplying the NHS are American (two of the remainder are Swiss). . . . The average profit on capital employed by eight American drug subsidiaries operating in the UK was 72.8 per cent. In a single case it was as high as 184 per cent.[8]

These developments relate, of course, to a recent period of history. The age of the chemical dynast ended long before the National Health Service was more than a dream and still longer before it became a nightmare. With the death, perhaps, of Lord Leverhulme (1925) the story enters a different and more purely technological phase.

11 Rubber

'I have seen a substance', wrote Dr Joseph Priestley in 1770, 'excellently adapted to the purpose of wiping from paper the mark of a black lead-pencil.' This was indiarubber: 'rubber' because it was used to rub out pencil marks and 'india' because it mostly came from the West Indies or Amazonia where it 'wept' out of the *hevea* or 'weeping tree'. The *hevea* grew wild in the jungle as did the similar *ficus elastica* of Sumatra. Rubber was, then, generally known to eighteenth-century scientists but they could make little use of it. The fact was that it was too suscept-ible to changes in temperature. Subjected to heat, even that of the sun, it became sticky; subjected to cold it became hard as a board. The stuff was almost useless until some means could be found of stabilizing it. This problem was still unsolved when Thomas Hancock was born in about 1796 and Charles Goodyear in 1800. To these two men, and to Charles Macintosh, the rubber industry was to owe its inception.

In about 1815 Thomas Hancock came to London from his native Wiltshire and set up in business as a coach builder. It is not clear why he chose to experiment with rubber, but he discovered that fragments of rubber will unite if minced up in a 'masticator' at a temperature of up to 300°F (150°C) and thereafter passed through rollers to produce a sheet or block. Contemporary with Hancock was Charles Macintosh, a Glasgow dyer, whose shop nearly adjoined the local gasworks. Trying to find a use for the by-products of coal gas, which were almost given away, he succeeded in producing naphtha, for which at first there was no obvious use. He discovered, however, that it was a solvent of rubber and promptly took out a patent for waterproofing fabrics with rubber which had been so dissolved. He established a factory near Glasgow which was soon swamped with orders for the 'Macintosh' textiles by which his name has been immortalized. Gasworks were not confined to Glasgow and naphtha was as cheaply available to Hancock in London as to Macintosh in Scotland. Under licence from Macintosh, therefore, and adding turpentine to the naphtha, Hancock began to manufacture a wider range of products, including the morocco-covered air cushions upon which King George IV reclined during his last illness. Hancock and Macintosh eventually formed a partnership upon which the future industry (in Britain) was to be based. In point of fact, however, the main problem remained unsolved: the rubber was still unstable. What would pass muster in industrial Britain, with little sun at the best of times and what there was now obscured by smoke and soot, was useless in Philadelphia or Boston. The Americans were compelled by their climate to develop a fabric to which their customers would not adhere.

Among the Americans working on rubber the genius turned out to be Charles Goodyear, of whom it was said: 'If you meet a man who has on an India-rubber cap, stock, coat, vest and shoes, with an India-rubber money purse, without a cent of money in it, it is he ...' Goodyear (1800–1860) had a chequered career. He was jailed more than once as a debtor, but devoted his life from 1832 to the study of rubber. In 1839 he discovered that rubber, if heated with sulphur, changes its nature and becomes firm, strong and stable. His patent held good in the USA but not in Britain, where Hancock had forestalled him and given the process the name 'vulcanization'. His firm was soon marketing vulcanized rubber for use in many forms: as washers, for example, as hose-pipe, tubing, pipe-joints and valves. Other uses multiplied, the most important being in steam engines, gas fittings and telegraphy.

All this time the crude rubber was being shipped from Para in Brazil, British imports rising from 464 cwt in 1830 to 22,000 cwt in 1857 and 129,163 cwt in 1874. Prices rose at the same time, for the supply was limited and the search for jungle trees must take the Brazilian tapper further and further from the nearest means of transport. The question was naturally asked whether rubber could not be made a plantation crop, planted where it would be accessible. As a first step Mr Henry Wickham obtained 70,000 rubber seeds from Brazil, bringing them to

Kew Gardens in 1876. Plants grown from these were then sent to places whose climate seemed suitable for their cultivation. Plants thus reached Singapore in 1877 and were first tapped there in 1889. There was no rush to plant the *hevea* nevertheless, for such local planters as there were had already planted coffee. They were working on a small scale in any case, for the world supply of coffee – like that of rubber – came mostly from Brazil. Having begun to trade in 1835–40, the Brazilians were exporting, by 1870, some three million sacks of coffee a year, aided by the employment of negro slaves. The sacks, shipped from Santos near San Paulo, were unblushingly labelled 'Mocha', 'Java', 'Martinique', or 'Bourbon', thus fetching a slightly better price. An apparent threat to this trade was the movement for the abolition of negro slavery which led to the slaves (107,000 of them) being freed in 1886. The Brazilians met the expected crisis by encouraging the immigration of 900,000 Italian peasants, some of the best workers in the world. The effect was to increase the average annual crop, 3.5 million sacks in 1870–75, to 12.5 million sacks in 1900–05. Efforts to restrain further planting were made too late and the moment came in 1906–7 when 20 million sacks of coffee were thrust upon a world which consumed only 17 million sacks annually, seven-tenths of the current requirement being already on offer and a surplus still on hand from 1901–2. The bottom fell out of the market. Nor did the fall in price have any appreciable effect in swelling the demand, for coffee is not like that – or not, anyway, beyond a certain point. People who prefer tea do not start to drink coffee just because of a fall in price. With a world surplus of the stuff the Malayan coffee planters – who hardly knew what had hit them – went out of business. The time had come to plant rubber instead.

The fact was, as we have seen, that the demand for rubber was rising as further uses for it were found. One important use was in making solid tyres for horsed vehicles. This business was entered by Harvey S. Firestone who took over an old run-down rubber factory in Chicago and had one man to assist him in the work. He bought the rubber in strips, cut it to size and fitted it on the steel rim of wheels, cementing the ends together. His invested capital amounted to $500 and he sold a set of tyres for about $40, using materials that had cost $14. Solid tyres were also being manufactured at this period for the penny-farthing bicyle (with a thirty-inch or sixty-four-inch wheel) which enjoyed a precarious popularity between 1870 and 1890. It was a machine for the bold and athletic and it began to be superseded by the smaller 'safety' bicycle first marketed in 1883. The pneumatic tyre was invented soon afterwards by Mr John Boyd Dunlop and manufactured at Belfast from 1890 onwards. The pneumatic tyre was almost universal by about 1894, the year in which the free wheel was perfected. The result of all this technical progress was a bicycle fashion which began in the USA in 1892 and spread to England in 1894. The Royal Cycle Repository and Riding School (Euston Road) flourished in the London of 1895 and was even visited by royalty. During the Season of that year ladies of fashion were to be seen cycling in Battersea Park, which they reached and left by carriage. The fashion passed but the bicycle did not. There were sixty million bicycles in use by 1943 and there must be many more today with new markets opening where roads improve. All are fitted with pneumatic inner and outer tubes and all contribute to the world demand for rubber. The pneumatic tyre was passed on to the horseless carriage or automobile but that will be the subject of a chapter to itself. For the immediate purpose, the salient fact is that rubber, which sold for 2s 10½d a pound in 1871, was priced at 3s 10d in 1901, 4s 6½d in 1904 and 6s 5½d in 1905. There were some wild fluctuations after that but the price reached 7s 0¼d in 1909 and 6s 9¼d in the boom year of 1910.

In following the further history of the rubber industry there are two separate aspects to consider. The rubber had to be grown in plantations established for the purpose. Shipped to Europe or the USA, it had then to be manufactured into the goods for which a demand had been created. Big Business was involved in both of these processes, but particularly in the second and final stage. Even the early planters, however, made fortunes which were not to be despised. Their success was conditioned by the fact that a rubber tree takes about five years to reach maturity. Only those who had planted rubber in 1895–1900 were in time to make big profits in 1905; only those who had planted by 1905 were placed to make big profits in 1910. So far as Malaya was concerned the first to plant rubber extensively would seem to have been R. C. M. and D. C. P. Kyndersley, W. W. Bailey, T. Heslop Hill, H. C. Rendle, C. Baxendale and a Chinese planter, Tan Chay Yan. A sort of primacy among the early planters belongs, however, to W. W. ('Tim') Bailey, who is thought to have made the biggest fortune that any working planter was ever able to accumulate. He retired in 1910 to breed horses near Limerick and won the Gold Cup at Ascot with his famous horse, Bachelor's Double. One of his estates, Seaport, was named after another of his racehorses. But Bailey was exceptional. Of the others who made money most of them probably lost it again. The difficulty in gambling is to know when to stop.

Rubber planting spread rapidly in the Malay states. The planters and their immediate assistants were British, their supervisors often Eurasian, their office and factory staff Chinese, their drivers Malay and their tappers mainly Tamil. Planting was not Big Business in the true sense but it was soon too big for the individual planter. The estates were sold to companies formed for the purpose, more rubber being planted as the railway lines were laid. The crop was highly profitable, especially for companies which existed before the boom began. Linggi Plantation, for example, had eight different estates in Negri Sembilan, 2,306 people on its pay-roll, and paid dividends on the following scale: 1908 – 60 per cent; 1909 – 165 per cent; 1910 – 237 per cent; 1911 – $131\frac{1}{4}$ per cent.

But Negri, with 17,656 acres all told, was far behind Perak and Selangor, the former state having 46,167 acres of rubber by 1907 and the latter having no less than 61,552. Rubber prices sagged in 1907 but soared again in the second rubber boom of 1910. Some shares stood by then at a premium of 600 per cent, 700 per cent or even 1,130 per cent and land values were rising as dramatically. Fortunes were made and as quickly lost but planting went on, rubber first taking the place of other crops like coffee or tapioca and then making inroads on the jungle itself. Malaya was not, incidentally, the only land to be planted with rubber. The same crop was appearing in Ceylon and still larger areas were being planted by the Dutch in Java and Sumatra. Malaya became, however, and has remained a principal source of plantation rubber. It was all the more important to Britain, in that rubber was a commodity which the USA lacked.

Behind the Malayan rubber estates, grouped under the different companies, stood the houses of agency. These were based in Singapore and mostly pre-existed the development of Malaya. Originally trading as merchants, in both import and export, these houses went on to become 'agents and secretaries' to rubber companies that were otherwise controlled by directors in London. Guthrie & Co. are the oldest and among the biggest of these firms. By 1952 their agency extended to nineteen estates covering 96,000 acres. Between the Board and the estate managers there also stood the local adviser, a planter of experience, and the visiting agents, whose tours of inspection were of great importance in the early days when the managers were often new to their work. It was through the house of agency that the planting equipment was supplied and through the same firm that the rubber was marketed. In nearly every instance the board of directors was strengthened by men with local knowledge, usually retired members of the Malayan civil service. Chief of these at one time was Sir William Hood Treacher, but he came to be rivalled by Sir Frank Swettenham. These were the men who interviewed and selected the European staff, recruited in London but often born in Scotland. One way and another the organization was created by which the rubber was planted, grown, tapped, processed, transported, sold and shipped, eventually reaching the factories in Britain and the USA where it would be turned into goods for actual use.

For the story of large-scale rubber manufacture we have to revert to the invention already mentioned (see page 185) of the pneumatic tyre. It was John Boyd Dunlop who in 1888 discovered this method of cushioning a vehicle's wheel. Next year he formed the Pneumatic Tyre and Booth Cycle Agency, a company which made bicycle tyres. A second factory was established at Birmingham in 1900, a centre for bicycle manufacture which was also the scene for some early development of the automobile. From then on the company became the Dunlop Rubber Company Ltd but quickly went on to make the wheels as well as the tyres. To secure its own rubber supplies the company began acquiring Malayan rubber estates, becoming the largest plantation owner by about 1920. It started its own textile factories at Rochdale and in 1916 acquired a three-hundred-acre site on the fringes of Birmingham where the factory complex is now called Fort Dunlop. From tyres the company moved on to golf balls and sports rackets. It merged with the Charles Macintosh group in 1925 and went on to produce the 'Dunlopillo' foam mattress in 1929. World War II deprived the company of its raw materials from the moment when the Japanese invaded south-east Asia, but there was a swift recovery afterwards and a rapid expansion both in Britain and overseas, especially after the merger with George Angus & Co. Ltd, of Newcastle. Dunlop have made synthetic rubber since 1953 in major factories set up at Grangemouth and Hythe. By 1970 the Dunlop directors were controlling a hundred and thirty factories spread over twenty-two countries, and employing 108,000 people of whom 56,000 were in the United Kingdom. They could then claim to be the thirty-ninth largest company outside the USA. In 1971, however, came the merger with the Italian firm of Pirelli, a pooling of assets valued at £343 million and the acquisition of another eighty-five factories and another 77,000 employees. The group, thus enlarged, is one of the largest in the world. It also has important subsidiaries in the USA which have captured a share of the American tyre-replacement business. The Dunlop Tire and Rubber Corporation of Buffalo was in operation long before Dunlop went into the golf ball market, opening a new plant in South Carolina which now produces 1.5 million dozen golf balls a year. Another plant followed in Georgia. Then the Buffalo plant began a new campaign to sell tyres, using the slogan 'Dunlop quality costs no more'. This was successful enough to encourage the group to establish another factory at Huntsville, Alabama. Small compared with the giant combines of USA, the Dunlop factories are holding their share of a highly competitive market.

Dunlop's continental partner was founded in Milan by Giovanni Battista Pirelli in 1872 and moved from electric cables, their original business, to tyres at the turn of the century. As the business expanded the group was reorganized with Pirelli & Co. as the central holding company controlling two main divisions, one comprising the fifty-one factories in Italy, the other (centred on Basle) comprising twenty-eight factories set up in places as remote as Turkey, Peru, Argentina and Brazil. A more recent regrouping (in 1960) has divided the factories into those which are in the EEC and those which are not. The products cover the whole range of production from hoses and conveyor belts to foam rubber goods and tyres. Rubber uses are still multiplying and recent products include adhesives, latex foam and vinyl asbestos floor tiles. Pirelli has been very much a family concern. Albert Pirelli (1882–

1971), son of the founder, president from 1956 to 1965, was succeeded by Leopoldo Pirelli. Alberto Pirelli was a diplomat as well as a business-man, and was prominent in the settlement of reparations and war debts after World War I. He was the first Italian to fly in an aircraft, as Wilbur Wright's passenger in 1908. He was also the first Italian industrialist to grant paid holidays to his workers. He lived to negotiate the alliance with Dunlop and to see the beneficial results of this move. Sir Reay Geddes, first chairman of Dunlop-Pirelli, pointed out at the time of the merger that one advantage of pooling resources was that research and development costs could be shared rather than duplicated. As one example of this one might instance the open-air test plant established by Pirelli at Vizzola near Milan, where tyre performance is measured by an elaborate system of instrumentation. To repeat these tests – as applied, say, to a radial ply tyre with a certain tread pattern – would be absurdly wasteful. Research needs to be centralized even where general administration can be dispersed.

While Dunlop's deserve early mention because the pneumatic tyre was a British invention, there are, of course, other and important rubber manufacturers in Britain. Avon, for example, was founded in 1885 and is well known today for its advanced design of radial tyres. But the biggest business in rubber must centre inevitably on the USA. The market there is dominated by the big five companies: Goodyear, Firestone, Goodrich, US and General. Biggest of these is the Goodyear Tire and Rubber Company, founded in 1898 to exploit the vulcaniza-tion process invented, in the USA, by Charles Goodyear (see page 183). The company had its factory at Akron, Ohio, and concentrated on tyres there until 1910 but then added other products to its catalogue. It was the market leader by 1916, one result of its success being to establish Akron as the rubber capital of the USA. Goodyear moved on, however, to make the wheels as well as the tyres, finally acquiring for this purpose a factory at Lansing, Michigan. From 1920 the Goodyear chemists were discovering still wider uses for rubber – as a base, for example, for paint. Later developments led to the production of paper, textiles, vinyl resins and plastics, and World War II hastened the improvement of synthetic rubber. Branches were established all over the world so that Goodyear factories now number over a hundred, with 135,000 employees and a capital value of over $3 billion. Goodyear comes twenty-fifth in *The Times*'s list of leading American companies. It represents, therefore, the biggest of Big Business but there would seem to have been no outstanding personality in its history, no one man responsible for its success. Its story is, to that extent, less dramatic than that of Firestone.

Mention has already been made (page 184) of Harvey S. Firestone, who started his career by making solid rubber tyres in Chicago. He moved to Akron in 1900, founding there the Firestone Tire & Rubber Company with James Christy as president. In describing this momentous event Mr Firestone explained:

I did not want to be president, and in fact did not become president until three years later. I have never cared much about titles – it did not bother me who had the title so long as I ran the company.

I cannot say that the new tire company was particularly welcome in Akron. The big rubber companies thought that there were already enough people making tires, but, at the same time, we were so small that they did not bother their head much about us. . . .[1]

The shift from solid to pneumatic tyres took place in 1904, the year in which Harvey S. Firestone made $71,043 on a capital of $200,000. He had now to begin again, devising new methods to manufacture a new article. When he obtained his first big order his pneumatic-tyre department had a staff of one, his whole factory offering employment to thirty-five. By 1905 he had a hundred and thirty on the payroll, a figure which reached a thousand in 1910, ten thousand in 1917 and 19,800 in 1920. Similarly the $150,000 turnover of 1902 had become $115,000,000, in 1920. Firestone commented afterwards that the financing of this growth was easier than the staffing. 'No one ever solves the labour problem,' was his sad conclusion. This may be true but Firestone managed to remain high in the list of the world's great rubber companies, outclassed only by Goodyear. To Goodyear will belong for ever the proud boast that the first vehicle tracks left on the moon's surface were those made by Goodyear tyres.

The B. F. Goodrich Company was founded by Dr Goodrich at Akron, Ohio in 1870 and there are now Goodrich factories in ten other countries apart from those in the USA. The United States Rubber Company was formed in 1892, an amalgamation of ten smaller firms. Goodrich tyres are mainly manufactured at Detroit, Michigan but the group has a score of other factories, some specializing in rubber chemicals, some in synthetic rubber, some in textiles and others again in artificial leather. The company now has subsidiaries in many other countries and its own rubber plantations in Malaya and elsewhere. There are many other rubber manufacturing companies in the USA, too numerous even to list, but those already mentioned and briefly described are certainly to be classed as Big Business, important in themselves and essential as an adjunct to the motor industry.

In France the rubber industry had its small beginnings in 1803 and 1828 but has a continuous history from 1832. The factory founded in that year by Aristide Barbier and Edouard Daubrée was situated at Clermont-Ferrand and owed its inception to Madame Daubrée who was a niece of Mr C. Macintosh. The business became the property of Barbier's two grandsons, Edouard and André Michelin. Their company was incorporated in 1863 and was well placed to take advantage of the later demand for rubber tyres. The company produced a detachable pneumatic cycle tyre in 1891, a first pneumatic car tyre in 1895, the importance of which development was its contribution to speed. So long as solid rubber tyres were used the automobile was restricted to about twenty miles an hour. Using pneumatic tyres a vehicle could travel at sixty miles an hour, a speed actually reached in 1895. The tyres, moreover, had a possible 'life' of 3,000 miles. They were advertised almost from the outset by a figure destined to become famous throughout the world.

BIBENDUM – THE MICHELIN MAN

Bibendum was born in 1898, the outcome of the creative vision of the two Michelin brothers, who had been struck by the almost human look of a pile of assorted tyres at a motoring exhibition at Lyons.

Since then the figure has been a feature of almost every piece of publicity and literature sponsored or produced by Michelin. Bibendum is adaptable, merely by a change of headgear he can be an English farmer or a Choctaw Indian.

Although habitually jovial he is able to express any emotion. As a baby he looks eminently bonny and, with a little ingenuity, he can even do female impersonations.

The ingenuity of Bibendum was matched from about 1900 by the informative standards of the famous Michelin maps and guides, a typically French contribution to the world of Big Business.

Michelin became and has remained Europe's largest tyre-making organization, concentrating exclusively on tyres and not diversifying its products in the manner of Dunlop and Pirelli. The Compagnie Générale des Etablissements Michelin, otherwise known as Michelin & Cie, made a trading profit of Frs. 90,454,000 in 1968. There was a reorganization, however, in 1971, as a result of which a new holding company was formed under the name 'Participation et Développement Industrielle'. This was to own approximately 53 per cent of Citroën SA shares, its own capital divided between Michelin (51 per cent) and Fiat (49 per cent).

Michelin companies have been set up in other countries both in Europe and Africa, the first British factory being opened at Stoke-on-Trent in 1927. There are now three others, two of them in Northern Ireland and a third, from 1960, at Burnley. Another Michelin factory has been established at Port Harcourt in Nigeria. In these factories, as in the original plant at Clermont-Ferrand, the emphasis has been on massive tyres for commercial vehicles, steel-based radial tyres for heavy trucks and excavators and, from 1966, the first asymmetrical radial tyres for high performance cars.

The largest German firm in the rubber business is the Continental Gummiwerke AG, founded in Hanover in 1871 and partly owned at one time by the B. F. Goodrich Company. Continental absorbed a number of other companies between 1927 and 1935 and it has, in addition, a subsidiary in Spain. Second largest German firm in this industry is the Deutsche Dunlop Gummi Co. AG, founded in 1893. There are other European rubber firms, notably in Holland, and some of their business might be described as big. In any discussion of the growth of the rubber industry one fact emerges as paramount: the motor industry, which is central to the whole of modern life, could never have been established without the help of rubber.

12 Photography

Photography began with a Frenchman, L. J. M. Daguerre, who created the 'daguerrotype' process in 1839. It was based on work done by the French physicist, Joseph Nièpce, work which was paralleled by that of an English inventor, W. H. Fox Talbot. The daguerrotype process was elaborate, expensive and slow. The image was captured on a silvered copper plate and required an exposure of about half an hour. A method was soon found of reducing the time of exposure to 90 seconds, and this discovery enabled an American, Alexander Wolcott to open a photographic portrait studio in New York in 1840. Other developments followed, the most important of which was the intro-duction of the glass plate negative, mass produced in Liverpool from 1878. The next step was the replacement of glass by celluloid, a plastic based on nitrocellulose and camphor. The credit for this (and the profit) went to the American firm of Eastman. The roll-film of 1889 was that firm's monopoly until the end of the century. It was George Eastman, moreover, who produced the Kodak camera in 1888, bringing photo-graphy within reach of the amateur. From that period there has been a vast and growing world market for cameras and films, and although improved lenses from Germany brought competition, Eastman retained an effective lead in what has remained an important industry. Mention must also be made of the enterprising Polaroid Group of Cambridge, Massachusetts, with a $466 million turnover in 1969, which is now in alliance with Eastman Kodak.

Other important manufacturers in this field are Agfa-Gevaert – the

German-Belgian group – and the Xerox Corporation of Rochester, New York. Xerox began as the Haloid Company, founded in 1906 for the manufacture of photographic papers. The photo-copying process known now as Xerography was invented by Chester Carlson in 1938 and marketed by Joe Wilson. The famous 914 photo-copier was first developed in 1957 and placed on the market in 1960. The result is that Xerox has now a $14 million laboratory complex with a research staff of 358. Its annual turnover exceeds $20 million and its future is more than promising. Much of the export business in Xerography is handled by Rank-Xerox in Britain, jointly controlled by Xerox and the Rank Organization.

Apart from ordinary photography the photographic business now developed in two new directions. First the illustrated newspaper emerged, of which the *Daily Graphic* (of 1890) was the first example. Second was the motion picture, exhibited at Paris in 1895. To take these in order: the photographic line-block came first, allowing the reproduction of line drawings, but it was soon followed by the half-tone process which permitted the reproduction of photographs. Photogravure followed and various processes for printing in colour, the eventual result being the illustrated newspaper of today and the magazine in which the pictures predominate. Compulsory primary education produced a wide public for newspapers, which came to represent an important business in themselves. Far more important, however, was the new advertising technique based upon photography. As from about 1900 it became possible to sell goods directly to the public through illustrated and coloured advertisements. The subsequent growth of Big Business has been based, to a large extent, on advertising, especially in the field of consumer goods. Without photography the modern sales campaign would not be possible, and without the sales campaign the manufacture of the goods would not be economic. It would be possible to trace the story of how magazines became advertising media, of how editorial matter came to lose its space if not its importance. This process is a story in itself and beyond the scope of the present work but it is the background to twentieth-century Big Business. For present purposes it is enough to note that photography prompted a new industrial revolution and one that made Big Business possible in the consumer industries.

Where photography became Big Business in itself was in the supply and exhibition of motion pictures. Credit for the invention of the cinematograph should go by rights to Thomas Edison who opened his Kinetoscope Parlor on Broadway, New York, in 1894. He failed to see the importance of his own discovery, however, and the first commercially successful films were produced in Paris and London. (The Derby of 1896 was filmed and the result exhibited that evening in London.) It was in these early days that the standard frequency was adopted of sixteen pictures a second, and the standard gauge of 35 millimetres. The earliest motion pictures were short, flickering and unambitious but a first cinema was opened in Paris at the end of 1895 with an attendance of two thousand each evening. Technically, some of the best work was done by the American, D. W. Griffith (1875–1948), who worked with the Biograph Company from 1908 and did much to establish the accepted techniques – cross-cutting, flashback, fade-in and fade-out. Commercially, the first important step was the formation in the USA of the Motion Pictures Patent Company of 1908. Organized by Jeremiah J. Kennedy, this group attempted to monopolize the new industry in both Europe and America, basing this operation upon an exclusive contract with Eastman Kodak. The Patent Company was soon attacked by two independent exhibitors, Carl Laemmle of Chicago and William Fox of New York, and these were presently joined in opposition by Adolph Zukor. While legal battles were fought over patent rights, the film-makers moved away from New York, finally showing a preference for the sunny and varied landscape of southern California. For the 'independents' the advantages of that region included the distance from the Patent Company's New York headquarters and the proximity of the Mexican border for those under the threat of legal action. Hollywood, a district of Los Angeles from 1910, had a first film studio in 1911 and was the site of a film made by Cecil B. De Mille in 1913. Up to this period there was comparable activity in Europe but the advent of World War 1 brought that to an end, allowing Hollywood to gain and keep a decisive lead. The early American films were short and comic, the best known of them using the acting talents of Mr Charlie Chaplin. The first full-length motion picture was the epic *The Birth of a Nation*, directed by D. W. Griffith, costing no less than $110,000 and exhibited in 1915. Its fantastic success pointed the way to other large-scale productions. These implied a big investment which demanded, in turn, a large organization. Successive mergers reduced major film corporations to a total of eight: the 'Big Five' and the 'Little Three'.

Oldest of the film companies, but never one of the Big Five, was Universal, founded by Carl Laemmle in 1912. It was followed by Paramount in 1915, the result of a merger between Famous Players and Lasky Features. Paramount centred upon the personality of Adolph Zukor but had Cecil B. De Mille as its most notable director and a specialist in biblical epics. William Fox, whose real name was Friedman, founded his studio in 1915 and reached his peak of prosperity in 1929, by which year he also controlled British Gaumont. He was supplanted in 1931, went bankrupt in 1936 and was imprisoned in 1942 for attempting to bribe a federal judge. The Fox Film Corporation was taken over by Twentieth Century Pictures in 1933, which became Twentieth Century-Fox, a corporation headed by Darryl F. Zanuck and Joseph Schenck. The Metro-Goldwyn-Mayer Corporation was formed by a merger in 1918 with Samuel Goldwyn as president. He quit, however, in 1922 and became an independent producer, having no part in the merger of 1924 which was brought about by Marcus Loew. When he died in 1927 MGM had Nicholas Schenk as president. This corporation was known for high-class films starring Clark Gable or Greer Garson, for homely films with Mickey Rooney, and for its outstanding success with *Ben Hur* in 1927. Jack and Sam Warner came to California in 1912 and formed their film company, Warner Brothers, in 1923. They specialized in sharp melodrama and crime stories with tough heroes like Edward G. Robinson and Humphrey Bogart and character actresses like Bette Davis. The brothers remained tenaciously in control and Jack Warner survived long enough to be the producer of *My Fair Lady* in 1964.

Columbia was founded by Harry Cohn in 1924. He, again, was a long-lived monarch, sometimes called King Cohn, who remained president of Columbia until he died in 1958. Columbia, however, was not one of the Big Five.

From 1912 to 1927 was the era of the silent film, an art form so successful that Hollywood came to represent the fourth largest industry in the USA. The effect of World War I was to discourage the nascent film industries of Europe, as we have seen, giving Hollywood an effective lead over the rest of the world. The fullest advantage was taken of this opportunity. The groups originally interested in the business were three: the makers, the distributors and the exhibitors, the folk severally recognizable as manufacturers, merchants and retailers. This pattern was not, however, of long duration. Films were costly to produce and costly to exhibit and the risks of producing a motion picture which no one would want, or owning a chain of cinemas for which no good films were obtainable, were unacceptable. The demand from the outset was for vertical integration. The key figures in the industry were practically all of them East European Jews who began as owners and managers of the halls in which motion pictures were first shown – penny arcades, amusement parks, nickelodeons and vaudeville music-halls. When they moved to Hollywood and entered production they already owned cinema circuits and film exchanges, thus preparing the way for the system by which the big production companies owned their own cinemas and decided what films should be shown. Among the leaders of Hollywood who had this sort of background were William Fox, Sam Katz, Carl Laemmle, Jesse E. Lasky, Marcus Loew, Louis Mayer, Joseph Schenck, Spyros P. Skouras (a lone Greek), Hal B. Wallis, the Warner Brothers and Adolph Zukor. The final picture was of manufacture, distribution and exhibition in the same hands. During the most prosperous periods these motion picture magnates were very wealthy indeed. When Louis Mayer, for example, became production head at MGM's Culver City studio he was for several years the most highly salaried individual in the United States.

It was during the era of the silent screen that the motion picture industry was marked with two characteristics which have proved more or less indelible. The first was the system by which leading players were given 'star' publicity. The motion picture advertisement offered the public the spectacle of A and B (the star players) in C (the title of the film), a drama or comedy featuring D, E and F (feature players) supported by G, H, K, L and M (the supporting cast). Everything possible was done to keep the spotlight on the 'stars' who eventually became a power in the industry. Men and women of 'star' quality were perhaps especially difficult to find in the early days when the acting was soundless. The idea was accepted, at any rate, that the star's talent was unique – which in some instances it clearly must have been. The other legacy of the silent screen was the musical accompaniment. For the unspoken film story was not really silent: each cinema had a pianist and the largest had even an orchestra of sorts, the musicians' task being to follow the action with such noise as might serve to illustrate the theme, add to the excitement or emphasize the suspense. This idea derived from the Victorian music hall in which the film was at first only a minor part of an evening's entertainment. The odd sequel is that the introduction of sound films with a spoken dialogue was unable to shake the established position of the Victorian pianist. Assisted latterly by a full orchestra and choir, he has been given full rein ever since, often to the point of ensuring that the dialogue is inaudible. This may be no great loss but it is interesting nevertheless, that the Victorian conventions (as in filmed swordplay) should so triumphantly survive.

The first stars were Buster Keaton, Charlie Chaplin, Mary Pickford and Douglas Fairbanks. Mary Pickford's contract of 1914 gave her what then seemed a fantastic salary of $104,000 a year. Chaplin (b. 1889) was a music-hall artist who came to the USA from London in 1910 and played in New York. His act was seen by Mack Sennett in 1912 and he was recruited into the Keystone comedies. The essence of his screen character was evolved in an afternoon and he went on to become the leading star of that early period. It was the measure of the stars' importance that he, Mary Pickford and Douglas Fairbanks were able to form their own film corporation, United Artists, in 1919. This move was their response to a threatened $40 million merger of the big studios. The interesting thing about this affair is that the artist with real business sense was 'America's sweetheart', Mary Pickford. As Chaplin complained, 'She understood all the articles of incorporation, the legal discrepancy on page 7, paragraph A, article 27, and coolly referred to the overlap and contradiction in paragraph D, article 24'.[1] Chaplin was no business man and this experience left him disillusioned and sad. His first film with United Artists was *A Woman of Paris* (1923), his second *The Gold Rush* (1925). It was soon apparent, however, that United Artists lacked the security of the chain of cinemas upon which the bigger film companies depended. It remained one of the 'Little Three' and Chaplin himself made only nine films for it and those spread over thirty years. He remained, however, a major figure in the film world and preferred mimed action to dialogue for the whole of his career. He is still, no doubt, one of the wealthiest men in the world.

In 1927 the era of the silent screen came to its end and it is surprising that it should have lasted as long as it did. Thomas Edison, who had invented both the motion picture and the phonograph, had tried to amalgamate them in 1913. Unfortunately for him, any failure to synchronize produces ludicrous results and it was 1925 before the technical problems were nearing solution.

Warner Brothers, then in a critical financial condition, saw the possibilities of the new Western Electric process and decided to gamble everything on it, signing a contract on 25 June 1925. Stanley Watkins of Maxfield's Western Electric sound staff moved a crew and equipment into the old Vitagraph studio in Brooklyn, which then belonged to Warner Brothers. Here experimentation was carried on until most of the more obvious difficulties were ironed out....

... On 6 October 1927, Warners presented the first full length talking picture, *The Jazz Singer*, featuring Al Jolson. This was the picture that sounded the death knell of the silent pictures.[2]

The Jazz Singer was primarily a musical but it included, almost accidentally, some dialogue. The era of the talking picture had begun, reviving the popularity of the cinema but adding enormously to the costs of production. *The Jazz Singer* cost $500,000 to produce but made a gross profit of $2,500,000. At the time of its release there were only about a hundred theatres wired for sound. The remainder of the Warner Brothers theatres (and they controlled 7,500 in all) had to be adapted during the run of this film. Before the run finished Warners (backed by Morgan) had bought control of another 500. The assets of this group, which had been almost insolvent in 1925, came to $16,000,000 in 1928 and $230,000,000 in 1929. Most of the other first-run cinemas were controlled by either Paramount, MGM, Fox or Universal and all these had to re-wire and re-equip at a cost of millions. This successful campaign posed a threat to gramophone and radio interests. Faced with this situation, the GE-RCA (General Electric and Radio Corporation of America) interests, Rockefeller backed, founded Radio-Keith-Orpheum, composed of RCA, American Pathé, and the Keith-Albec-Orpheum theater chain, for the purpose of producing sound pictures.[3]

RKO was the last of the eight major studios and it was created by

Mr Joseph Kennedy in 1929. There were frequent changes in management but a good head of production was finally found in David O.
Selznick, a deserter from Paramount, where films, he complained, were
produced on the assembly line. Selznick later became an independent
producer, in which capacity he was responsible for *Gone with the Wind*
(1939) but this was released through MGM. RKO later allowed Orson
Welles to produce *Citizen Kane*, an acknowledged classic of the screen
and an identifiable portrait of William Randolph Hearst. Of the minor
studios the most important was Republic Pictures, specializing in the
less ambitious type of western (latterly, from 1957, for sale to television).

More than anything else Republic is remembered for the frequent starring
vehicles provided for the Czech skating star Vera Hruba Ralston (runner-up to
Sonja Henie in the 1936 Olympics) whose sole quality off the ice was a sense of
chilly detachment. After declaring their unwavering devotion to her, many a
Republican hero went off to face Indian arrows or Axis artillery, and invariably
with a desperation born of disbelief.[4]

Vera was the wife of the company's president, Herbert Yates – and
forty years his junior, which made the whole situation a disheartening
one for the stockholders.

Separate from the other Hollywood studios was that founded by
Walt Disney, whose medium and market were quite distinct. Disney
was a commercial artist who came to Hollywood in 1923 and went into
the production of cartoon films. His first major success was with his
third Mickey Mouse film in 1928, presented with sound accompaniment. All his early cartoons were short and were intended, like the
news feature, for use before the main film in making up the programme.
His first feature-length cartoon, and his most successful, was *Snow
White and the Seven Dwarfs*, first shown in 1938. Others followed but
without invariable success. As a form of art the cartoon film had two
serious limitations. In the first place, the film was colossally expensive
to make. In the second place, Disney was the only man who could make
it. The first difficulty was overcome by his brother, Roy Disney, who
was the business manager. It was he who more than recovered film
losses by the marketing of clothes and toys with the brand image of
Mickey Mouse and Donald Duck. The second difficulty, a result of
Disney's undoubted genius, was overcome by the establishment of

Disneyland, the amusement park, which could continue to flourish after Walt's death in 1960. Disney's later efforts to blend cartoon and living characters, thus diluting the high-cost part of the production, were never very satisfactory and he turned from them to make nature documentaries for the young. Walt Disney Productions must still be classed as a big and expanding business with a vitality which outlives that of many organizations headed by founders who are still technically alive.

Just as the sound track came to save an industry which had rather slumped in the nineteen-twenties, so the advent of the colour film revived its fortunes again in 1932. Before the effect of novelty wore off completely there was World War II bringing a new demand for escapist entertainment among men and women whose real lives were at once dangerous and dull. For a few wildly profitable years any film would succeed. Following the war, however, came the advent of television, which swept the world in 1946 – and, but for the war, would have done so in 1940. Up to this point there had existed a reliable public which would go to the cinema every week, frequenting the same theatre much as they had once attended their parish church and often without particular concern about the motion picture currently on show. With the coming of television that uncritical public was replaced – but scantily and fitfully replaced – by a public which wanted to see a particular film like *My Fair Lady* or wanted, at least, to be away from home at a particular time. As Samuel Goldwyn asked: 'Who wants to go out and see a bad movie when they can stay at home and see a bad one free on television?' To this the answer was 'Young men and their girlfriends when in search of (relative) privacy'. But even these were mobile enough to prefer one film to another. By this time the big film corporations had practically ceased to make motion pictures at all, their function being merely to lend money and hire out studio facilities to independent producers. These in turn had to cater for special interests and age groups. Their technical advantage over television still lay in the possibilities of colour and, after 1952, in the possibilities of the wide screen and stereo sound. Scope thus remained for lavish musicals and enormous battle scenes, as for stories of sex or horror. The great days, however, were over, and the spectacular profits were a thing of the past except for a handful of stars who owned their own companies or bargained for a share of the takings. Some of these are now very wealthy indeed.

Such have been the fluctuations of the film industry that established wealth has tended to avoid it. There were interventions, as we have seen, by Morgan and Rockefeller but these were no part of the normal scene. There were, however, three millionaires who campaigned in Hollywood and all three represented the biggest of Big Business. These were William Randolph Hearst (1863–1951), Howard Hughes and Joseph Kennedy. Hearst's father, George (1820–91) had made a fortune in mining and became US Senator for California. He left William Randolph the San Francisco *Examiner*. Not content with that, William acquired the New York *Morning Journal* and thirty other daily newspapers, not to mention a number of magazines. He was so important in federal politics that he dreamed at one time of securing nomination as a presidential candidate. He came to Hollywood in 1924, bringing with him his own company, Cosmopolitan Pictures, and his own star (and mistress) Marion Davies, formerly of the Ziegfeld Follies. Hearst was central to Hollywood society for a number of years but his role was to spend money on films, not to make money out of them. Even Charlie Chaplin was rather shocked by Hearst's extravagance, remarking that 'Rockefeller felt the normal burden of money, Pierpont Morgan was imbued with the power of it, but Hearst spent millions nonchalantly ...'[5] He is less interesting, therefore, than Howard Hughes of Texas, a millionaire by inheritance, who first went into films at the age of twenty, his third film winning an Oscar when he was still only twenty-two. There followed *Hell's Angels*, with Jean Harlow, which cost $4,000,000 – it had to be re-shot as a sound picture – and made double that amount. Then, with *Scarface*, a gangster film, he ended his career in motion pictures, at least for the time being, and went into aircraft production. The Hughes Aircraft Company was of great importance during World War II but this did not prevent him from returning suddenly to his film career in 1939. The result, after two years' effort, was a western, *The Outlaw*, in which the lead was played by the then unknown Jane Russell:

... The movie did poorly (at its premiere in a San Francisco cinema) until a sustained attempt by Hughes and his press agent to have the film banned reached its climax in the cinema manager's arrest. He was acquitted after a sensational trial; the public flocked in; Hughes withdrew the picture. Not until 1946 did he finally release it after a further sensational campaign. *The Outlaw* broke box-office records everywhere.[6]

Thus encouraged, Hughes acquired the RKO Radio film company in 1947, concluding the deal by signing a personal cheque for $23 million. He was more interested, however, in Trans-World Airlines, which he formed and controlled, RKO receiving little of his attention until he finally sold it to a television producing company. He then sold his TWA stock for $546.5 million and acquired 30,000 acres of real estate at Las Vegas where his total property was soon valued at a figure in excess of $2,000 millions. From this bare outline it will be apparent that he had only a passing interest in motion pictures. His interventions howed, however, that motion pictures were at one time an attractive investment for even the most powerful financier.

As for Joseph Kennedy (1888–1969), his interests were so widely spread that it would be quite misleading to describe him as a film magnate. He was originally a banker but made his first millions on the Stock Exchange. After World War I he acquired a chain of cinemas in New England, moving on from there to acquire the Film Booking Office of America Inc. in 1927, the first step towards the complicated manoeuvres which finally established the RKO Radio organization in 1929 (see page 199). Although a Harvard graduate, Kennedy had no cultural interest in the cinema. Under his guidance the FBO produced nothing but second-feature cowboy thrillers costing $30,000 each and produced at the rate of one a week. When he sold RKO in 1957 he had made five million dollars on the deal – not a vast sum for a man whose current fortune was estimated by *Fortune* magazine at $250 million. His only other venture into the film industry was when he lost money on a never-completed film called *Queen Kelly* with Gloria Swanson, going on to recoup his losses on another Swanson film called *The Trespasser*. Apart from that one exceptional venture into epic production, he showed no interest in anything but money. That, however, was not to be an aim in itself for his vast fortune was designed to further his political and social ambitions, at first for himself and later for his nine children.[7] His hopes centred initially on young Joe, the brightest of them, who was killed in 1943. John Kennedy was the next candidate for high office, becoming successively congressman, senator and finally president of the United States. What the presidential election cost John Kennedy's father has often been estimated but may never be known finally and accurately.

The motion picture industry has been established in countries other than the USA but not on the same scale. With its English dialogue the American film has access to a large part of the world, including Britain and the British Commonwealth. Motion pictures made in Germany, Japan or France have no such worldwide market but must depend on 'dubbed' interpretation from the outset, not an invariably satisfactory process. Films made in Britain have access, in theory, to the USA, but lack the vast home market in which to recover the costs of production. So the golden era of Hollywood was – and is likely to remain – unique. Some reference to the British film industry is worth making, however, for purposes of comparison. The basic fact is that in Britain, as in the USA, the final power rests with the groups which own or control the cinemas: the Rank Organization and Associated British Cinemas. Until 1958 there were three release systems for first-run motion pictures, but two of them, the Odeon and the Gaumont circuits, were already owned by Rank. The amalgamation of these systems left the industry effectively divided between Rank and ABC. There are one or two local circuits like Granada, and a fair number of independent cinemas, but the first-run theatres, above all in London, are mostly controlled by one combine or the other. There are plenty of small theatres but these are for second-run films and specialized audiences. They have no influence on film production.

Central to the British film industry has been the personality of Joseph Arthur Rank (b. 1888), the nonconformist flour miller. His original business lay with the Riverside Milling Co. Ltd and Rank-Hovis-McDougall Ltd. His approach to the world of cinema was through Religious Films Ltd in 1933, and with his obtaining control of Gaumont British, Ltd, Odeon Cinema Holdings Ltd, Odeon Properties Ltd, Odeon Associated Theatres Ltd and Rank Television and General Trust Ltd. The boom period for British films was from 1944 to 1949. British films were then being made at Elstree, Ealing, Denham and Shepperton, weekly attendance rose from thirty to thirty-five million and the numbers employed in the industry reached a total of 7,700. About 330 cinemas had been destroyed by enemy action but some notable films had been produced, varying from Sir Lawrence Olivier's *Henry V* to *Whisky Galore* and *The Third Man*. At that point (1949), however, the audiences began to dwindle. The fall in receipts continued and the Rank Organization closed seventy-nine cinemas in 1956, the year in which Ealing Studios were sold – significantly – to BBC Television. Thenceforward weekly attendances fell by 17 per cent each year, the total attendances in 1959 being less than a third of the figure for 1949. The future seems to offer only the making of films for television but the Rank Organization is also interested in the idea of the cassette, the film which could be sold to the individual for replaying through a television set.

Neither Rank nor ABC are directly involved in the making of motion pictures. They merely control what films shall be shown of those which exist. The story of film production is much more complicated, involving personalities like Sir Michael Balcon, the Boulting Brothers and John Schlesinger. It is clear, however, that the British film industry has never ranked as Big Business on its production side. The same would be broadly true of France, Germany and Japan. Motion pictures have been a potent medium for advertising and propaganda, a useful tool in education and technical instruction and an adjunct to the much larger tourist industry. They have seemed to verge on Big Business when some mammoth film has been launched like, say, *Cleopatra*. But that sort of epic is the work of a temporary alliance, not of a solid industrial organization. The backers, the producer, the director, the agents and the stars, all have somehow reached agreement on the making of that one film. Their association ends when the film is released or, at latest, when the profits (if any) are shared. It remains to be seen whether any new form of entertainment will arise to take the place of the motion picture. It could be argued that television has done so and that organizations like CBS are in Big Business today. That they are extremely influential is beyond question but the big money is not made by those who devise the programmes – or, even by the entertainers who, more than fleetingly, take part in them. It is Big Business to manufacture the television sets and Big Business again to replace them by others which screen the programme in colour. It will again be Big Business if the video-cassette – a prerecorded programme of sound pictures, probably on hire, to be

screened on a television set by means of a converter – can be manufactured at a price which the public can afford. But television sets, like
high-fidelity record players and radio are the product of another
potent industry, that concerned with the world of electricity and
electronics, which deserves a chapter to itself.

Part III   THE TECHNOCRATS

13   Electricity

The origin of the electrical industry can be traced to Michael Faraday's demonstration of electromagnetic induction before the Royal Society in 1831. As we have seen, however, the earlier uses of electricity were in telegraphy and telephony. There followed the development of electric lighting, due largely to the Edison Electric Light Company in the USA (1878) and the Edison & Swan United Electric Light Company Ltd, founded in Britain in 1883. Electric lights became fairly common after 1880 but their usefulness depended upon the supply of electricity itself and upon the mass production of electric light fittings and bulbs. One of the first power stations was built by Edison himself in Pearl Street, New York (1881). It was also he who marketed the carbon filament lamp. It was natural, therefore, that the leader in this field of manufacture should be the Edison Electric Light Company, which became the Edison General Electric Company of New York. Its chief rival was the Thomson-Houston Electric Company of Lynn, Massachusetts. These two companies amalgamated in 1892, with the blessing of J. P. Morgan, to form the General Electric Company under the presidency of Charles A. Coffin, with its principal factory at Schenectady. In his first annual report Coffin told his stockholders: 'While your Company has about 6,000 customers included in the different departments of its business, the interesting and important development is in the direction of local lighting and railway enterprises.'

Railway enterprises were streetcars for the most part, or tramways as they were called in Britain, each system centred upon a power station driven by water power (where it was available) or by coal or oil (where it was not). Over the next few years most of the bigger cities of the world acquired a streetcar system. London's Metropolitan Electric Tramways, United Tramways and associated companies had thus 123 miles of track by 1913. But supply of electric motors for streetcars was only one aspect of a rapidly expanding business and one which was to penetrate every branch of industry. The General Electric Company is now the largest manufacturer of electric equipment in the USA. It employs 305,165 men and women, has an annual turnover of about $8,448 million and a net income of $278 million after taxes. It has an enormous headquarters on Lexington Avenue, New York, and works through eleven groups with specialities varying from aerospace to domestic appliances, from information systems to television.

Parallel with General Electric is the Westinghouse Electric Corporation, founded by George Westinghouse (1846–1914), the pioneer of the alternating current and of the steam turbine as a source of electric power. He was a prolific inventor and discovered a method of transforming direct into alternating current, the latter being capable of transmission over a greater distance. He founded a company at Pittsburgh in 1886 which finally became the Westinghouse Electric Corporation, worth $200 million and employing nearly 30,000 people at the time of its founder's death. The company today has 160,000 employees and an annual turnover of about four billion dollars. Like General Electric, the Westinghouse Company devotes a part of its efforts to research, seeking to develop mass transit to relieve the world's traffic-choked cities; seeking also to produce abundant fresh water, food and minerals from the seas, and rescue urban centres from the flood of refuse they create. Westinghouse is more internationally-minded than many other American corporations, having founded its own international company in 1919. The Westinghouse World Corporation controls a variety of enterprises which include the manufacture of elevators and heavy electrical equipment in Belgium, transformers in Australia, power equipment in Spain, semi-conductors in France, air conditioners in Italy and lighting products in Venezuela. Westinghouse products are made in eight countries outside the United States and are marketed throughout the world. Chairman of Westinghouse is Mr Donald C. Burnham, who took office in 1963 and initiated the overseas movement of the company's activities from 1965 onwards. Among the more recent acquisitions are plants in Italy, Amsterdam and Belgium.

Level with the USA in the development of their electrical industries were Germany and Britain. Werner von Siemens, of the famous German engineering family, is credited with the invention of the dynamo in 1866. The Berlin Potsdamerplatz was first lit by arc lamps in 1882 and Siemens, now in partnership with Halske, set up in Berlin the first German plant for the manufacture of filament lamps. It had a rival in the German Edison Company but the two merged to form the Allgemeine Elektrizitäz Gesellschaft, known today as AEG-Telefunken. Siemens Aktiengesellschaft (founded 1847) is now the second biggest company in West Germany, with a capital investment of over five thousand million marks, employing 301,000 people, and recording a growth rate of over 12 per cent per year. Within the EEC Siemens has a number of rivals, headed by Brown Boveri of Switzerland, but its relations with AEG-Telefunken are friendly – so much so that three other companies, including Osram Lamps, are jointly controlled. In the telecommunications field Siemens has a rival in ITT-Ericsson of Sweden. This company was founded by Lars Magnus Ericsson who set up a workshop in Stockholm in 1876, and it is to this firm that the world owes the invention in 1956 of the 'all-in-one' telephone instrument in which the speaking device, receiver and dial are combined in one unit. Sweden offers only a small market and much of the Ericsson sales activity has been directed towards France, Italy, Norway and Denmark. The group now comprises more than a hundred companies with a total of about 60,000 employees and annual sales exceeding $600,000,000. Although the telephone is no novelty the number of instruments used in many countries is still quite small so that this is an industry still capable of great expansion. Only in North America has the market been fully exploited.

In Britain the electrical industry owes a great deal to Sebastian Ziani de Ferranti (1864–1930) who was appointed in 1881, by Alexander Siemens, to the Siemens works at Charlton. He was, by 1882, the inventor of a generator more powerful than any hitherto known. He was soon afterwards chief engineer to the London Electric Supply Corporation Ltd, which built, under his direction, an impressive power station at Deptford, able to generate 120,000 hp and to transmit the current over 10,000-volt cables. There were differences of opinion which led to his resignation in 1891, but he went on to design and install street-lighting systems for a number of other cities including Glasgow, Paris and Barcelona. In later life he concentrated on the factory he set up at Hollinwood in Lancashire, where he did valuable work in the development of the turbine generator. The Ferranti Company which he set up in 1882 was incorporated in 1905 and is still in existence, specializing in power transformers, computers and electronic goods. Its chief plants are around Manchester but there are other factories in Scotland, Canada and the USA. In 1967–70 it sold its scientific control instruments division to Hilgers & Watts Ltd and its machine-tool control division to Plessey. Even after these changes Ferranti remains an important firm, with a turnover (1970–71) of over £57 million and 17,274 people on the payroll. The English Electric Company, founded in 1900, is of more recent date, but has since acquired a vast complex of companies and subsidiaries all over the world. With a capital of £295,406,000 and with some 128,000 employees, and with Lord Aldington as chairman, it is a large organization. It later merged, however, with General Electric.

Electricity leads to electronics and this process is well exemplified in the story of the Plessey Company Ltd, the creation of Sir Allen Clark, who joined the firm immediately after World War 1, and who has been described as 'dynamic, human, tough, twinkling and generous'. He was certainly enterprising because the original factory, for making jigs and tools, was little more than a shed situated at Holloway in North London. Early British wireless installations were all made by the Marconi Company (see page 96), which was quite unable to cope with the post-war demand for domestic crystal sets. They passed the orders to Allen Clark who quickly perceived that the radio manufacturers needed to buy ready-made components. Plessey began to supply these parts to the trade, making relatively few sets for sale and those marketed by other firms. The company moved on, inevitably, to television, and to the manufacture of telephone equipment.

Plessey maintained the original concept of service to industry and government. It never sold direct to the consumer but concentrated on serving authorities and manufacturers with just the capacity they needed. This was the main reason that Plessey remained largely unknown to the general public for many years. Allen Clark used to say wryly: 'You take the publicity and I'll take the cash.'

By the time of World War II Plessey, its main factory at Ilford since 1921, had become a very important firm. The effect of the war was to multiply its importance overnight. It was a war in which many of the victories were more technical than tactical. So vital were Plessey components that the main factory was moved into a five-mile section of the Central Line of London's Underground. After the war the various wartime discoveries had to be applied to more peaceful activities, and this absorbed the company's major efforts until 1960, the year in which Plessey took over the Garrard Engineering Company, which had begun with range-finders and ended by manufacturing record players. Within the year Plessey also took over the two main telephone companies in Britain: the Automatic Telephone & Electric Company Ltd (founded at Helsby, Cheshire, in 1884) and Ericsson Telephones Ltd, the British firm exploiting the Ericsson patents at Beeston in Lincolnshire. These mergers were the last achievements of Sir Allen Clark, who died of cancer in 1962, working autocratically to the last. His death was the signal for a boardroom conflict which led to the resignation of three directors and the emergence of Sir Allen's two sons, John and Michael. The immediate vacancies were filled, however, by two ex-Ministers, Lord Kilmuir (as chairman) and Lord Watkinson, together with Field Marshal Lord Harding who was destined to succeed Kilmuir in the chairmanship. John Allen, however, has been chairman since 1970. In 1965 Plessey acquired Decca Radar for £4 million, thus completing their coverage of the whole field of electricity and electronics. This led to a reorganization of the group into four main product divisions: telecommunications, electronics, dynamics and components, each under a managing director and each run as a largely independent concern. The telecommunications division, working mostly for the Post Office, has a turnover of £83 million and provides 46 per cent of the total business. There is still room for expansion in this field but there is greater scope for development in data-processing. Plessey came to public notice for the first time when the company made a £263 million bid, which failed, for English Electric; a move which seems to have driven EE into its merger with GEC. With a net turnover of £179 million and a trading profit of nearly £28 million, with about 60,000 employees, Plessey is a strong contender in a highly competitive field but is still only a quarter the size of GEC. 'In an era when managements want increasingly to be lovable and loved, Plessey wants first and foremost to win and has no sympathy, time or love for losers.'[1]

John Clark has no illusions about expansion. 'To develop at 10 per cent per annum or 15 per cent in this area of technology and competition calls for a massive weight of management effort, continuous and highly professional. It is our objective to achieve such a target. But it isn't easy.'[2]

A comparable story in Europe is that of the Dutch firm of Philips Gloeilampenfabriken of Eindhoven in North Brabant. This Company was founded by Gerard Philips with the object of manufacturing electric light bulbs, but its growth began when Anton Philips joined his brother in running the business in 1895. The first problem was in marketing light bulbs in a world where electric power was scarce and the earlier sales campaign took place in the Ruhr, in Westphalia and Russia. The German firms, AEG and Siemens-Halske, tried to exclude their Dutch competitor but finally reached an agreement with him. It was from Germany and Austria, incidentally, that Philips obtained their glass bulbs, they themselves adding the electrical components. Philips ceased to be a purely family affair in 1912, becoming NV Philips Incandescent Filament Lamp Factories. The first effect of World War I, in which the Netherlands were neutral, was to prompt Philips to set up their own glass factory. The second was to stimulate interest in radio, the transmission of Dutch programmes beginning in 1924. Philips began to manufacture radio components but went on to make radio receiving sets. These were first exhibited at the Utrecht Trade Fair in 1927 and were soon in such demand that the number of Philips' employees rose to ten thousand in that year and to twenty thousand by 1929, some of them daily migrants from Belgium. Subsidiary companies were set up, moreover, in New Zealand, Rumania, Algeria, South Africa, Ireland and India. It was these, incidentally, which were still expanding when the Dutch factories were suffering from the slump of 1930. Recovery followed, leading up to the moment when Anton Philips retired in 1939. When the Netherlands were invaded in

1940 the technical staff of Philips, led by Anton, were moved to England and later to the USA. Recovery and expansion of the business after the war brought the number of employees to 99,000 by 1951 and the annual sales to £116,500,000. This was the year of Anton's death. Since then the company's products have diversified, including the Philishave (dry shaver), television and colour television receiver sets, stereophonic systems, deepfreezers and microwave ovens. By 1970, under the leadership of the founder's son, Fritz Philips, the group had a turnover of £1,750 million, with a prospect, as it seemed, of further expansion. At that point Philips NV ran into financial difficulties due to industrial disputes, overproduction in the USA and a costly attempt to break into the computer business. 'The concern has grown too fast,' Fritz Philips complained, but that was only one aspect of the situation. One has also to understand the nature of the competition.

Plessey and Philips are alike overshadowed by International Business Machines or IBM, an institution in the forefront of modern progress. Awestruck by its scientific reputation we might expect to find that it was founded by white-coated physicists and German-accented mathematicians. Its actual founder was Thomas J. Watson, an American salesman of Scottish-Ulster descent who was born as long ago as 1874, and whose business was done from a waggon or horse-drawn buggy. He became a traveller for the National Cash Register Company in 1896. This meant working for John H. Patterson, the father of modern salesmanship, the man of genius who first proclaimed that the art of selling rests upon motivation, education and technique. At Dayton, Ohio, Watson rose in NCR to become acting sales manager, a post made substantive when he doubled the sales record, marketing a hundred thousand machines in 1910. By 1912 the National Cash Register Company was thought to have a virtual monopoly of the cash register business, having killed most of the opposition by questionable methods. There was a prosecution under the Sherman Anti-trust Act and Patterson, Watson and Joe Rogers were convicted and each sentenced to a year in jail. While their appeal had still to be tried Patterson dismissed the other two. At the age of thirty-nine Watson, who was newly married, had to begin all over again, seeking a new career.

At forty he seemed a failure: disgraced, under jail sentence, with no job, no home, little money. And what success he had achieved in the past was modest for what was the National Cash Register Company compared to giants like US Steel, General Electric, and Standard Oil? And who was a sales manager, however brilliant, compared to men like Rockefeller and Morgan and Ford?[3]

Who indeed? That Patterson had used unfair methods to drive competition out of business is certain. That Watson had implemented Patterson's policy is clear. That they had made enemies in the process is manifest, and their trial and conviction was the result. But Watson was a religious man with a high code of ethics and he had been unhappy about the firm's practices, which were in fact no better or worse than those of other American companies at this period. His own code was very different from Patterson's – and would have been in any case – but the whole episode gave strength to his more puritanical outlook. His standards of conduct were never again in question.

The cash register which Watson had been selling was, after the abacus, the world's first calculating machine. So useful was it to the retailer that it remains in use to this day, improved but not superseded. Its eventual effect was to replace the skilled tradesman by the relatively uneducated shop assistant. The keys, moreover, of the cash register were reminiscent of the piano and – like the typewriter – suggested female rather than male employment. Its implications were more profound than was immediately apparent. It was not, however, the only calculating machine in use. There were typewriters fitted with adding attachments. There was also – and this was more important for the future – the pianola or mechanical piano-player which depended for its effect on holes punched in a roll of paper. Watson was no technician but his experience was with cash registers and Charles R. Flint offered him the presidency of the Computing-Tabulatory-Recording Company, the CTR, a group of small factories with a total of twelve hundred people on the payroll. One company in a tiny and discordant group of dissimilar enterprises was the Tabulating Machine Company. This had been formed to exploit the commercial use of the tabulating machine invented by Herman Hollerith to compile statistics based on the US census of 1890. The essence of his invention was to record information by punching holes in electrically non-conducting material and count the totals by means of mechanically operated electromagnets. The idea was a good one but needed improvement. An effective model, which printed results from a flow of cards, was designed by Clair D.

Lake and was demonstrated in 1919. The company began to progress and Watson, now chairman as well as president, renamed it, choosing the title International Business Machines or IBM.

Inevitably Watson's ideas gave the IBM spirit a religious tone. Company meetings, especially in later years, were usually opened with a prayer, often delivered by the official IBM chaplain, Reverend John V. Cooper, an old NCR salesman, who, to Watson's admiration, had given up a profitable territory for the ministry.[4]

In setting the tone of IBM, Watson laid emphasis on moral character so that no employee's conduct should discredit the organization. Business should never be mixed with alcohol. Following Watson's Episcopalian examples, IBM executives wore dark suits and white (usually stiff) collars. They developed an IBM manner, great ceremony at conventions, and their own anthems and marching songs, one of them with a rousing chorus which ran:

> Leader of our noble cause, his precepts high and true
> Building men in IBM, he's taught us how to do,
> Honor him and follow him, he'll guide us safely through,
> The IBM marches onward.[5]

March on it did but its early progress was slow and there was much competition in the office-equipment industry. When the slump came, however, in 1929, Watson grasped the opportunity to extend his factory and laboratory space. All capacity would soon be needed for the New Deal and the social security legislation of 1935 created a vast problem of accounting on the national scale, a problem which without IBM equipment would have been insoluble. By 1935 Watson was publishing the magazine *Think* as a means of gaining publicity. He had by then the highest salary of anyone in the USA – a thousand dollars a day. By 1940 he had a $50-million turnover and by 1942 it was IBM machines which helped organize the American effort in World War II. As the historians of the company claim, 'IBM machines helped break the Japanese code before the Battle of Midway and predicted the June weather over the English Channel.' It was the war, in fact, which brought IBM into Big Business, tripling its gross income to reach $140 million in 1945. It was, however, the Korean War which brought IBM's 701 computer into worldwide prominence, making electronic data-processing a function of modern society. The company now employs about 260,000 people and has assets of higher value than all the gold in Fort Knox. Its gross income for 1968 reached $6,888,549,209. The £1,000 we should have used (why didn't we?) to buy IBM shares in 1930 would be worth more than £9 million today. Annual computer sales in the USA amount to £5,500 million, of which £3,750 million goes to IBM. Watson handed over the business to his son in 1956 and died soon afterwards of a heart attack. His son resigned the chairmanship in 1971, following a heart attack, and was succeeded by T. Vincent Levison. Another son, Arthur K. Watson, remained chairman of the IBM World Trade Corporation.

Thomas J. Watson's place is secure in the history of business and his achievement compares with that of Henry Ford, Charles Schwab and John D. Rockefeller. But he differed from earlier giants in that IBM never belonged to him. His own fortune was at one time near $100 million – a great deal of which went in charity. So far, however, as IBM was concerned, he was always, in theory, a salaried executive, owning only a small percentage of the stock and holding office only with the shareholders' approval.

It is a peculiarity of IBM that its overseas branches may be financially independent of the parent company. In this way IBM (UK) is in fact a separate enterprise. While this may be so, however, the British IBM, a staggeringly profitable business with 13,000 employees and four subsidiary companies, has absorbed a full share of the Watson tradition. Here, too, is a world of dark-suited executives whose lives are dedicated to the company. Such is the internal discipline, moreover, that no member of a trade union is hired and no trade union can recruit members on IBM premises. The employees' loyalty to the firm is to be absolute and not confined to office hours. The prospects in an expanding enterprise are good, the salaries are above average and the fringe benefits exceptional. The employees are content with their conditions of service and have no good reason to attempt collective bargaining with the management. Nor would it be easy to argue with a manager who had used the company's own computer to establish the median rate for the industry as a whole. But apart from that, IBM have set up their own methods of detecting and dealing with unrest before it becomes vocal. As Vincent Hanna points out:

(IBM) has a communications system which has virtually eliminated the need for collective bargaining or group grievance.

It possesses the resources and the expertise to select and train the sort of men who will identify not only their work goals with the company but their life goals as well. IBM combines the fervour of the old style evangelist (believe in capitalism and the company will sustain you) with the fluid dialectic of the Jesuits. Viewed from any angle it is awesome firepower.[6]

As awesome again is the company's return – nearly 50 per cent – on the capital invested. With profits on this scale it may be supposed that competitors are anxious to share the market. Leading contenders in the USA include Honeywell, but its computer interests are already merged with General Electric. There is also the Addressograph-Multigraph Corporation of Cleveland, Ohio, with 24,600 employees, and many other companies of note. In Britain, for example, the government-aided International Computers Limited (ICL), supplies 45 per cent of the computers sold. In Germany, by contrast, IBM has supplied two-thirds of the computers in use and the German electronics industry has had only a small share of the business. One German group active in this field were Siemens but they relied on collaboration with the American RCA, which afterwards lost interest in computers. Siemens were successful, nevertheless, in their 1970 tender for computerizing traffic flow in central London. The other big German electrical firm, AEG, has been even less successful, its chief product being the TR 440, a £3-million scientific computer of which only thirty-five models have been sold since 1968. AEG has now gone into partnership with Heinz Nixdorf, who heads a company which specializes in visible record computers, the sort of machines used in branch offices of organizations possessing a more elaborate machine at head office. There can be no doubt that there is a big potential market for computers in Europe, especially in chemicals, the oil industry, aviation, engineering, banking and insurance. The opinion is gaining ground that there should be a European computer organization and that nothing more local can hope to compete with IBM. It is significant that Britain, the European country least overshadowed by IBM, still turned to that American giant to provide the equipment for BOAC's computer centre at London Airport. Boadicea – the name given to this centre, meaning British Overseas Airways Digital Information

Computer for Electronic Automation – has proved a great success: ... all of which is very satisfying for BOAC, which plunged into computers in a big way seven years ago. While other airlines held back, it has spent £43 million on Boadicea, which is housed in a low building about 400 yards from where the jets sweep in down one of the flight paths to Heathrow Airport. The five computers, all IBM equipment, are estimated to have saved the Corporation some £69 million in wages and other overheads.

That airline installation is not recent, however, and it is arguable that ICL, the government-supported British firm, is in a stronger position today as the result of a merger (1968) between ICL and English Electric which gave it a 45 per cent share of the market in the United Kingdom. This is partly the result of government contracts in a welfare state, but the company is an active one and likely to play a key part in any European project that may be undertaken. Other companies likely to be involved in any joint effort are the French Compagnie Internationale pour l'Informatique, the Dutch Philips and the German Siemens. Another important group is the Turin firm of Olivetti, founded in 1908 to make typewriters and now employing 73,000 people throughout the world to make all sorts of office machines. Their computer side, nevertheless, is partly owned by General Electric. The USA and Europe, however, are not the only fields for electronic enterprise. In Asia there is a possible rival in Hitachi, which was founded in 1920 as an electrical engineering company and now stands second among the leading groups in Japan.

Apart from computer manufacturers, the world's larger industrial organizations have all become aware of the computer's importance. With the computer come a number of problems, first, in finance, second, in the provision of sufficiently trained technicians and third, in the application of the right machine to the right phases of industrial activity. It cannot be denied, however, that the general tendency of the computer is to strengthen the giant combine against the smaller firm. The computer may cost millions to buy or hire, and, rightly applied, can make or save millions in turn. But all this expenditure and profit is on the large scale and is only justifiable when the scale of operations is large. It is the Big Business, therefore, that is likely to be computerized and this is a trend which we cannot expect to see reversed. It is important to remember, however, that even the biggest organizations will often depend upon a crowd of small firms to supply components; and this is true of the computer industry itself. It would be wrong to think of the most sophisticated business as one in which only the giants can survive.

The other obvious effect of the computer has been to professionalize management. With the computer comes the theory that modern management is a science, that the right decision can be reached mathematically and that the age of the individual genius has passed. According to this theory the great opportunists must follow the merchant princes and robber barons into extinction, leaving the stage to the graduates of the business school. We must also agree, if we accept this theory, that Thomas J. Watson's achievement was to abolish the class of businessman that he himself represented so that none could do again what he had done. Whether this is to be the trend of the future may be matter for argument, but it is not yet the trend of our own time. While we see examples of the family concern in which the son follows the father – and for these we need look no further than Philips, Plessey and IBM itself – we can still see examples of a new industry producing its own leaders, essentially the men who dared when others were holding back. There would seem to be no rational grounds for doubting that this pattern will be repeated and that there is room still for men of originality, courage and flair. Situations change too quickly for the textbook solution to apply for more than a decade. There may well be room for the science of management but there is also room at the top for something else: we have not yet found for it a better word than genius.

14   The Automobile

In the process of forming the mechanized world of today the later steps are represented, as we have seen, by steel, petroleum, rubber and electricity. All these products and processes came together to create the automobile, the central invention and prime influence in our industrialized society. Although some later inventions are more dramatic, more sophisticated and infinitely more scientific, the vehicle on pneumatic tyres, driven by the internal combustion engine, remains essential to our way of life. There are scores of other activities which might seem more significant than the mere driving of a car but they all presuppose a car as our first step towards participation. Without the motor vehicle we should be virtually debarred from church or airfield, from the laboratory or the space rocket, from political office or public acclaim, from love or crime, from burial or war. Whatever the occasion it is the car which brings us to or from the scene of action. The way for its coming was unwittingly prepared by roadmakers who thought only of the waggon or carriage. The cities between which it would travel were, many of them, the creation of the railroad. The methods by which it would be produced were devised for the manufacture of firearms and financed by previously developed systems of stock markets and banks. Its sales were and are promoted by the use of photography and its paintwork reflects all the scientific skill put into chemistry and plastics. Its engine is electrically ignited, its headlamps and interior electrically lit. It is, finally, the symbol and the product of the Biggest Business of all.

For all practical purposes the motor car was the invention of Karl Benz (1844–1929) of Mannheim, who designed, manufactured and drove the first successful car in 1885.

... His predecessors, such as de Rivay, Lenoir, Marcus, Butler, Delamare-Debonneville et Malandin and others, all made highly praiseworthy efforts to build a successful road vehicle propelled by an internal combustion engine, but they all failed, and had none of them been born, the development of the motor-car would not have been retarded in point of time by a single hour, nor in point of development by an inch. Karl Benz succeeded, whereas the efforts of those who came before him led to nothing at all. Save Daimler and one or two experimentalists who achieved nothing, not a hand in Europe was at work on the automobile when Benz was designing his first car.[1]

Karl Benz did more than invent a car. He also founded an organization and a factory which still exist. Contemporary with him was Gottlieb Daimler (1834–1900), a distinguished engineer who worked in close association with Wilhelm Maybach, a designer of great ability. Daimler was originally a gunsmith but studied engineering both in Germany and Britain, working for two years with Armstrong Whitworth, with Robert & Co. in Manchester and in Coventry. After holding various engineering appointments he set up his own workshop at Kaunstadt in 1882. There he made the world's first motor-cycle and the world's first motor-boat. He followed up these successes by building automobiles, his third (of 1889) being more than a motorized horse-carriage. It was exhibited and demonstrated at the Paris World Fair of 1889 with the result that the French manufacturing rights in the Daimler engine were granted to the Parisian firm of Panhard & Levassor. It was Levassor who designed a new type of vehicle in which the engine would be in front of the driver but would transmit its driving energy to the rear axle. A Frenchman Armand Peugeot, developed a car with the engine in the rear, but he relied for the engine itself on Panhard et Levassor and came round in the end to the forward position of the engine. At much the same time the agency for the Benz cars in France was given to Emile Roger. He assembled Mannheim-built Benz cars under the trade name of Roger-Benz and one of these reached Britain it is thought in 1894. Inspired by these German engines a French nobleman Comte (later Marquis) Albert de Dion went into partnership with M. Bouton and produced the first high-speed motor. It is worthy of note that, so far, other countries – Britain and the USA included – had contributed practically nothing to the development of the automobile.

With hindsight, knowing what the future was to hold, we tend to forget that the internal combustion engine was merely one possible answer to the problem of mechanical road propulsion. Many other experimental vehicles were being made, some driven by electricity, some by steam, others again by compressed air or clockwork. It was the Comte de Dion who proposed that all should be put to the trial on an endurance test over 732 miles from Paris to Bordeaux and back. The date was 11 June 1895 and of the hundred or so entrants twenty-one actually appeared.

The race was a triumph for the petrol-car, particularly for Panhard-Levassor and Peugeot but most of all for Emile Lavassor himself. His car, No. 5 was first and he drove every yard of the way himself ... Although undeniably the winners, Panhard et Lavassor were not awarded first prize as the rules stipulated that this should be for a car with four seats – and the Panhard had but two. First prize therefore went to Peugeot, No. 18, and the following list of finishers shows the order of arrival.[2]

Place	Entry No.		Hours	Minutes
1	5	Panhard-Levassor	48	$47\frac{1}{2}$
2	15	Peugeot (2-seater)	54	35
3	16	Peugeot (4-seater)	59	48
4	18	Peugeot (4-seater)	59	49
5	12	Roger-Benz	64	30
6	7	Panhard-Levassor	72	14
7	28	Panhard-Levassor	78	7
8	13	Roger-Benz	82	48

It should be added that No. 16 in third place, was disqualified for fitting a new wheel and that the first steam car to finish came in ninth in 90 hours and 3 minutes. Levassor's average speed was 24.4 mph compared with the failure of most other drivers to reach an average of 20 mph. The other steam and electric cars failed to finish or were not timed. It was this event which established the Panhard-Levassor engine as the pattern for the future. Whether this was wholly fortunate is a matter of dispute. For the moment it is important to remember that the Panhard-Levassor was essentially a Daimler engine, ancestor of the first Mercedes which raced in the Grand Prix of 1901. The name Mercedes was that of the daughter of Jellinek, a director of the Daimler Motoren Gesellschaft. The two great German firms were in competition for many years but amalgamated to become Daimler-Benz in 1926. The Daimler-Benz Aktiengesellschaft of Stuttgart ranks currently as the sixth largest company in Germany. The group as a whole employed 136,376 people in 1969, over 99,000 of them in the Daimler-Benz AG. In the same year the company produced 256,713 cars and an increasingly large number of commercial vehicles. The total for 1970 was 280,000 to which must be added the production of a Mercedes plant in Brazil and the 300,000 Moskvitch cars produced in USSR. Mercedes policy has generally been to concentrate on heavy trucks and luxury cars, leaving the cheaper price ranges to other firms. Under the guidance of Dr Joachim Zahn, Mercedes has built up one of the most modern plants in Europe.

The motor car assumed in 1895 the form it has retained until today. It has been argued that crystallization of the idea in that guise was a technical disaster. On this subject one critic has written:

No one designed the automobile – it was merely put together, more or less by chance, in 1895, when a Frenchman installed a German's engine in a wagon by means of a series of typically Gallic compromises with reality. The engine was one of Germany's few failures in an otherwise exemplary technical history. The piston thrice went up and down within the cylinder before an explosion moved something worth moving. The Frenchman, one M. Levassor, placed this monstrosity before his cart, apparently on the theory that it would replace the horse. . . . Since the rear wheels were to supply the push (God knows why) the drive shaft had to be carried from the front of the wagon to the rear axle. . . .

The sound reason for this state of affairs is that not one of the automobile's first builders – neither the Europeans not their American imitators – was an inventor of the least repute. . . . The bleak fact is that our automotive engineers were merely a gaggle of village pipefitters.[3]

Some think this judgement over-harsh. It has substance, nevertheless, and our lack of progress in this field of enterprise may well be due, in part, to mistakes made at the outset. Our motor engines, 'lugubrious Teutonic devices', are even now mostly cumbered with the drive shaft, the manual gears and the clutch. These examples of misapplied ingenuity have the merit of being funny in a quiet way but any other merit they may have is far from obvious.

The car, as thus devised and technically frozen, was not everywhere regarded in exactly the same light. There was a basic difference between the European and American attitudes towards it. The cars which raced from Paris to Bordeaux and back in 1895 were able to do so because the roads had been made by Napoleon I and widened in Paris by Napoleon III. In Britain the roads had been made for the royal mail coaches and these highways, although disused in the railway age, were more or less intact. They were not really suitable for motoring because the dust caused by suction from the rubber tyres, which tended to blind the driver, could make the going extremely dangerous, but they were a great deal more suitable than the cart tracks in use elsewhere. Bridges and cuttings were in existence and a technique was already known for improving the surface with asphalt or tar. This was improved in the early twentieth century and the true motor road came into existence. The European highways were soon to offer motorists the chance to drive with dignity and elegance. But Europeans mostly lived in a social hierarchy to which the carriage had been important for reasons distinct from those of convenience. Theirs was a world in which 'carriage folk' patronized the shops which catered for 'the carriage trade'. Not only was a carriage the symbol of prestige but its exact form and appearance allowed of precise gradations and sharp distinctions. There were broughams, phaetons, landaus and victorias, the basket chaise and the governess cart, all horse-drawn vehicles, assuming myriad forms for as many specialized purposes. The cars which replaced the gigs and dog-carts tended, therefore, to reflect the same social distinctions. Far from aiming at uniformity the European car manufacturers sought to illustrate all the niceties of social rank and individual taste. There were two hundred and twenty-one car makers in the Britain of 1900 and there soon emerged such distinct types of vehicle as the Wolseley (1901), the Vauxhall (1904), the Napier (1904) and the Lanchester (1905). British motoring was established and popularized by the Automobile Club's 1,000 Miles Reliability Trial in 1900. Winner of the Gold Medal was the Hon. C. S. Rolls (1877–1910) driving a Panhard which averaged 37.63 mph in the speed trial. Rolls met F. H. Royce (1863–1933) at Manchester in 1904 and they founded the Rolls-

Royce Company in 1907. That company's 'Silver Ghost' model of 1908 remained in production, with slight variations, until 1924. There was no continental rival to the Rolls-Royce but there were many prestigious European cars from the Renault to the Lancia, from the De Dion Bouton of 1901 to the Italian Isotta-Fraschini of 1910. There was little attempt at first to provide for the needs of folk who would not earlier have possessed a carriage.

The United States offered the motor manufacturer a different sort of challenge. The distances were vast, the roads were primitive and the society one in which democratic sentiment had become traditional. As in Europe the inventive period was from 1895 to 1905. The first important car manufacturer was Ransom E. Olds of Lansing whose Oldsmobile appeared in 1904. This was quickly followed, however, by the Buick and the Model 'A' Ford. The American car industry centred on the middle-west and on the state of Michigan, encouraged by the fact that Detroit was already established as a manufacturing city and one noted for its output of carriages. Almost from the outset the lead was taken by Henry Ford (1863–1947) who had been chief engineer of the Edison Electric Company but who resigned in 1899 and produced his first automobile in 1900. He was working then for a group of businessmen who had formed the Detroit Automobile Company but the association was short-lived. Ford parted company from his partners who now formed the Cadillac Motor Car Company, the president of which, Mr Henry M. Leland, later resigned in order to form the Lincoln Motor Car Company. Ford now rented a workshop in his own name and there built a racing car. With this vehicle he entered a ten-mile race against Alexander Winton, who had made the first American track record in 1897. Winton's car had engine trouble and Ford won by three-quarters of a mile, thus becoming the new track champion. This success enabled him to form the Henry Ford Company of Detroit with six shareholders, Mark Hopkins being one. The enterprise also ended in disagreement, however, and Ford went on to build another racing car, the '999' which achieved a spectacular victory in 1902. This led to the formation of the Fordmobile Company of 1903 and the production of the Model 'A', followed in 1904 by 'B' selling at £2,000 and 'C' at $950. Business boomed from the start but various stockholders lost their nerve during a period of declining profits. By acquiring their shares in 1906 Ford obtained control of the company. At about the same time the company acquired the Highland Park Race Track outside Detroit, with sixty acres of ground and a mile of track. Even before the new factory had been opened (1910) the famous Model 'T' was on the market, the first car in which the driver's seat was shifted from the right (where the coachman had always sat) to the left. It was a simpler, lighter and yet stronger machine than the earlier models, doing 22 to 25 miles – instead of 10 – to the gallon of petrol, fitted with tyres good for 10,000 miles, giving a better performance than cars costing $2,000 or more and yet offered at the low price of $950. The claims made for the Model 'T' seemed impossible but there was a gruelling test in 1909 from which a Model 'T' emerged triumphant. A prize had been offered to the winner of a 4,106-mile race from New York to Seattle. Five cars attempted it but a Ford came in first, proving that the cheapest car was also the best. There followed the announcement that the Ford Motor Company would in future market only the one model – that known to history as the 'Tin Lizzie'.

With the opening of the Highland Park factory on 1 January 1910, there began a new era in the history of mass production. The aim was to produce 25,000 cars in the first year. Although it fell short of that target, the conveyor-belt system produced 34,528 cars in 1911 and 248,307 cars in 1914, by which year the receipts came to $120,000,000 and the profits to $25,000,000. In that same year Henry Ford doubled the wages of his 7,000 workmen and reduced their daily hours of work from nine to eight. His policy was now to reduce the cost of the car itself. Retaining the same design, with only minor improvements, he gradually brought the price down to its final figures of $345, $290 and (for the smallest version) $260. He had by then (1927) sold fifteen million cars of the same model. The time had long since come for a new design but Ford, in the meanwhile, had revolutionized the world, making a bigger and more immediate impact than any political reformer one could name.

. . . He thus freed the peasant from his Kansas clods, enabled the wage slave to live miles from his useful toil, brought the Bronx to the Catskills, took the front porch off the house in favour of the Sunday drive, substituted the back seat for the village haymow, simplified the problem of the bank robber's getaway, and changed the whole pattern of American life. By 1929, there were nine million more automobiles in America than there were telephones and the automobile industry was already the nation's largest. Today, 10,000,000 Americans are directly or indirectly employed in the manufacture, sale or maintenance of automobiles.[4]

While Henry Ford's achievement was astonishing and while he was at one time pre-eminent, he was not the only car manufacturer of his time. Contemporary with him was William C. Durant, who had been the leading wagon and carriage producer in the USA and who took over the Buick Motor Company in 1904. He then formed the General Motors Company in 1908, a merger of Buick, Olds, Oakland (now Pontiac) and Cadillac, the separate factories to operate under the control of the central holding company. To these assembly plants he added a number of factories which manufactured component parts. The company was presently in financial difficulties and Durant, losing control of it, joined with Louis Chevrolet to establish the Chevrolet Motor Company in 1911. General Motors, meanwhile, came under Du Pont control and so remained until Durant recaptured the company in 1916. Works Manager of Buick was Walter P. Chrysler who later became president and general manager. He resigned, however, and later (1925) formed his own company, the Chrysler Corporation, which acquired the Dodge Brothers Motor Company Inc. in 1928 and added Dodge trucks to a range of cars which included the De Soto and Plymouth. When Durant resigned again from General Motors in 1920 Pierre S. du Pont became president and Alfred P. Sloan soon afterwards became executive vice-president, replacing du Pont as president in 1923 and serving as chairman of the board from 1937 to 1956. In the history of the motor car Sloan played almost as important a part as Ford. While Ford revolutionized the techniques of mass production it was Sloan who was the founder of corporate strategy, product planning and market research.

When Sloan took the helm at GM, Ford dominated the world motor industry almost completely. The Ford Motor Company held over 60 per cent of the American market which was easily the largest in the world and had licenced production of its vehicles in Canada, Britain and France. Its only real competitor was GM which consisted of seven small companies, mostly making luxury cars, which fought each other for custom more than they fought Ford. No other manufacturer could possibly match Ford's productivity on the Model T which consequently was the only really cheap car on the market.[5]

If GM's weakness lay in the multiplicity of its models the weakness of Ford lay in the obstinacy with which old Henry adhered to the one model, complete with starting handle, and indeed to the one colour scheme (black). It might be true that nearly every American motorist would begin with a Ford but the proof of his success in business lay in the promptness with which he acquired a more expensive car. Sloan reduced the ten competing models of GM to five, one in each price range and one produced by each of five companies: Chevrolet, Pontiac, Oldsmobile, Buick and Cadillac. In ascending order, these cars represented so many steps in social consequence, even the Chevrolet (at $795) being priced about $300 above the price level of the Model 'T'. Sloan completed his system by introducing the annual model change, a further refinement in status symbolism. By clinging to the lowest price market, Ford was producing customers for General Motors. He was also ignoring the improvement of the road surface. The Model 'T' was a wonderful replacement for the farmer's horse and buggy, bumping happily over puddles and cinder track. On level tarmac there was scope for something more stylish and this was what General Motors had to offer. The result was that GM's share of the American market increased from 12 per cent in 1921 to 60 per cent and while Ford's share of the market has varied, nothing that Ford could do has made much impact on GM. The first effort to break into the more expensive market – the Ford Edsel of 1957 – was a disaster. There followed, however, the Ford Cortina of 1962, the successful Mustang of 1964 and then the Capri of 1967 which spearheaded a Ford invasion of Europe. In 1970 General Motors and its foreign subsidiaries manufactured 4,700,000 cars, while Ford's comparable total was 3,950,000. The third group in the USA is Chrysler, producing among other models the Plymouth, Dodge and Simca, and that group's total output in 1970 came to 2,100,000. There were originally in the USA such well-known firms as Studebaker and Packard but these and others were unable, in the end, to compete against General Motors. Even the continued existence of American Motors, with an output of 276,000 cars in 1970, seems to be precarious. Quite secure, by comparison, is General Motors, which is probably the biggest Big Business in the world with a million shareholders, 600,000 people on the payroll, £3,000-million assets and £5,000-million sales. GM's chairman is said to be the most highly paid man in the world. In the world of Big Business there is good reason to regard General Motors as in every way the summit.

In Europe the Ford epic is paralleled by the story of the Volkswagen. This project began in 1932 when Ferdinand Porsche was instructed by Adolf Hitler to design a 'Strength-through-Joy' 'people's car' which would cost less than 1,000 Reichsmarks (or £50). The Leader's order was obeyed but the first prototype did not appear until 1937 and World War II prevented it from coming on the market. It was developed instead for military purposes, to be driven through the sand of the desert and the snow and mud of the Russian front. Originally designed for the German roads before the days of the *autobahn*, intended above all to be cheap and reliable, the Volkswagen had an air-cooled engine placed behind the rear axle and independent suspension for each wheel. Production was confined originally to the one design. Porsche, a genius who had invented an electric helicopter in 1918 and a score of other ingenious machines, from fire-engines to airships, died in 1951. After the war the Volkswagen plant at Wolfsburg was reopened by Dr Heinz Nordhoff in 1948. His policy was to produce for export, first building up a service organization and an adequate supply of spare parts.

Volkswagen was soon the market leader in Switzerland, Holland and Belgium – helped perhaps by the fact that the British industry was unable to support its home demand and could not divert resources to satisfy the Continent as well. Output at Wolfsburg virtually doubled each year for almost a decade and reached a million cars a year by 1961. Until 1966 sales increased every year without faltering. The tremendous German economic boom of the late fifties and early sixties carried Volkswagen along with it, as the workers in the steel mills, coal mines and shipyards became affluent enough to buy their first car.[6]

Having conquered post-war Europe, which rather resembled the USA of the Model 'T' Ford era, the manufacturers of the Volkswagen went on to invade America. This movement began with members of the US armed forces who had been stationed in Germany. Having met the 'beetle' there, they brought word of it (if not the car itself) to their homeland, where a market for the family's second car was developing, and some of the Volkswagen's success may have been due to that.

Meanwhile Nordhoff maintained his standards of service and his cars retained their name for reliability. There were minor improvements but the original design lasted for twenty-five years. By 1970 the Volkswagen output, from the world's largest automated motor factory, reached two million cars a year, twice the number produced by any European rival except Fiat. But history repeated itself and the growth of European prosperity began to change the nature of the demand. Buyers were in a position to demand something better, such as the Opel Kadett produced by General Motors. More than that, the Fiat 850 and the Renault 4 came to challenge the Volkswagen at its own price level. Sales began to decline (except in the USA) and a basic reorganization was begun by Dr Kurt Lotz in 1968. To break into higher-level price brackets, his policy was to acquire smaller firms with experience of manufacturing for that market. Volkswagen had already bought Audi from Daimler-Benz in 1965 and to this Dr Lotz added NSU. The result has been a number of new types including the VW Porsche and the 'Super-Beetle'. The future of Volkswagen would seem to turn on its success with more expensive cars.

Although Volkswagen has played a vital part in the European car industry it is now eclipsed in size by the Fabbrica Italiano Automobili Torino (Fiat), the organization founded by Giovanni Agnelli at Turin in 1905. It is now run by the two brothers, Giovanni and Umberto Agnelli, brilliant men and enormously wealthy. Fiat prosperity grew with the recovery of Europe after World War II, Milan and Turin having the advantage of recruiting cheap labour from the impoverished areas of southern Italy. As the new industries developed, each worker wanted a car and the Fiat 500 was the car he bought. With the Italian market secured, Fiat moved into countries which had been hitherto neglected: Spain, Yugoslavia, Poland, Bulgaria and Russia. The differences which exist between these different countries – geographic, climatic and even ideological differences – have led Fiat to develop a wide range of cars. Since the dawn of the European Economic Community this has given the company an advantage in entering new markets. Unlike some other motor firms, however, the Fiat empire extends to other forms of enterprise, to ships and aircraft, to general engineering and to nuclear power. This diversification has not checked its progress in its original field, however, and it took over Lancia and a half-share in Ferrari in 1969. Even before that came the alliance with the French Citroën company which finally gave it a joint control (with Michelin) by 1970. The Fiat-Citroën organization now dominates a market which extends, as Ensor points out, from the Atlantic to the Urals.

In France Citroën's traditional rival was Renault, which was later (1966) to form an alliance with Peugeot. But Louis Renault died in prison, accused of collaboration with the Germans, and President de Gaulle nationalized the company in 1945. Its first attempt to enter the world market was represented by its Dauphine model of 1956 which had great success in the USA until the appearance of the Corvair and Falcon. Renault sales slumped but the company was saved by Pierre Dreyfus and the Renault 4, itself eclipsed later by the Peugeot 204, the most popular car in France. The effort of present European car manufacturers is to aim at the European market as a whole, not forgetting countries like Rumania, while maintaining links with South America and Asia. They have to share the European market, however, with the subsidiaries established in Europe by General Motors, by Ford and by Chrysler.

Great Britain, as we have seen (page 226) produced a variety of cars before World War I. The slump of 1920, however, eliminated a number of firms, leaving only five of any size: Wolseley, Morris, Singer, Austin and Rover. When things were at their worst Mr W. R. Morris cut the price of his Morris Cowley by £100 (to £425) and that of the two-seater version by £90 (to £375).

The immediate consequence for him was that whereas for the national industry 1921 was a slump year, the total of vehicles produced falling from 1920 to 1921 by one-third to 40,000, or several thousand below the 1913 peak, his output had increased by over 50 per cent from 1,932 to 3,076. The following year that output again was to be more than doubled, a total of 6,956 cars being produced. These figures, seen in the light of later progress, make it clear that Morris virtually gained the leadership of his industry in the year of the great slump.[7]

Morris had begun to reach out for a wider market. He was no engineer in the technical sense and his factory was at first a mere assembly plant for purchased components. His gift was for producing what he thought that the public would want at the price he guessed they would pay. He soon discovered, however, that he had to control the sources from which his components came. In 1923 he bought the firm which supplied his radiators, the Coventry firm which made his car bodies and the Hotchkiss factory which made his engines. These and other concerns were afterwards absorbed into Morris Motors Ltd (1926) and Morris also acquired the Wolseley Company in 1927.

Chief rival to Morris Motors was the company founded by Herbert Austin, the manufacturers of the Austin 7 of 1922, which sold at £225 and was eventually reduced in price to £130. Another rival was the Singer 10 which appeared in 1921 and cost £250 in 1923. Destined for a still bigger future were the Rootes Brothers, William and Reginald, who acquired two Coventry car firms, the Humber and Hillman companies, from which came eventually the Hillman Minx. But these British concerns were all tiny when compared with the giants of the USA. They were reminded of this fact when Henry Ford set up his enormous factory on a five-hundred-acre site at Dagenham, his base for an invasion of Europe. At much the same time the British firm of Vauxhall was acquired by General Motors. The competition was always intense but the slump of 1929-32 made it cut-throat. The Morris Minor, designed at Wolseley's, had appeared just before the slump but a new and cheaper version followed in 1930-31 under a telling slogan: '100 mph, 100 miles per gallon and £100 the price.'

By 1937, Britain had become the second largest producer of vehicles in the world; by 1938 there were more than three million on British roads. 1937 was the high point in production, with 379,000 cars coming off the assembly lines, and further nationalization meant that by the time war broke out only about twenty independent car-producing firms had survived, six of them controlling 90 per cent of the market.[8]

On 22 May 1939 the millionth car was driven from the Cowley works, making a notable day for W. R. Morris (later Lord Nuffield) and a notable day for British industry. There followed World War II and a transfer of manufacturing effort into other fields of enterprise. After the war there was a great drive to recover the pre-war levels of production. Main contenders for the market were Austin, Morris, Standard, Jaguar and Ford. To the wholly British firms the main threat came from Ford. The answer to this was the merger of Morris with Austin in 1951, forming a new group called the British Motor Corporation. An immense effort followed in the standardization of components and in the automation of processes, one BMC product being the Austin-Healey sports car and another the Mini-Minor, designed as much to park as to drive. Smaller companies went out of business and British annual output approached the million mark, reaching its peak of production in about 1955.

In 1950, Britain ran a confortable (if poor) second to the United States as a producer of cars and was easily the greatest exporting nation in the world. We sold three times as many cars as the Americans in overseas markets, six times as many as the West Germans. By 1956, however, West Germany had ousted us from second place, both as producer and exporter; they overhauled us in the African and Asian markets as well as in America and by 1961 Britain had slipped still further down the ladder. In that year France also produced more cars than Britain, and Japan jockeyed us out of second place in the output of commercial vehicles.[9]

Mention of commercial vehicles brings us naturally to the subject of Leyland Motors Ltd. If the British were slow in taking to the road as car-owners they were proportionately quick and competent in their approach to trucks and public transport. From an early date the London General Omnibus Company had bought its double-decker omnibuses from Leyland and the same company was producing a variety of lorries for road transport. The business soon extended to long-distance single-decker buses and heavy vehicles for export. Leyland built up an enviable reputation for studying the needs of each country and industry. Dominating the profitable heavyweight market, Leyland took over Rover and Triumph and was still digesting those acquisitions when it became apparent that BMC – which had taken over Jaguar – was itself in difficulties. Its best-selling models were past their peak of popularity and it had no ace to play. Faced with growing competition from Vauxhall's Viva, Ford's Cortina and finally, Ford's Escort, BMC's share of the British market dropped from 44 per cent to 29 per cent in little over a year. The result was the merger which led to the creation of British Leyland in 1967, led by Sir Donald (now Lord) Stokes from January 1968. A major reorganization followed of a group which had sixty plants, too many products and far too many employees. The first visible result of the merger was the Austin-Morris Marina, followed by Triumph's Toledo and Dolomite. Second was the move into Europe, especially into Belgium and Spain. The hope at British Leyland's headquarters is that market planning and computerized supply of spare parts will allow the group to hold its own against Ford, Fiat and Renault.

Since 1966 all established motor industries have begun to feel the pressure of Japanese competition. This began in the motor-cycle field with the Japanese Honda and Yamaha but these were followed by the major car manufacturers, Toyota and Nissan. These existed before World War II but their later prominence was due to the Korean War of 1950-53. American industry had reverted to peace-time production and could not meet the new demand for trucks and jeeps. Orders went, therefore, to Japan, which was, in any case, nearer to the scene of conflict. Using American production methods and market planning but employing Japanese labour, the Japanese built up a formidable industry which went over to peacetime production when the war ended. Cars were at first supplied to the well protected Japanese market but cars for export followed in 1965, beginning with the Corona designed for sale in the USA and followed up by cars destined for Europe and Asia.

In just four years, between 1966 and 1969, production of cars in Japan tripled from 880,000 to 2.6 million and Japan became the world's third largest producer. By 1974 it is estimated that car output will reach five million, still well behind the twelve million cars which will be produced in the US but easily outdistancing German production of four million.[10]

With an output of 1.2 million cars and 70,000 workers on the payroll, Toyota is certainly Big Business, and even Nissan, the makers of the Datsun range of cars, had an output of 800,000 cars in 1970. In order of size, measured by output, the car makers of the world are General Motors, Ford, Chrysler, Fiat-Citroën, Volkswagen, Renault-Peugeot, Toyota, British Leyland, Nissan and Daimler-Benz. And if it is significant that the three largest companies are American, it is at least noteworthy that the seventh and ninth should be Japanese.

15   Aircraft

It has been claimed that man first left the earth in powered flight on 17 December 1903, when the aviator, Orville Wright, of Dayton, Ohio took to the air. It is arguable that this feat had already been performed by Hiram Maxim whose flying machine flew for two hundred yards on 5 July 1894. But Orville Wright's achievement was the more significant for at least two reasons. In the first place it led at once to his further flights, one of them lasting thirty-three minutes in 1905. In the second place, his success stimulated a host of imitators, one of whom, Louis Blériot, flew from France to England in 1909. From that date the main problems had been solved and the construction of useful aircraft had become technically possible. It was not generally admitted, however, that what was possible was necessarily desirable. The more obvious uses for the aeroplane were military but little of the experimental work was done with official encouragement, perhaps because the armies of the day were already provided with balloons and kites – the British, for example, had their army balloon school from 1878 and an army airship factory at Farnborough from 1907.

When war began in 1914 Britain had four air squadrons in process of formation and the Royal Aircraft Factory was able to produce about two new machines a month, and beyond this there was not a single organized aircraft factory in England and no single engine in production.

The manufacture of aircraft was open to private enterprise and one of the first men to enter this new business was Geoffrey de Havilland

(1882–1965), the descendant, like his cousins Olivia de Havilland and Joan Fontaine, of a distinguished Guernsey family, who was trained as an engineer and who, in 1905, joined the Wolseley Tool and Motor-Car Company in Birmingham. The managing director was Herbert Austin, who left and founded the Austin Motor Company. His successor was John Siddeley, another man with a future, but de Havilland left the company and resolved to build an aircraft. With a thousand pounds given by his grandfather, with Frank Hearle as assistant and with an engine built by the Iris Car Company at Willesden, he completed a biplane in December 1909. It crashed and he built another in 1910, which he flew. De Havilland was then offered, and accepted, a post as aircraft designer at Farnborough. He left Farnborough in early 1914 and joined the Aircraft Manufacturing Company at Hendon as designer. After World War I began the company, known by now as Airco, was told to produce a fighter aircraft with a higher performance than the German Fokker. This was the DH2, four hundred of which were supplied to the Royal Flying Corps. It was followed by a bomber, the DH4, powered by a Rolls-Royce engine. Airco did good work during the war but collapsed afterwards, selling their buildings and plant to BSA. Geoffrey de Havilland at this point (1920) founded the De Havilland Aircraft Co., using the key men from Airco to form the basis of his team. The site for the factory was a war-time aerodrome at Edgware, three miles from Hendon, where the first British civil transport aircraft were built. Most important of these was the Moth, a small two-seater plane used by private owners and flying clubs and sold originally for £650. This was a commercial success and the company moved to a better site at Hatfield. During World War II it was this factory which produced the Mosquito, a versatile 'plane which did good service as bomber, fighter, (both day and night) high-altitude fighter and reconnaissance aircraft. Before the war ended 7,781 Mosquitoes had been produced, some in Canada and Australia, and 75,000 people were employed by the original firm. Other de Havilland war planes were the Sea Venom and Vampire, while the firm also produced two civil planes which have been in very general use: the Heron and the Dove. After World War II the same team went on to produce the Comet, Britain's first jet-liner, which went into service in 1952. Two disasters in 1954 proved a serious setback but the fault was remedied by 1958 when the Comet 4 provided the first jet service across the Atlantic.

Other wartime aircraft firms included the Avro Company of Manchester, the British & Colonial Aeroplane Company Ltd. of Bristol, the Blackburn & General, Fairey (at Eastchurch), Handley Page and Short Brothers. It was Fairey Aviation which founded the aerodrome which later became London Airport, Heathrow. Two leaders of importance were Sir Thomas Sopwith and Harry Hawker, who formed the Hawker Engineering Company. After World War I this company acquired three other aircraft firms, Armstrong Whitworth, Gloster and A. V. Roe, becoming the Hawker Siddeley Group of Kingston-on-Thames. Another important company was that of Vickers-Armstrong, destined to make such well known aircraft as the Supermarine Swift, the Valiant, the Supermarine Attacker and, finally, the Viscount. British aircraft manufacturers did splendid work during the general period of World War II, producing many famous aircraft, but they were not in Big Business until successive mergers – a rationalization was approved by Mr Duncan Sandys (now Lord Sandys) in 1959 – had reduced their number to three. These were the Hawker Siddeley group, already described, the Westland Group, comprising Fairey, Bristol and Saunders Roe and the British Aircraft Corporation which was formed in February 1960. This last group brought together the aircraft and guided weapons interests of the Bristol Aeroplane Company, English Electric and Vickers. Since then the Bristol Aeroplane share (20 per cent) has been acquired by Rolls-Royce, which has also acquired Bristol Siddeley Engines, and English Electric has been absorbed (see page 212) by Sir Arnold Weinstock's GEC. When first formed, BAC had four wholly owned subsidiaries in Bristol Aircraft, English Electric Aviation, Vickers-Armstrong (aircraft) and BAC (guided weapons), and these, too, were amalgamated and brought into the group. Taking the three major groups in order, the Hawker Siddeley Group have been the builders of the Argosy (1961–6), the Comet (1952–67), the HS-748 (1962–70) and the Trident (1965–70); the Westland Group of Yeovil were the builders of the Shackleton (1949), the Vulcan (1952), and the Britannia (1952) but have since specialized in building helicopters like the Gazelle and the Lynx, while BAC have built the Lightning (1952), the Viscount (1953–63), the Vanguard

(1961–4), the VC-10 (1964–70) and the BAC1-11. This last-named aircraft, over two hundred of which had been sold by 1971, has been used throughout the world and has been in service with such US airlines as American Braniff and Mohawk. BAC war planes include the Lightning and Strikemaster and the total of its products in service were valued at $3,500,000,000 in 1971.

While these British firms have done brilliant pioneering work and produced some technically remarkable aircraft, their sales have been small when compared with the giant firms which dominate the aerospace industry in the USA. To illustrate the difference in scale one might quote the figures of aircraft currently in operation with major airlines which read something like this:

Boeing aircraft (707 to 747 inclusive)	9,174
Douglas aircraft (DC-8, DC-9, etc.)	3,747
Bristol Britannia	734
Viscount (turbo-prop.)	459
Caravelle (French jet plane)	272
VC-10	54

To complete the picture one might add that whereas Boeing aircraft are used by Air France, BOAC, Lufthansa and Quantas, the Viscount – outside Britain – is used only by Air Canada and Lufthansa, and by one American airline (United). The French Caravelle is used – outside France – by Sabena, Alitalia, Swissair and also by United. There is, in other words, no comparison between the part played by American and European aircraft in the world's transport system. As regards war planes the picture is different, partly because of the USA's delayed participation in World Wars I and II. Some of the world's most advanced war planes are still made in Britain and France but the development of the airliner has so far been the achievement, mainly, of the Big Business of the USA.

Whereas World War I did much to create the aircraft industry in Europe, the United States lacked that stimulus until rather late in the conflict. In 1915, nevertheless, Messrs Boeing and Westervelt began making seaplanes on the shore of Lake Union at Seattle in Washington State. This partnership became Pacific Aero Products in 1916 and the Boeing Airplane Company in 1917, with contracts from both navy and army. Boeing obtained a share of the US airmail service in 1927, flying a Wasp aircraft with a Pratt & Whitney 420 hp engine. This led to the formation of Boeing Air Transport, which absorbed Pacific Air Transport and other airlines, eventually becoming the enormous group since known as United Airlines. On the construction side, Boeing's main rivals have been Douglas, Lockheed and Corvair but it is worth bearing in mind that the aircraft industry is not confined to the biggest production lines. Besides the production of giant airliners there are diverse markets for specialized aircraft, for trainers, for private planes, for executive jets, air-taxis and helicopters. There are major firms which can exist alongside the giants, the names which come to mind including Fairchild, Grumman, North American, Northrop and Piper. The same is true of Europe, where it would be wrong to ignore such firms as Fiat of Italy and Saab of Sweden. It is notable, however, that firms making aircraft are more numerous than the firms which make engines. Even in the USA the latter business is tending to concentrate in the hands of Pratt & Whitney and Westinghouse.

The Douglas legend begins with the birth of Donald W. Douglas in 1892. He was president of the Douglas Co. of Santa Monica, California from 1920 to 1928. It became the Douglas Aircraft Company Inc. in 1928, with the same president until 1957 when the founder was succeeded by a son of the same name, the elder Douglas remaining chairman and chief executive until 1967, and honorary chairman of McDonnell-Douglas since the merger of that year. The success story, as distinct from the legend, begins with United Air Lines ordering sixty Boeing 247s in 1933. The reaction of Transcontinental & Western Airlines (now TWA) was to ask the other manufacturers whether they could improve on the Boeing design. Responding to the challenge, Douglas produced its design for the DC-1. Only one DC-1 was ever produced, however, for the Wright Company at this point produced a new and more powerful engine. Consequent changes of structure produced the DC-2, which was a commercial success, coming second to the de Havilland Comet in the air race from London to Melbourne in 1934. Encouraged by this result, Mr C.R. Smith, president of American Airlines, asked Douglas to produce an enlarged version of the DC-2, capable of carrying twenty-one passengers instead of fourteen. The result was the DC-3, one of the most successful aircraft ever made. It came into service on 25 June 1936, on the New York–Chicago route. Such was its popularity that United Airlines ordered DC-3s to replace its 247s that very year. The DC-3 was economical to buy and maintain, carried a good payload over short stages, was able to operate from small airfields and had variable-pitch propellers and a usefully slow landing speed. It was, from the beginning, a commercial triumph, there being 360 in use on American domestic air routes by 1941. Before that, in 1938, DC-3s were carrying 95 per cent of all commercial air traffic in the USA and were also used by thirty foreign airlines. It was in this steady and reliable aircraft that the American and European public acquired the habit of flying.

When the United States came into World War II there was a tremendous and instant demand for transport aircraft. The DC-3 was the answer, ready to hand, and it was quickly adapted to a score of specialized purposes, over 10,000 being produced in the USA alone. Thousands more were produced under licence elsewhere – as the Dakota, for example, in Britain and as the PS-84 in Russia – making a world total of 13,000 or more. When the war ended the USA alone had four thousand to dispose of at a bargain price. They were sold to a swarm of small airline operators, men whose wartime experience had been gained on this particular plane. They were shipped all over the world and turned up in unexpected places, where many of them are still in service. There were said to be over three thousand still flying in 1963, with replacements and spare parts still available, and while the total must be reduced each year there can be no doubt that many will have had a life of thirty years or more. In the total build-up of the industry the local feeder services and the non-scheduled flight operators have played an essential part. Through their activities whole populations have become accustomed to the idea of flight. Psychologically, more-over, as well as physically, the local flight (Penang to Singapore) is the first step towards the greater adventure (Singapore to Perth). It was on these local services, incidentally, that the DC-3 won its reputation for safety. In the USA or Europe a plane in difficulties can often make an emergency landing on a service or disused airfield. Over a country like Malaya there may be nowhere to land between point of departure and destination, with nothing below the aircraft but virgin jungle, the habitat of terrorists and tigers. For a lifetime, however, no aircraft was ever lost. The same reputation was acquired by the DC-3 in many remote areas, encouraging people to use aircraft who may never before have boarded a steamship or travelled in a car.

The DC-3 was followed by the DC-4 and successive types, leading to the long-range jet-propelled DC-8 of 1959 and the short-range and extremely successful DC-9 of 1965. Each of these has been modified in later series, increasing the number of passengers that can be carried. Next in line is the DC-10, some 243 of which tri-jets had been ordered up to March 1971. This aircraft, costing £8,340,000 is designed to carry 253 passengers at 551 mph. It will rather closely resemble its rivals, the Boeing 747 and Lockheed's L-1011 with its RB-211 engine. In other respects, however, Douglas has its own distinctive character. As the London *Times* pointed out on 25 March 1971, it remains a conservative and canny organization:

... the Scots–American family tradition is still strong in the company and is seen in a roll call of the four-man executive committee of its board of directors – Mr James McDonnell, Mr Donald Douglas, Jun., Sanford McDonnell and Mr Dolor Murray.

In its pride and tradition it is in some ways an American equivalent of Rolls-Royce, and when a 50-strong band of kilted pipers saluted Mr James McDonnell and Mr Donald Douglas, Sen., at an emotional fiftieth anniversary celebration last year many of the staff had tears in their eyes.

There was at least no occasion for tears of grief whether at Santa Monica or at St Louis, the former McDonnell Company's headquarters, for the 1970 before-tax profit of $173 million would seem to leave room for encouragement and hope.

Only thirty miles from the Douglas plant at Santa Monica is the Lockheed base at Burbank. The first notable aircraft to come from Burbank was the ten-passenger Electra of 1934, used extensively by American Airlines. The early Lockheed successes have also included some notable fighter planes, the Lightning of 1942, the Shooting Star and the later F104 or Starfighter of 1956. There can be no doubt that Lockheed (like Boeing and Douglas) gained much from the agreement reached during World War II which left the manufacture of transport (as contrasted with combat) aircraft to the USA. The result was to give the USA a considerable lead in freight- and passenger-carrying aircraft. Between them, Britain and the USA produced no less than 380,000 aircraft during World War II[1] but those with commercial possibilities were mostly American. Lockheed was well placed when war ended, the more so in that this firm had produced, in 1937, the first aircraft with a pressurized cabin. In the same year came a development of the Electra, the Lockheed 14, a technically successful machine but overshadowed by the still greater success of the DC-3.

The result of the American lead in transport aircraft was that other countries had nothing available for commercial use when the war ended. Second only in importance to the DC-4 Skymaster was Lockheed's Constellation, 'one of the most graceful aircraft ever to fly'. It was designed in 1939 for TWA and first flew in 1944, carrying fifty-one passengers in a pressurized cabin at a cruising speed of 280 mph. Britain had nothing comparable, as BOAC's wartime service between Whit-church and Lisbon had to rely on five rescued DC-3s originally supplied to KLM. It was on one of these that the film actor, Leslie Howard, lost his life in 1943, when the plane was shot down over the Bay of Biscay by a Junkers 88. After the war, in 1946, BOAC had government permission to purchase five Constellations for their Atlantic route, flown via Shannon and Gander between London and New York. The same aircraft was afterwards used on the BOAC service to Singapore and Australia, a few surviving as late as 1959. The change to jet propulsion, however, began in Britain rather than in the USA. Whittle jet engines reached the USA in 1941 and were copied there. The Lockheed XP-80, fitted with a de Havilland engine, was the proto-type of what became the Shooting Star, used in the Korean War. The new Electra of 1957 was a turbo-prop capable of carrying ninety-nine passengers at 405 mph. Nearly two hundred of them were manu-factured, many for KLM. More recently Lockheed effort has been put into freighter aircraft, such as the Galaxy-1100 which can carry a hundred tons of payload at 600 mph, container-loaded for easier handling at the airport.

Mention has already been made of William E. Boeing, founder of the Boeing Airplane Company of Seattle in Washington State. It was he who flew passengers on the first international airmail flight, from Vancouver to Seattle, on 3 March 1919. There was a period, as we have seen, when Boeing operated the aircraft they built. That period ended with anti-trust legislation, including the Air Mail Act of 1934, which prevented aircraft or engine manufacturers from having a financial interest in airlines. Boeing had to part with the system which became United Air Lines and has since then concentrated on the building of aircraft. During World War II the greatest Boeing achievement was probably the B-29 or Superfortress, a heavily armed bomber capable of carrying a 20,000 lb bomb load at a maximum speed of 360 mph. The B-29 dropped 171,000 tons (HE and incendiary) on Japanese targets, ending with the atomic bombs dropped on Hiroshima and Nagasaki. The B-29 had a post-war civilian equivalent, the Stratocruiser of 1949, which could carry up to a hundred passengers. The post-war development of the jet engine led to the B-52 or Stratofortress of 1952, for many years the backbone of the long-range force under the US Strategic Air Command. In parallel, however, with this line of development, Boeing was also designing a jet airliner. The lead in this field should have gone to the British Comet (1949) but two disasters grounded that aircraft and it took years to discover and remedy the defects. In the meanwhile Boeing was designing its larger and now famous 707 of 1954. This was the aircraft, carrying up to 189 passengers, which created the jet age. No less than 3,009 of these were sold, and another 800 to the US airforce. It was the standard jet-plane used by the major US airlines – Pan-American, American, TWA, Braniff United – and it became standard with BOAC, Air France, Lufthansa, Air India and Quantas, too. The 707 was followed inexorably by the 720 (of 1960), the 727 (of 1964) and the 737 (of 1967). Then the series was crowned by the Boeing 747 or 'jumbo-jet', designed to carry 490 passengers but carrying, in the first place, no more than 350. The maximum cruising speed is 640 mph and its range is 4,600 miles. Its distinctive feature in appearance is the raised flight deck, giving it a humped profile. At the time of writing no fewer than eight hundred and fifty six of these airliners have been sold, a success equivalent, certainly, to that of the 707. Boeing have had difficulties, nevertheless, and have had to reduce their workforce in 1970 from 108,500 to 66,500. This reflected the recession and a consequent reduction in the number of air travellers. The Boeing 747 was initially easier to sell than it has since been to fill.

At 640 mph the 727 is approaching the speed of sound (760 mph) but it moves more slowly than military machines flying at a higher altitude and with a lighter payload. Supersonic speeds were thus nearly reached by the Vulcan B Mk2 of 1952 (Mach 0.94), far surpassed by Britain's BAC Lightning of 1952 (Mach 2.0), and again by the American Phantom II of 1958 (Mach 2+) the Russian Mig-23 of 1965 and the Swedish Viggen of 1967 (Mach 2+). Britain dropped out of this race by cancelling the TSR-2 but the stage was set, nevertheless, for the production of a supersonic airliner, a machine to combine (eventually) the accommodation of the Boeing 747 with the performance of Phantom II In even remotely approaching this target the air manufacturer is confronted by problems which are at least partly new in kind. A large airliner flying at Mach 2 must be extremely complex and appallingly costly. Faced with such a project, manufacturers are haunted by memories of past failures, the worst of which have involved a vast expense, a seemingly endless delay and the final launching of a machine which was already obsolete. Not the least daunting factor is the cost of design – the millions spent at the drawing board – before anything is built at all. Design teams number up to five thousand and development costs for a single aircraft can reach £200 million, with as much again for the engine. Nor are costs even predictable for many attempted solutions of a given problem must fail – and who is to guess how often this will happen? The original estimate (£100 million or £150 million, say) can be exceeded and indeed doubled. Faced by the need for an initial outlay of this order, the manufacturing firms have turned to governments asking for subsidies or loans and pointing out that a cancellation of their plans will lead to immediate unemployment and an eventual loss of national prestige. Governments responded at first to this sort of appeal but have latterly come to the conclusion that the more ambitious projects are beyond the means of a single country. Two recent rejections have emphasized this change in attitude, one being the refusal of the US Senate to support the plan for an American supersonic airliner, the B2707, the other the refusal of the British Government (December 1970) to subsidize the BAC3-11, the British subsonic 300-seat airbus backed by GEC and Vickers for sale, in the first place, to BEA. In the latter instance, preference was given to the A-300 B, the European airbus with wings by Hawker Siddeley, planned between Britain and France in 1965-6 but now shared also with Germany and Holland. Similar international efforts are being put into combat planes like the Jaguar, the MRCA or Q-Stol and the American Tri-star airbus with its British RB 2-11 engine. Countries are no longer so eager to go it alone.

At the time of writing the story of aircraft construction has reached a dramatic climax in the technical success of the Anglo-French Concorde. This was planned between Aérospatiale and BAC in 1962, the aim being to carry 120 passengers at Mach 2, (1,520 mph) at an original estimate of £100 million. Government support was forthcoming on either side of the Channel and the estimate was changed to £150–£170 million. The work was directly to involve some 25,000 technicians for at least ten years, with four hundred other firms providing components. When the extent of the under-estimate began to be realized (in 1964) the British Labour Government tried to cancel the project but was held to its bargain by the French. Costs mounted to £730 million by the time the first two prototypes were airborne and estimates now vary from £825 million to £900 million. Technically, the success of Concorde has been complete: the French prototype, built at Toulouse, was first in the air; the British prototype, constructed at Filton, reached 1,210 mph (Mach 1.78) in October 1970. The Concorde is now regularly in service but doubts are still expressed about its commercial success. Further machines are already being built, with improvements on the first, and the assumption is that these will be the parents of a new generation, perhaps touching higher speeds and probably carrying a bigger payload. It was originally supposed that these aircraft would sell at £10 million each. It is now believed that the price will be far higher and that this higher cost will be reflected in the fare.

With Concorde it might seem that we are moving away from earlier patterns of Big Business in the aircraft industry. BAC and Aérospatiale do not represent private enterprise in the old sense. There is no patriarch in this field, no Vanderbilt or Henry Ford, no Thomas Watson or Anton Philips. Government finance has been needed from the outset and even this proves insufficient, governments themselves having to pool their resources and co-ordinate their efforts. While this is true, however, of supersonic air travel, we must remember that an effort of this kind is based upon a broad industrial foundation. In the supply of components there is scope for private enterprise and often for enterprise on the largest scale. It would be wrong, therefore, to think that this task has been wholly entrusted to two more or less nationalized corporations. There is reason to think, however, that private enterprise is changing in character. This is especially evident in the design and construction of aircraft, a business in which the major firms are few and of an increasingly international character. Predictions have been made that the European aircraft industry will end as only two groups. That has certainly been the trend in the USA although North American Rockwell (with 86,000 employees and sales of $26,000 million), the builders of the Apollo spacecraft, can be regarded as a third. But here again the figures are daunting, the cost of the proposed space-shuttle vehicle being estimated at $4,500 million, a figure beyond the scope of private or even national enterprise. This is Big Business indeed, but not the sort of business we have previously seen.

Postscript

In the industrial world of the later twentieth century the great corporations stand out like the high-rise buildings of Manhattan. Each has its satellites and subsidiaries and all relate to each other in a bewildering and changing pattern of co-operation and rivalry. In this book we have tried to explain how some of these great organizations have come to dominate our economic landscape. This story has brought us to the present day and to new situations which are difficult to describe and almost impossible to analyse. These are the subject of another book, *Big Business*, to which this may serve as the historical prelude, the two together forming a contribution to the epic story of business enterprise. It may be convenient for teachers to make politics the main subject of history and current affairs. It may make for simplicity to treat economic history as a branch of socialist propaganda and applied statistics. It is arguable, however, that our lives are far more closely affected by other things – by the electric lights in the home, by the car in the garage, by the refrigerator in the kitchen, by the telephone on our desk. For these items of equipment we are indebted, as we realize, to the great inventors, a few of whom we may even know by name. We are just as beholden however, to the businessmen who put these things on the market, planning their mass production and persuading the public to buy. No one device of this sort is an unmixed blessing and some appear to create as many problems as they solve. The fact remains, however, that these are an essential part of the world we have created, a world more influenced by the businessman than by the politician. If we are to understand that world, we do well to study Big Business, not as an exercise in the worship of wealth nor as a prelude to the castigation of the capitalist, but simply as part of an effort to grasp the realities of the society in which we live and work. If this volume should help to explain the world of Big Business it will have served its purpose. Faced by Big Business, we can give voice to our admiration or, if we prefer, to our outspoken condemnation. What we must not do, surely, is to ignore it.

Notes

CHAPTER 1

1 John Langton Sanford and Meredith Townsend, *The Great Governing Families of England*, 2 vols (London, 1865), pp. 15–16.
2 Douglas Sutherland, *The Landowners* (London, 1968).
3 Christopher Trent, *The Russells* (London, 1966), pp. 12, 160, 167, passim.
4 Sutherland, *The Landowners*, p. 33.
5 G. S. Thomson, *Life in a Noble Household, 1641–1700* (London, 1937).
6 G. E. Mingay, *English Landed Society in the Eighteenth Century* (London, 1963), p. 227.
7 Mingay, *English Landed Society*, pp. 159–60.
8 David Spring, *The English Landed Estate in the Nineteenth Century: its Administration* (Baltimore, 1963), pp. 28–9.
9 H. H. Smith, *Principles of Landed Estate Management* (London, 1898).
10 G. Millerson, *The Qualifying Associations* (London, 1964), pp. 55, 83.
11 E. L. Jones and S. J. Woolf (eds), *Agrarian Change and Economic Development: The Historical Problem* (London, 1969), p. 16.
12 Mingay, *English Landed Society*, p. 113.
13 Sutherland, *The Landowners*, p. 29.
14 Sutherland, *The Landowners*, p. 48.

CHAPTER 2

1 W. S. Lindsay, *History of Merchant Shipping*, 4 vols (London, 1876), IV, p. 187.
2 Charles Hadfield, *The Canal Age* (Newton Abbot, 1968). See also Robert Payne, *The Canal Builders* (New York, 1959).
3 Spring, *The English Landed Estate*, pp. 93–4.
4 Stella Margetson, *Journey by Stages: Some Account of the People who Travelled*

by Stage-Coach and Mail in the Years between 1660 and 1840 (London, 1967), pp. 60–1.

5 C. W. Scott-Giles, *The Road Goes On: a Literary and Historical Account of the Highways, Byways and Bridges of Great Britain* (London, 1946), p. 158.

6 Margetson, *Journey by Stages*, pp. 60–1.

7 Hugh McCausland, *The English Carriage* (London, 1948), p. 23 et seq.

8 J. W. Gregory, *The Story of the Road* (London, 1931), pp. 170–71.

9 McCausland, *The English Carriage*: description of the park phaeton on pp. 61–2.

10 Margetson, *Journey by Stages*, pp. 152–4.

CHAPTER 3

1 Malacky Postlethwayt, *The Universal Dictionary of Trade and Commerce*, 3rd ed. (London, 1766), I (article on Holland).

2 Lord Braybrooke (ed.), *Diary and Correspondence of Samuel Pepys* (London, 1924), II, p. 21 (entry for 13 June 1667).

3 John Giuseppi, *The Bank of England: A History from its Foundation in 1694* (London, 1966).

4 See C. R. Fay, *Great Britain from Adam Smith to the Present Day* (London, 1928), chapter four on Currency and Banking.

5 E. H. Coleridge, *The Life of Thomas Coutts, Banker* (Edinburgh, 1919).

6 Frederic Morton, *The Rothschilds: A Family Portrait* (London, 1962).

7 Sir Charles Oman, *The Coinage of England* (Oxford, 1931), p. 361. The Duke of Wellington's receipt is still displayed in the offices of N. M. Rothschild & Sons.

8 Joseph Wechsberg, *The Merchant Bankers* (London, 1967).

9 See *Eight European Central Banks*, published under the auspices of the Bank for International Settlements (London, 1963).

10 Martin P. Mayer, *Wall Street: the Inside Story of American Finance* (London, 1959).

11 Gustavus Myers, *History of the Great American Fortunes* (New York, 1936).

12 See Edwin P. Hoyt, *The House of Morgan* (London, 1968).

13 John Gunther, *Inside U.S.A.* (New York, 1945).

14 H. E. Raynes, *Insurance* (Toronto, 1960), pp. 8–10.

CHAPTER 4

1 Francis Trevithic, *Life of Richard Trevithick*, 2 vols, (London, 1872), I, p. 108.

2 E. Berghaus, *The History of Railways* (London, 1964), p. 19.

3 George Dodd, *Railways, Steamers and Telegraph* (London, 1867), p. 52.

4 J. B. Snell, *Early Railways, Pleasures and Treasures* (London, 1964), p. 31.

5 R. S. Lambert, *The Railway King 1800–1871: A Study of George Hudson and the Business Morals of His Time* (London, n.d.), pp. 164–7.

6 Lambert, *The Railway King*, pp. 158–60.

7 Quoted by R. S. Lambert, *The Railway King*, pp. 261–2.

8 Berghaus, *The History of Railways*, p. 125.

9 J. C. Hemmeon, *The History of the British Post Office* (Harvard, 1912), p. 62.

10 Hemmeon, *The History of the British Post Office*, p. 70. There was no agreement with the USA until 1904.

11 W. L. Randell, *Messengers for Mankind* (London, 1940), p. 42.

12 Randell, *Messengers for Mankind*, p. 52.

13 D. Hunter, *Papermaking: The History and Technique of an Ancient Craft* (London, 1947), pp. 355–6.

CHAPTER 5

1 Dodd, *Railways, Steamers and Telegraphs*.

2 Dodd, *Railways, Steamers and Telegraphs*.

3 Hemmeon, *The History of the British Post Office*, p. 217.

4 Dodd, *Railways, Steamers and Telegraphs*, p. 261. The Western Union was formed in 1865.

5 Randell, *Messengers for Mankind*, pp. 80–1.

6 G. L. Lawford and L. R. Nicholson, *The Teleon Story, 1850–1950* (London, 1950), p. 28.

7 A. C. Clarke, *Voice Across the Sea* (London, 1958), pp. 126–7.

8 A. H. Morse, *Radio: Beam and Broadcast* (London, 1925), p. 22.

9 Randell, *Messengers for Mankind*, p. 157.

10 Norman Wymer, *From Marconi to Telstar* (London, 1966), pp. 12–13.

11 Admiral Sir R. H. Bacon, *The Life of Lord Fisher of Kilverstone*, 2 vols (London, 1929), II, p. 144.

12 Captain Vladimir Semenoff (trans. A. B. Lindsay), *The Battle of Tsu-Shima* (London, 1906), pp. 25–7.

13 Wymer, *From Marconi to Telstar*, pp. 33, 35, et seq.

14 B. L. Jacob and D. M. B. Collier, *Marconi – Master of Space* (London, 1935), p. 163.

15 Stanley Jackson, *The Savoy* (London, 1964), p. 109.

16 Jacob and Collier, *Marconi*, p. 218.

17 Wymer, *From Marconi to Telstar*, p. 65.

CHAPTER 6

1 Sir Arthur Helps, *Life and Labours of Mr Brassey* (London, 1872; new edition, 1969), p. 329. For a portrait of a railway contractor, see also *Doctor*

Thorne by Anthony Trollope, in which Sir Roger Scatcherd is supposed to typify the contractors of that day.

2 Helps, *Mr Brassey*, p. xiv.

3 S. E. Morison, *The Oxford History of the American People* (Oxford, 1965), p. 701.

4 J. T. Watson Newbold, *The Railways 1825–1925* (London, 1925), pp. 55–7, with quotation from Myers's *History of the Great American Fortunes*, II, p. 32.

5 Edwin P. Hoyt, *The Vanderbilts and their Fortunes* (London, 1963), pp. 169–71.

6 Hoyt, *The Vanderbilts*, p. 171.

7 W. S. Griswold, *A Work of Giants* (London, 1962), p. 89.

9 Matthew Josephson, *The Robber Barons: the Great American Capitalists 1861–1901* (London, 1962), p. 229.

10 E. R. Johnson, *American Railway Transportation* (New York, 1910), pp. 28–33.

11 Joseph Husband, *The Story of the Pullman Car* (Chicago, 1917), pp. 33–4.

12 Rudyard Kipling, *Captains Courageous* (London, 1897), p. 206.

13 J. B. Snell, *Early Railways, Pleasures and Treasures*, pp. 108–11.

14 Josephson, *The Robber Barons*, pp. 165–6.

15 Nathaniel Burt, *The Perennial Philadelphians: The Anatomy of an American Aristocracy* (London, 1963), p. 162. Jay Cooke was not himself a true Philadelphian. He came from Ohio but managed to establish himself among the elect, known to, if not quite the equal of, the Wanamakers, Biddles and Drexels.

16 Hoyt, *The House of Morgan*, pp. 158–61.

17 Michael Conant, *Railroad Mergers and Abandonments* (California, 1964), p. 134.

18 Josephson, *The Robber Barons*, p. 331.

19 Cleveland Amory, *Who Killed Society?* (New York, 1960), p. 469.

20 Amory, *Who Killed Society?*, pp. 485–6.

CHAPTER 7

1 D. A. Fisher, *The Epic of Steel* (New York, 1963), pp. 16–17.

2 R. Ewart Oakeshott, *The Archaeology of Weapons* (London, 1960), pp. 166–7.

3 P. S. Rawson, *The Indian Sword* (London, 1968), pp. 19–22.

4 Oakeshott, *The Archaeology of Weapons*, p. 106.

5 Henri L. Joly and Inada Hogitaro (trans.), *The Sword Book* (London, 1913).

6 Joly and Hogitaro, *The Sword Book*, p. 117

7 W. K. V. Gale, *Iron and Steel* (London, 1969), pp. 26–7.

8   Fay, *Great Britain from Adam Smith*, p. 274.
9   Gale, *Iron and Steel*, pp. 71-2.
10 W. H. G. Armytage, *A Social History of Engineering* (London, 1961), p. 182.
11 J. F. Wall, *Andrew Carnegie* (New York, 1970), pp. 263-5.
12 Wall, *Andrew Carnegie*, pp. 265-6.
13 Arundel Cotter, *United States Steel* (New York, 1921), pp. 14-15.
14 Cotter, *United States Steel*, p. 15.
15 D. A. Fisher, *Steel Serves the Nation 1901-1951* (New York, 1951), p. 26.
16 G. von Klass (trans. J. Cleugh), *Krupps: The Story of an Industrial Empire* (London, n.d.), p. 184.
17 Armytage, *A Social History of Engineering*, p. 192.

CHAPTER 8

1   L. T. C. Rolt, *Great Engineers* (London, 1962), p. 92.
2   Rolt, *Great Engineers*, pp. 97-9. Models of these machines are preserved in the National Maritime Museum at Greenwich, London.
3   Herta E. Paull, *Alfred Nobel, Dynamite King etc* (London, 1947), p. 52.
4   H. Busk, *The Navies of the World* (London, 1859).
5   Admiral Sir R. Custance, *The Ship of the Line in Battle* (London, 1912), p. 14.
6   William Manchester, *The Arms of Krupp, 1857-1968* (London, 1969), p. 163.
7   See A. M. Low, *Musket to Machine-Gun* (London, 1942), p. 71. The Maxim was the first real machine-gun, firing up to six hundred rounds a minute. Hearing of this expenditure of ammunition, the king of Denmark objected that it would bankrupt his kingdom in about two hours.
8   Manchester, *The Arms of Krupp*, p. 252.
9   David Dougan, *The Great Gun-Maker* (Newcastle, 1970).
10 Manchester, *The Arms of Krupp*, p. 846.
11 David Dougan, *The History of North-East Shipbuilding* (London, 1968), pp. 134-5.

CHAPTER 9

1   Jules Abel, *The Rockefeller Millions: The Story of the World's Most Stupendous Fortune* (London, 1967), pp. 13-14.
2   Robert Henriques, *Marcus Samuel* (London, 1960), p. 70.
3   Christopher Tugendhat, *Oil, the Biggest Business* (London, 1968), pp. 35-6.
4   Henriques, *Marcus Samuel*, pp. 338-9.
5   H. Longhurst, *Adventure in Oil* (London, 1959), p. 32.

6 Bacon, *The Life of Lord Fisher*, I, p. 157.
7 Longhurst, *Adventure in Oil*, p. 57.
8 Henriques, *Marcus Samuel*, pp. 258-9.
9 Tugendhat, *Oil, the Biggest Business*, p. 96. Gulbenkian's son, Nubar, inherited the 5 per cent, which on an investment never exceeding £1 million has yielded between £5 million and £6 million a year since 1955. See also Ralph Herrins, *Mr Five Per Cent* (London, 1957).

CHAPTER 10

1 W. J. Reader, *Imperial Chemical Industries: A History*, (Oxford, 1970), I, pp. 104-5.
2 *The Autobiography of Margot Asquith*, 2 vols (Harmondsworth, 1937), pp. 14-17.
3 Reader, *Imperial Chemical Industries*, pp. 193-4.
4 Harley Williams, *Men of Stress* (London, 1948), pp. 281-2.
5 Harley Williams, *Men of Stress*, pp. 316-7.
6 Reader, *Imperial Chemical Industries*, p. 456.
7 Herman Kogan, *The Long White Line* (New York, 1963), p. 94.
8 James McMillan and Bernard Harris, *The American Take-over of Britain* (London, 1968), pp. 47-9.

CHAPTER 11

1 Harvey S. Firestone and Samuel Crowther, *Men and Rubber: The Story of Business* (New York, 1926), pp. 55-6.

CHAPTER 12

1 Charles Chaplin, *My Autobiography* (London, 1964), p. 239.
2 Oliver Read and Walter L. Welch, *From Tin Foil to Stereo: Evolution of the Phonograph* (New York, 1959), p. 286.
3 Read and Welch, *From Tin Foil to Stereo*, p. 287.
4 Philip French, *The Movie Moguls* (Harmondsworth, 1971), p. 35.
5 Chaplin, *My Autobiography*, p. 334.
6 French, *The Movie Moguls*, p. 128.
7 See Joe McCarthy, *The Remarkable Kennedys* (London, 1962).

CHAPTER 13

1 *Management Today*, January 1970.
2 *The Director*, July 1965.
3 T. G. and M. R. Belden, *The Lengthening Shadow: the Life of Thomas J. Watson* (Boston, 1961), p. 88.

4 Belden, *Thomas J. Watson*, p. 127.
5 Belden, *Thomas J. Watson*, p. 137.
6 *Sunday Times*, 10 October 1971.

CHAPTER 14

1 David Scott-Moncrieff, *Three-Pointed Star* (London, 1955), pp. 9–10.
2 Anthony Bird, *The Motor Car* (London, 1960), pp. 60–3.
3 John Keats, *The Insolent Chariots* (New York, 1959). The exception to his rule was F. W. Lanchester, LLD, FRS, whose unorthodox cars have, in some ways, never been surpassed.
4 Keats, *The Insolent Chariots*, p. 24.
5 James Ensor, *The Motor Industry* (London, 1971), p. 12.
6 Ensor, *The Motor Industry*, p. 131.
7 P. W. S. Andrews and Elizabeth Brunner, *The Life of Lord Nuffield* (Oxford, 1955), p. 105.
8 Graham Turner, *The Car Makers* (London, 1963), p. 28.
9 Turner, *The Car Makers*, p. 56.
10 Ensor, *The Motor Industry*, p. 173.

CHAPTER 15

1 Charles H. Gibbs-Smith, *Aviation: An Historical Survey* (H.M. Stationery Office: Science Museum Publication, London, 1970).

Index

California, 24, 105, 107, 110–11, 114,
158
Calthorpe, Lord, 7, 11
Cambridge University, 168–9
Cammell & Co., 147, 148
Canada, 94, 103, 153, 169, 238
canals, 31–3
Cannell, Charles, 133
Canyng, William, 44
Capell family, 44
car industry, 158, 162, 163, 222–36
Caravelle, 240
Cardiff, 11, 33
Carinthia, 44
Carnegie, Andrew, 102, 134–8, 142,
155
Carnegie Company, 136, 137
Carron Works, 131
Caucasus, 123, 124, 157, 160
Cavendish, Henry, 168
Cavendish family, 10
CBS, 205
Cecil family, 6
Central Bank of London, 50
Central Pacific Railroad, 109–10, 114
Ceylon, 186
Chamber of Assurance, 62
Chamberlain family, 152
Chandos, Duke of, 13
Channel Tunnel, 75
Chaplin, Charlie, 195, 198–9, 202
Chaplin, William, 38, 40–1
Charing Cross Bank, 17
Charles I, King of England, 35
Charles II, King of England, 6–7, 15,
35, 46, 49, 51
Charles V, Emperor, 44, 45
Chartered Bank of India, 51
Chase Manhattan Bank, 61
Chatham, William Pitt, 1st Earl of,
16
Chatham, 2nd Earl of, 16
chemical industry, 169–81
chemistry, 168–9
Chester and Crewe Railway, 103
Chevrolet, Louis, 229
Chevrolet Motor Company, 229, 230
Chicago, 106, 108, 109

Chicago, Burlington & Quincy Railroad, 116
Child, Francis (1642–1713), 47
Child, Sir Francis (?1684–1740), 47
Child, Sir Josiah, 15–16
Chilworth Gunpowder, 173
China, 24, 80, 123, 124, 148, 149, 160
Chrysler Corporation, 229, 230, 233,
236
Churchill, Winston, 108, 159
CIBA, 170
cinema, 195–206
Citroën SA, 192, 233, 236
Clark, Sir Allen, 212–13
Clavel, Alexander, 170
Clement VII, Pope, 45
Clement, Joseph, 144
Cleveland, 155
Cleveland, Mrs Stephen Grover, 138
Clinton family, 6, 11
Clyde, 25, 27, 29
Coalbrookdale, 130–1
Cockerill, John, 140
Coffin, Charles A., 209
Colls & Sons, 10
commerce, development of, 15–16,
43–4
Commercial Union Insurance Company, 63
Compagnie Internationale pour
l'Informatique, 220
computers, 216–21
Computing - Tabulatory - Recording
Company (CTR), 216
Concorde, 247
Connecticut Steamboat Company, 58
Consolidated Mining Company, 137
Constantinople, 45, 75
Continental Gummiwerke AG, 192
Cooke, William Fothergill, 85, 87
Corn Laws, 16
Cort, Henry, 132
Corvair, 241
Cosmopolitan Pictures, 202
Cotton Powder Company, 173
Coutts & Co., 47
Coutts family, 47, 51
Coventry family, 44